rebar

modernfoodcookbook

rebar

modernfoodcookbook

made from scratch by:

audrey alsterberg + wanda urbanowicz

photographs by david ellingsen

bigideaspublishinginc.

Big Ideas Publishing Inc.
1324 Minto Street
Victoria, British Columbia, V8S 1P4

Cover and interior design by Audrey Alsterberg
Written and type-set by Wanda Urbanowicz
Photographs by David Ellingsen

Printed and bound in Canada, by Hemlock Printers, Vancouver, B.C.

Alsterberg, Audrey D.
Urbanowicz, Wanda T.
The rebar modern food cookbook
Includes index
ISBN 0-9688623-0-6

First Edition

dedication

For Christopher, whose enthusiasm for life has changed mine; for my son Shamus, my pride and joy and best cooking buddy; for all of my sisters who keep me strong and from taking life too seriously; for Marion, Jodi and Becky who are always there for me; for Billy, forever by my side and for Wanda, who made this book happen. — a.a.

This book is for Trevor, whose old soul and big heart helps put everything into perspective. — w.u.

contents

Adele Chong Akihiko Sakagami Alan Black Alan McEachern Alan Miceli Alika Stobo Allegrta Pitt Amy Dunaway Amy Neal Andrea Dawn Mohl Andrew Crossley Andrew Engelleder Andrew Kinnear Andrew Malcolmson Andy(boy)Impett Ann Wilson Arran Scott Asa Nilsdotter-Swan Athanasia Tsavalas Becky Hay Ben Pardy Beth Tarasof Betsy Lamarche Billy(the Bavarian)Hilton Blair Macdonald Brandy Buchanan Brian Cheng Bridgette Brodi McRae Brook Cameron Brookes Hogya Bruce Ployart Carly McMahon Carol Dolbel Carol Harris Carol Madsen Catherine Smith Catherine Weyman Cathie Street Chad Genres Chelsea Woods Cheryl Hemstad Chris Boss Chris Highes Christie Howes Christina Meade Christine(baby-g)Nagasawa Christine Babichuk Christine Woodward Christopher Fleet Christopher Parker Cindy Schafer Claire MacMahon Colin MacRae Connie Daniels Cordelia Horsburgh Corrine Erwin Corrine Irwin Cory Baker Cory Gagnon Craig Drummond Cynthia Milton Dagmar Bandiera Dale Ajas Dan Wear Daniel Arsenault Daniel Bier DanielHBrown Daniel Macdonald Danika McDowell Danyel Price Darren(darla)Upshaw Darren Ball Daryl Grant Dave Antoniou Dave McKnight David(homey)Ellingsen David Adams Davida Dean Buscher Dean Mollon Debbie Brown Debbie Lelievre Debbie Saber Deborah Cox Del Brown Denise Brend Denise Cox Derek LaFramboise Desmond Carpenter Doug Cabana Elizabeth Blake Elizabeth(possum)Rooke Emilie Shaneman Erin Kendall Erin Rae Hervieux Erin Scott Fergus Haywood Fernando Jiminez Fiona Howlett Fran Lynott Francis Redford Fred Simpson Gary Abersek Genvieve Laplante Glen Morris Gord Sih Gordon Martin Graham Duffy Graham Sherwood Grant Hartley Grazia Watson Greigh Sanderson Guln Dubois Haim Behar Harbans(harby)Dosanjh Heather Campbell Heather MacLaren Heidi Fink Heidi Gues Holger Bush Ian Wilson Iliana Rooke JD Courtney Anderson James(jay-bird)Nelson James Bray James Cove James Dean Lloyd James Nelson Janine LM Johnstone Janna Hills Jason Chapple Jason Rosina Jayme McKillop Jayne Ireland Jeannie Puritch Jenna Hills JenniferAMRosina Jennifer Benner Jennifer Charles Jennifer Cox Jennifer Farrell Jennifer Harrington Jennifer James Jennifer Karagianis Jennifer Knight Jennifer Pritchard Jeremy Robinson Jess Nichol Jesseca White Jessica Lefebvre Jessica Lovelace Jessica Munroe Jessica Rea Jessie

Penny JillKElliott Jody Barned Johanna Hestler John Bill Jonathan Pulker Josh Hoekeme Joshua Lovelace Joyita Rubin Judy Walker Julia Decker Julia Young Karen Jones Karen Ralph Karrie Hill Katerina Smylitopoulos Katherine A Paul Katie Twohig Kees Schaddelee Kelly Deering KendraGPowell Kenny Kempster Kirsty Dickson Kristin Scott Larissa Pelletterio Laura Marsden LeighAnnRowlandson Leigh Nielsen Leslie Quilty Levi McKechnie Lil' Al+Big Al Baird Lisa Hoover Lisa Murray Lisa Wietzke Liza Lizzy(possum)Rooke Lorna Potter Louise Krohman Lucy Lestage Lynndie Dzuris Majit Dhalliwal Malkin Sahota Marc Swan Marcel Bertrand Marcia Hewett-Hicks Marion Selfridge Mark Brossland Marketa Jurcak MarnISCraig Mary Patterson Maureen Kelly Meghan Magee Meghan(shmeg)Wardel Melanie Crowe Melanie Parker Michael Herman MichaelPaulHopkins Michaelah Fox Michelle Daniels Michelle Gagne Michelle Magnone Michelle S Michelle Williams Mike Stoutely Morgan Bardat MorganMCChisholm Murray McConaghy Naomi Harding Naomi Thornton NiallCMaclachlan Nick Tooke Nigel Blackhall Noah Quillevierve Pam Ewasiuk Pamela Hamilton Patricia Rebel Patrick Garland Patrick Love Paul Torresan Peter Green Rachael(rae)Carrol Rachel Hoole Ravinder(ravi)Bains Rebecca Games Rebecca Lind Rebecca Smith Reed Chudley Regan Kirkland Regan Lawrence Rhonda Sarnum Richard Adams Richard Crellin Rick Pambrun Rob Alford Rob Bellamy Robin Edgar Ron Welch Russell Green Ruth Anderson Sahra Nudge Sally Adams Sally Tippett Sam Jones Sandeep Kalkat Sarah H Sarah Jennings Sarah Wendt Sarah Winn Sarina(bean)L'Esperance Sascha Gait Sasha Lees SeanSMcCulloch Sean Spellacy Senz Hamilton Shamus McDougal Shandra Crow Shannon Cunningham Shannon Robin Shanti Jucknat Sharlene Grue Sharon Richer Shawn Resatz Shayni Sherman Shellie Green Sheridan T Sheri-Lynn Thomson Shoshannah Buck Sian Richards Simon Castle Simon Myttenar Stephanie Enns Stephen Fosker Stephen Jenks StevePBrake Steve Ras Allen StevenLKravitz Stuart L Sue Perello Suzannah Kelly Suzanne M Dupuis Tamara Jones Tara Mitchell Tara Tudor Terry Theresa(T)Kosk Tiffany Jowitt Tom Holliston Tosh Hayashi Tricia Berg Truna Shivilo Varinder(dooble)Singh Verocnica Graham Virginia Bray WadePallister Yuana H Zeb Baranyai Zia Sutherland Zoe Dominiak IfWeMissedYouWe'reSorry

acknowledgements

The help and support of many people have made this book possible. First and foremost, we'd like to thank Trevor Davis, whose technical support and computer wizardry saved us time and time again, and made this project a reality from the first step to the last. A great big thank you to David Ellingsen for his keen eye in capturing the mood of rebar and it's people in his photographs throughout the book. Thanks also to Dawn Dorigo for her photo contributions. A heartfelt thanks to Becky Appleton, Rachael Carroll, Darren Upshaw, Cathie Street and Shoshannah Buck for holding down the fort at rebar and Cascadia while we were occupied with the book. Thanks also to Sarina L'Esperance and Emilie Shaneman for much-needed help in the recipe-testing department and to Jean Sproule for her eagle-eye editing. Special thanks to Silk Questo, Noël Richardson and Carolyn Bateman for some very sage advice early on in the game and to Ann Urban, whose "thumbs up" at several critical junctions gave us the confidence we needed to forge ahead. Also thanks to Francis Sullivan of Graphic Knights for technical support and Grant Forrest of Hemlock.

We'd like to express deep gratitude to those that came to our aid in times of need: Anna Vi, the Lyles, the Bumps, the Appletons, and Jodi Skiba for her continual emotional support, and to all of our family and friends for their love and faith in us.

rebar would never exist today without the dedication, energy and enthusiasm of many people who were, and continue to be, instrumental in keeping rebar and Cascadia going strong. Special thanks to Chris Parker for his commitment to excellence and hard work in setting up and maintaining the "bar", and overseeing bakery operations. Thanks to Joe Kubinek and Bonnie Olesko for coming up with the name "rebar modern food". Thank you to all in our community for your patronage and support. Finally, thanks to the many many people, from dishwashers to suppliers, who put in so many hours of hard work—Shamus, Cheryl, Andy, Billy, Lizzy, David, Harbans, Ravi, and all the others who have left their special mark on **re**bar.

introduction

there's an unmistakeable feeling you get upon entering rebar. Your senses are instantly engaged as the door opens and you find yourself on a raised landing facing a bird's-eye view of the restaurant. Light streams in through the street-level windows and reflects warmth from the boldly painted walls. As you descend into the room and stand before the busy bar, you might, depending on the moment, experience a chlorophyll-laden scent of freshly extracted wheatgrass juice, the refreshing fragrance of peeled citrus or a heady whiff from a just-pulled shot of espresso. As you weave your way to your seat, intriguing aromas from the kitchen waft by— roasting garlic, fresh rosemary. Tables covered in festive Mexican tablecloths and a downright decadent dessert case catch your eye and create an exciting sense of anticipation. The friendly staff, funky music and cheerful off-beat decor are charged with a genuine spirit of health and vitality. It's clear from the start—this is no ordinary restaurant.

It's this unique combination of elements and special energy that draws people to rebar, be it a first visit from unwary travellers, or a regular foray by our very loyal customers and friends. Continuity also plays a big part. In a business notorious for high-turnover, it is uncommon for a restaurant to survive for more than a decade and even more unusual for original employees and clientele to still be a part of it all. Some staff date back to the early days and have become familiar faces and friends to our regular patrons. Over the years this "extended family" has seen life-long friendships form, babies born, wedding celebrations, friends passing and many memorable Christmas feasts and celebrations. For all these reasons and more, we felt compelled to capture some of this spirit in a book.

rebar's original concept sprang from humbler beginnings. Thanks to a few old friends, who were too naive to know any better, we opened the original rebar in 1988. At the time, the "fresh food" revolution that has since shaken the restaurant world was still very much in its' early stages. We found inspiration in restaurants like the Greens in San Francisco, the Gravity Bar in Seattle and in people like Alice Waters, John Robbins and Ann Wigmore. The traditional Western cooking methods that many of us were accustomed to in restaurants, using high-fat, processed, enzyme-depleted and over-cooked foods, no longer fit in with our new ideas and modern lifestyle. This, combined with the allure of starting a new business and the desire to spread the concept of food as nourishing and health-supporting, set the mould for "rebar modern food". We wanted a restaurant with a conscience and Victoria seemed ready for this concept.

Few people were aware of the invigorating health properties of wheatgrass or familiar with the accompanying industrial-strength centrifugal juicers that greeted them when they entered the original rebar location at the foot of Johnson St. in downtown Victoria. The cozy 500 square feet, with it's galvanized sheet metal-covered walls, was charged with an atmosphere that spelled out VITALITY loud and clear. The energetic music of James Brown and Grace Jones combined with an upbeat, wise-cracking staff who served up delicious fresh and vibrant food hooked a steady and growing clientele. It wasn't long before we outgrew those four walls.

Maybe because we were young and feeling like we had a "hit" on our hands, we took some wild, against-the-odds risks and expanded to a space just vacated by the "Badge Kingdom" memorabilia shop in the heart of the city's historic Bastion Square. An enthusiastic staff helped set up shop, paint brushes in hand, covering the walls with a shade of green paint that prompted one passer-by to comment, "that colour would give me indigestion!" (We've never been able to live down the colour of our walls. Many restaurant reviews written about rebar mention the walls!) We had no idea how receptive and supportive our customers would be, but were soon encouraged when our regulars didn't bat an eye to walk an extra four blocks to get their favourite chock-full-of-flavour baked goods and coffee. In our on-going search for quality local products, we were the first in the city to have our coffee shipped from a small roasting company in Seattle named Starbucks—goes to show our customers know a good thing!

Since those early days, rebar has evolved into something of a West Coast institution. The opening of our sister bakery "Cascadia" in 1995 marked a new era for rebar and we haven't looked back since. With more space, a larger staff and expanded menus, we worked hard to rise above the "fresh juice and veggie burger" level and to offer eclectic, seasonal fare with a touch of class. This led to some favourable attention from the outside—an honourable mention in Bon Appétit magazine, excellent Zagat survey ratings and a constant stream of good press in national travelogues and newspapers over the years. Combined with the appreciation shown by loyal and enthusiastic fans, we were able to keep the momentum going.

Our recipe for success is easy—serve good coffee, good bread and good soup (and we don't stop there). Most hungry diners' look for a meal that is fresh, carefully prepared with quality ingredients, well seasoned and healthy. Our aim is to satisfy that elusive "home-cooked meal away from home", but with a pleasing twist that mother would never have thought of. We offer a menu that is predominantly meat-free, although most customers would be hard-pressed to notice that anything is missing! Still, with growing concern over the impact of large-scale meat production on the land, water and people around the world, eating less meat has become a very sensible choice.

rebar is all about a certain energy, good food and a communtiy of people—anyone who works there can tell you that. Wanda & Audrey feel driven to show that rebar is about more than just funky green walls and almond burgers. We want to share what we've learned over the years and share some of the stories behind the scenes of restaurant life. As self-taught cooks working in a professional environment, we've been inspired by contact with a stream of people in the food business, books and magazines we've amassed, and years of cooking experience in diverse situations and kitchens. Above all we feel the need to show something for the countless hours of chopping onions and all of the missed hours at home cooking for and being with our dear partners, for our "labour of love"—rebar.

☯ – a vegan recipe

salads

eat your greens! Salads make up the bulk of our menu at **re**bar. They are the source for fresh raw vegetables, rich in vitamins, minerals and enzymes, which are essential to a healthy diet. Not only do salads serve to supplement a meal, but regularly replacing a meal with a salad gives our systems a rest from complex, cooked meals. It should go without saying that you should use the freshest available ingredients, preferably organic, to make a salad. Differences in the quality of vegetables are more pronounced when they're eaten raw, so don't hesitate to pay a little extra for organic produce—it's well worth the price in terms of taste and food value (not to mention all the land-based benefits of eating organic).

Better still, if you have a garden, salad greens are easy to grow. Arugula, for instance, is often difficult to find or expensive to buy, but is very easy to grow, particularly in our West Coast climate, where it can thrive well into the winter months. We use fresh herbs in all of our recipes. They're easy to grow too, but are also widely available in supermarkets. Finally, use fine quality, cold-pressed oils for all the same reasons—they're healthier, taste better and will ultimately increase your enjoyment of "eating your greens".

Saigonsalad

with rice vermicelli, vegetables and spicy lime sauce

fat-free is a term that seldom inspires the taste buds. Here we proudly present an exception! If you're not averse to a bit of fish sauce, adding some to the dressing contributes an authentic Southeast Asian kick that takes this dish to another level. (If you've never tried fish sauce, just remember that it tastes much better than it smells.) This dish is filling enough to make a substantial lunch or dinner for two.

serves 2

☯ replace fish sauce with all soy for a vegan salad.

dressing

1 cup (240 mL) hot water

4 tbsp (60 mL) brown sugar

2 garlic cloves, minced

1 jalapeño pepper, seeded and minced

1 tsp (5 mL) sambal oelek

4 tbsp (60 mL) fish sauce

2 tbsp (30 mL) soy sauce

6 tbsp (80 mL) lime juice

salad

2 cups (480 mL) shredded lettuce

1/2 package rice noodles, 1/4" wide

4 scallions, minced

1/2 cucumber, seeded and sliced

2 carrots, grated

2 tomatoes, chopped

4 tbsp (60 mL) chopped fresh herbs
   (cilantro, basil or mint)

2 tbsp (30 mL) peanuts, roasted and
   chopped (optional)

1 Dissolve sugar in hot water and let cool. Stir in garlic, chiles, soy and/or fish sauce and lime juice. Whisk thoroughly to combine and set aside while preparing the rest of the recipe.

2 Follow noodle package instructions; strain in a colander and rinse with cold water. Shake excess water from the noodles and gently toss with a light drizzle of oil (sesame is ideal).

3 To assemble salads, place 1 cup (240 mL) shredded lettuce in the bottom of each serving bowl. Mix 1 tbsp (15 mL) chopped herbs into each bowl. Next, divide the noodles evenly and nest them on top of the lettuce/herb mix. Ladle 4 tbsp (60 mL) of dressing into each bowl. Arrange vegetables on top of the noodles and sprinkle with remaining herbs. Drizzle with more dressing and top with roasted peanuts.

4 Serve with chopsticks. Have each diner use them to mix everything together from the bottom up in their own bowl. Serve with extra dressing and fresh lime wedges on the side.

cooltofu&watercresssalad

with toasted sesame-miso dressing ☯

this nutritious salad was inspired by a chilled tofu and ginger sauce dish at Futaba, a favourite local Japanese restaurant. Convincing customers to order this salad from our menu has not been easy. While eating chilled, uncooked tofu may seem strange to Western palettes, it is common in the East. Many who try this dish soon grow to love it. The creamy soft tofu cubes contrast the crunchy, peppery watercress, silky miso dressing and pungent pickled ginger. It's a great combination to serve with sushi (p. 104), or to have on it's own for a healthy, fresh lunch.

serves 4 - 6

1 Process the first nine ingredients in a food processor or blender until smooth. Slowly drizzle in the oil while the motor is running. Season to taste.

2 Divide watercress among serving plates. Arrange even amounts of cubed tofu on top of the watercress and drizzle with dressing, followed by a light glaze of soy sauce.

3 Garnish with shredded pickled ginger, toasted sesame seeds and thin cucumber slices or tomato wedges.

dressing

(yields 1 1/2 cups - 360 mL)

1 garlic clove, minced

1 tbsp (15 mL) minced ginger

1/2 cup (120 mL) mirin

1/4 cup (60 mL) genmai miso

1/8 tsp (.5 mL) cracked pepper

1/8 tsp (.5 mL) Szechuan peppercorns, toasted and ground

1 tbsp (15 mL) sesame oil

2 tbsp (30 mL) sesame seeds

1/4 cup (60 mL) rice wine vinegar

3/4 cup (180 mL) vegetable oil

salad

2 blocks medium-firm tofu, drained
and cubed

4 cups (960 mL) stemmed watercress

1/4 cup (60 mL) pickled ginger (p. 12)

3 tbsp (45 mL) soy sauce

1 tbsp (15 mL) sesame seeds

kasha & summer bean salad

with roasted beets and dill-sunflower vinaigrette

traditional recipes and combinations are fun and challenging to re-create and "modernize". Though we like to tinker, it's important to us that the results remain true to their old-world essence. This salad was conceived with the hope of impressing my Polish relatives, who are happiest with the foods most familiar to them. They may not recognize the dish by looking at it, but one mouthful will readily put them back in their comfort zone.

serves 4 - 6

vinaigrette

juice of 1/2 lemon
zest of 1/2 lemon, minced
2 tbsp (30 mL) apple cider vinegar
1 garlic clove, minced
1 tsp (5 mL) Dijon mustard
2 tbsp (30 mL) minced fresh dill
1/4 tsp (1.2 mL) cracked pepper
1/2 cup (120 mL) sunflower oil

salad

1 cup (240 mL) buckwheat groats (kasha)
2 bay leaves
1 tsp (5 mL) salt
2 cups (480 mL) water
2 medium beets, roasted (p. 10)
1/2 lb (225 g) green and/or yellow beans, blanched
2 tbsp (30 mL) sunflower seeds, toasted
2 hard-cooked eggs for garnish

☯ omit the egg garnish for a vegan salad.

1 To make the vinaigrette, combine lemon zest, juice, vinegar, garlic and Dijon mustard and whisk to blend. While whisking, slowly drizzle in the oil. Add 1 tbsp (15 mL) dill and season to taste with salt and pepper. Set aside.

2 Next, spread kasha in a single layer on a pan and roast in a 350°F oven for 5 minutes, or until golden and fragrant. Remove from the oven and cool. Bring water to boil in a small pot and stir in the roasted kasha, bay leaves and salt. Cover and reduce heat to low for 15 minutes. Remove pot from the heat and leave it covered for an additional 5 minutes. Fluff kasha with a fork and cool to room temperature.

3 Peel and dice the roasted beets into 1-inch cubes. Toss with a small amount of vinaigrette and set aside to marinate. Trim the ends of the blanched beans and slice each bean into three pieces on the bias.

4 To assemble the salad, toss kasha and beans with enough vinaigrette to coat. Gently mix in the marinated beets, the remaining dill and toasted sunflower seeds. Turn onto a serving dish and garnish with an arrangement of sliced eggs and dill sprigs.

suichoyslaw

with snow peas, carrots and black bean vinaigrette ☯

oriental greens, such as sui choy and baby bok choy, make an excellent base for building a slaw. Sui choy, or Chinese cabbage, is lighter than regular cabbage and makes a more delicate dish. The black bean vinaigrette was introduced by Heidi, one of our chefs who took a cooking class from the renowned Vancouver chef, Karen Barnaby. It was originally meant as a sauce for salmon, but after readjusting the recipe, we tried it as a dressing and received rave reviews at the restaurant. Since then we've found a number of great uses for it. Here is one of them ... and kudos to Karen for the inspiration!

1 Add all of the dressing ingredients, except the oil, into the bowl of a food processor and pulse to break up the chunks. Let the motor run while drizzling in the oil and blend until smooth.

2 Finely shred the sui choy. Cut the butt end off the bok choy, separate the leaves and rinse in cold water. If the leaves are wilted, leave them in a bowl covered with cold water for 15 minutes. Shake off excess water and thinly shred each leaf or group of leaves on a sharp angle.

3 Wash and string the snow peas and thinly julienne along the length of the pea. Peel the carrots and slice thin coins on a diagonal. Lay each coin flat and julienne into long, thin matchsticks. Finely julienne the red pepper.

4 Mix all of the vegetables together in a bowl and toss with enough vinaigrette to coat well. Sprinkle with finely minced scallions and toasted sesame seeds. Serve.

serves 4

vinaigrette
(yields 1 1/2 cups - 360 mL)
3 garlic cloves, minced
1 tbsp (15 mL) minced ginger
1/2 cup (120 mL) pickled ginger (p. 12)
1/3 cup (80 mL) fermented black beans
2 tbsp (30 mL) pickled ginger juice
2 tbsp (30 mL) rice vinegar
1/4 cup (60 mL) mirin
1/4 tsp (1.2 mL) roasted and ground
    Szechuan peppercorns
1/4 tsp (1.2 mL) cracked pepper
1/2 tsp (2.5 mL) salt
3/4 cup (180 mL) vegetable or peanut oil

salad
1/2 small head sui choy
4 baby bok or Shanghai choy
6 oz (180 g) snow peas
2 carrots
1/2 red sweet pepper, seeded
1/2 bunch scallions, thinly sliced
1 tbsp (15 mL) sesame seeds

freshfig&chèvresalad

with fresh mint and lavender honey-balsamic vinaigrette

dreams of travelling to Provence inspired this salad. Imagining a
centuries-old stone farmhouse amid fruiting olive groves and fields of blooming lavender is enough to make a kitchen-bound restaurant cook cry. Nothing that a chilled
bottle of Chassagne-Montrachet and this lovely salad can't cure. Bon appétit!

serves 2 - 3

vinaigrette

(yields 1/2 cup - 120 mL)

1 tbsp (15 mL) lavender-infused honey

3 tbsp (45 mL) balsamic vinegar

1/4 tsp (1.2 mL) cracked pepper

1/4 tsp (1.2 mL) salt

1/2 cup (120 mL) extra virgin olive oil

salad

4 oz (120 g) assorted salad greens

4 fresh figs

4 oz (120 g) chèvre

2 sprigs of fresh mint

1 To make the vinaigrette, prepare the lavender honey well in advance and cool. Combine all of the ingredients, except oil, in a bowl and whisk them together. Slowly drizzle in the oil as you whisk. Correct seasoning to taste.

2 To serve, divide greens among serving plates. Slice figs into 6 sections, arrange them among the greens and crumble chèvre over top. Drizzle vinaigrette over each salad and garnish with chopped mint leaves and cracked pepper.

lavenderinfused honey

1 cup (240 mL) honey

1 tbsp (15 mL) dried lavender blossoms
  or 2 tbsp (30 mL) fresh lavender

Heat honey in a small pot over low heat until it turns to liquid. Add lavender and continue to heat gently for 10 minutes. Remove from heat and allow the honey to infuse for a few hours. Reheat the honey to a liquid and strain out the flower blossoms.

mesclun and fresh pear salad

with Brie, hazelnuts and blackberry-thyme vinaigrette

blackberries grow wild all around Victoria, so by mid-August

we're always looking for ways to include them in everything from desserts to baked goods and savoury dishes. This vinaigrette is tart, fruity and delicious paired with creamy mild Brie cheese, ripe juicy fruit, toasted nuts and slightly bitter salad greens.

1 Purée blackberries and strain through a fine mesh sieve. Combine berry purée, vinegar, orange juice and honey in a bowl and whisk while slowly drizzling in the oil. Stir in minced thyme and season with salt and pepper to taste.

2 To serve, divide greens among plates. Quarter the pears lengthwise and remove the seeds and stems. Slice each quarter into thin wedges and arrange them among the greens. Chop Brie into small pieces and scatter evenly. Drizzle with vinaigrette and garnish with chopped hazelnuts and fresh thyme leaves.

serves 6

vinaigrette

(yields 1 1/2 cups - 360 mL)

1 cup (240 mL) blackberries, fresh or
   thawed frozen
1/4 cup (60 mL) raspberry or white
   wine vinegar
juice and zest of 1 orange
2 tsp (10 mL) honey
1 tbsp (15 mL) minced fresh thyme
1/2 tsp (2.5 mL) salt
1/4 tsp (1.2 mL) cracked pepper
3/4 cup (180 mL) vegetable oil

salad

8 oz (240 g) assorted salad greens
2 ripe pears
4 oz (120 g) Brie cheese, at room
   temperature
1/3 cup (80 mL) hazelnuts, roasted
   and coarsely chopped
2 tbsp (30 mL) thyme leaves

babyfieldgreenssalad

with garlic croutons, shaved Parmesan and lemon-thyme vinaigrette

simple and refined salads like this are perfect as a first course for a special meal, or as part of a romantic, late-night dinner served with a warm rustic loaf, a favourite cheese and a chilled bottle of Pinot Gris. The vinaigrette is also delicious tossed with potatoes, fresh artichoke hearts and whole shallots that have been roasted together in the oven. Serve warm on a bed of greens.

serves 4

vinaigrette

(yields 1/2 cup - 120 mL)

3 tbsp (45 mL) lemon juice

1 tsp (5 mL) minced lemon zest

1 shallot, minced

1 tsp (5 mL) minced fresh thyme

1 tbsp (15 mL) honey

1/4 tsp (1.2 mL) salt

1/4 tsp (1.2 mL) cracked pepper

1/2 cup (120 mL) extra virgin olive oil

salad

6 oz (180 g) assorted salad greens

1 cup (240 mL) garlic croutons

4 oz (120 g) Parmigiano Reggiano

1 Whisk together all of the vinaigrette ingredients, except oil, in a bowl. Continue whisking while slowly drizzling in the oil. Correct seasoning to taste.

2 Just before serving, toss greens with croutons and just enough vinaigrette to lightly coat. Divide among serving plates and garnish with shaved or grated Parmesan cheese and cracked pepper.

garliccroutons

5 slices bread, cubed 1/2" x 1/2"

3 tbsp (45 mL) olive oil

3 garlic cloves, minced

1/4 tsp (1.2 mL) salt

Toss bread cubes with oil, garlic and salt. Spread out on a lined baking sheet and bake in the oven at 350°F for 8–10 minutes, or until evenly browned and crisp on the outside.

honey**ginger**dressing

sweet honey and pungent ginger make this our second most popular house dressing (after basil vinaigrette). Try it on your favourite salads or mix it with grated beets, carrots and fresh mint for a refreshing side dish. In late spring, toss it with steamed baby carrots, beets and sweet peas sprinkled with fresh chive blossoms.

☯ replace honey with maple syrup for a vegan dressing.

1 Combine all of the ingredients, except oil, in a food processor or blender and process until smooth. Keep the motor running and slowly add oil in a thin steady stream. Taste and adjust seasoning.

yields 1 1/2 cups (360 mL)

1 1/2 oz (45 g) ginger, minced
2 tbsp (30 mL) fresh ginger juice (see hint)
2 tbsp (30 mL) honey
5 tbsp (75 mL) rice vinegar
1/8 tsp (.5 mL) ground white pepper
1/2 tsp (2.5 mL) salt
1 cup (240 mL) vegetable oil

helpful**hint** ✳

If you don't have a juicer, use a garlic press to extract juice from the ginger. Or, an extra ounce of minced ginger may be added in place of the ginger juice.

asparagus&beetsalad

with hazelnuts and orange-raspberry vinaigrette ☯

spring brings asparagus season, and with it, a renewed sense of enthusiasm for cooking after a long winter of serving root vegetables. The novelty eventually wears off after several months of exhausting every possible use for asparagus, but before it does, we make sure to get plenty of mileage from this beautiful salad. The complimentary flavours and contrasting colours make an impressive opener to an elegant spring meal.

serves 4

vinaigrette

(yields 1 1/2 cups - 360 mL)

1 cup (240 mL) fresh orange juice

zest of 1 orange, minced

1 shallot, minced

2 tbsp (30 mL) raspberry vinegar

1/2 tsp (2.5 mL) salt

1/2 cup (120 mL) hazelnut oil or
vegetable oil

salad

6 oz (180 g) assorted salad greens

4 small beets, roasted (see "hint")

1 lb (450 g) asparagus spears

2 tbsp (30 mL) chopped hazelnuts,
roasted and skins removed

1 Pour orange juice into a small non-reactive pot and bring to a simmer over medium-high heat. Continue to simmer until the liquid is reduced to measure 1/2 cup (120 mL). Cool to room temperature. Combine reduction with the next four ingredients and whisk while slowly drizzling in the oil. Set aside while preparing the vegetables.

2 Peel and slice the roasted beets into rounds or wedges. Steam or blanch asparagus until just tender. Shock in a bowl of ice water, drain and spread out on a clean kitchen towel to dry.

3 Divide greens evenly among individual salad plates. Arrange beet slices and asparagus spears among the greens, drizzle with vinaigrette and garnish with chopped hazelnuts.

helpfulhint ✳

Roasting beets is a great way to preserve their sweet flavour and gorgeous colour. Wash, dry and securely wrap each beet individually in foil. Roast in a 375°F oven for 40 minutes to an hour, depending on size. Cool, unwrap and slip off the skins before using.

Szechuan noodle salad

with soba, avocado and cashews

spicy chilled noodle salads really hit the spot in warmer weather. They are filling but not heavy, and make great leftovers or picnic additions. At the restaurant we use buckwheat "soba" noodles for this popular salad, and raw vegetables for their cooling nature and crunch. The dressing is worth whipping up on it's own to use as a dipping sauce for salad rolls or potstickers, a light marinade for grilled salmon or shrimp satay, or as a sparkling low-fat sauce to drizzle on steamed vegetables.

☯ replace honey with maple syrup for a vegan dressing.

serves 4

1 Heat oils in a pot over medium-low heat. Add garlic and chiles and sauté briefly, being very careful not to let them burn. Stir in vinegar, soy sauce and water and bring to a boil. Reduce heat to a simmer. Add honey and stir to dissolve. Mix cornstarch with a few tablespoons of water in a bowl and whisk into the simmering liquid. Continue to simmer for 5 minutes. When the sauce has thickened slightly, remove it from heat and let cool. Stir in lime juice and minced cilantro and set aside.

2 Meanwhile, cook the noodles according to package directions in plenty of salted, boiling water. Drain in a colander and rinse with cold, running water. Shake off excess water. Toss with a light coating of sesame oil. Refrigerate the noodles until ready to use.

3 Before serving, combine chilled noodles and prepared vegetables (except avocado) in a large serving bowl. Add dressing to liberally coat the ingredients and toss well. Garnish with avocado slices and roasted cashews. Serve immediately.

dressing
(yields 2 cups - 480 mL)

2 tbsp (30 mL) sesame oil
1 1/2 tsp (7.5 mL) chile oil
3 garlic cloves, minced
1/2 tsp (2.5 mL) red chile flakes
2 tbsp (30 mL) rice vinegar
1/2 cup (120 mL) soy sauce
1 cup (240 mL) water
1/4 cup (60 mL) honey
1 tsp (5 mL) cornstarch or arrowroot powder
juice of 2 limes
2 tbsp (30 mL) minced cilantro

salad
1 lb (450 g) soba noodles
2 tbsp (30 mL) hijiki seaweed, soaked
4 scallions, minced
1 carrot, shredded
1 sweet red pepper, julienned
1/2 long English cucumber
1 avocado
1/4 cup (60 mL) roasted cashews

sunomono salad
with sweet sake dressing

cool low-fat rice noodle salads are a staple in Japanese restaurants here in the West. Silky rice vermicelli, crisp vegetable garnishes and chilled sweet and sour dressing make a refreshing appetizer or light lunch—perfect on those sweltering summer days when turning on a burner is unthinkable.

☯ omit honey and replace with all mirin for a vegan dressing.

serves 2

dressing
(yields 1 1/4 cups - 300 mL)
1/4 cup (60 mL) sake
2 tbsp (30 mL) honey
1/2 cup (120 mL) rice vinegar
1/4 cup (60 mL) tamari
1/4 cup (60 mL) mirin

salad
3 oz (90 g) rice vermicelli
8 slices cucumber
1/4 cup (60 mL) shredded daikon
2 tbsp (30 mL) pickled ginger
1 small tomato, cut in wedges
fresh shrimp or crab (optional)
1 tsp (5 mL) sesame seeds

1 Bring sake to boil in a small pot. Immediately remove from the heat, stir in honey and let cool. Add remaining liquid ingredients and chill until ready to serve.

2 Cook rice vermicelli according to package instructions. Drain and rinse under cold running water. Shake off excess water and divide among serving bowls. Pour enough chilled dressing over the noodles to just barely submerge them.

3 Attractively arrange the garnishes over the noodles, sprinkle with sesame seeds and serve.

make your own pickled ginger

1/2 lb (225 g) fresh ginger
1 cup (240 mL) unseasoned rice wine vinegar
1/2 cup (120 mL) cider vinegar
1/2 cup (120 mL) sugar
2 tbsp (30 mL) salt

Peel the ginger and cut into paper-thin slices. Place in a bowl and cover with boiling water for 4 minutes. Drain and cover with a heated mixture of the vinegars, sugar and salt. Transfer to a clean glass jar, cool, cover and refrigerate. Use within 4 weeks.

summergreens&nectarines

with chèvre, wholegrain croutons and honey-balsamic vinaigrette

pairing nectarines with soft, mild goat's cheese may not be the first combination to come to mind, but you'll have to trust us and try this delicious summery salad. Multigrain croutons add a rustic touch to the otherwise delicate ingredients. You can easily replace these with roasted almonds or pecans for a more upscale crowd.

1   In a small bowl, stir together the vinaigrette ingredients, omitting the oil. Slowly drizzle in the oil while whisking. Season to taste.

2   To make croutons, cut bread into 1/2" cubes. Heat olive oil in a skillet and sauté the bread until golden on all sides. Just before serving, slice nectarines. Toss greens with nectarines, croutons and vinaigrette to lightly coat. Place in a salad bowl or on individual plates, crumble chèvre and crack fresh pepper on top; serve.

serves 4

vinaigrette

(yields 1 1/3 cups - 320 mL)

2 tbsp (30 mL) honey

1/3 cup (80 mL) balsamic vinegar

1 shallot, minced

1/4 tsp (1.2 mL) salt

1/4 tsp (1.2 mL) cracked pepper

1 cup (240 mL) extra virgin olive oil

salad

4 thick slices wholegrain bread

2 tbsp (30 mL) olive oil

6 oz (180 g) assorted salad greens

2 ripe nectarines

4 oz (120 g) chèvre

helpfulhint ✳

When whisking up a vinaigrette, keep the bowl in place by spreading a damp kitchen towel under the bowl.

warmvegetablesalad
with sesame-maple dressing ☯

east meets west combinations are more popular than ever. This dressing blends maple syrup, balsamic vinegar and Dijon mustard with sesame oil, garlic and chiles to make a smooth and punchy dressing that has been a favourite on our menu over the years. The dressing is also delicious tossed with roasted new potatoes and fresh watercress sprinkled with toasted sesame seeds.

serves 2

dressing

(yields 1 cup - 240 mL)

2 tsp (10 mL) Dijon mustard
2 garlic cloves, minced
2 tbsp (30 mL) pure maple syrup
2 tbsp (30 mL) sesame oil
2 tbsp (30 mL) balsamic vinegar
2 tbsp (30 mL) red wine vinegar
1/4 tsp (1.2 mL) red chile flakes
1/4 tsp (1.2 mL) salt
1/2 cup (120 mL) vegetable oil

salad

2 cups (480 mL) broccoli florets
2 cups (480 mL) cauliflower florets
1 small zucchini
2 medium carrots
1 small red pepper
1/2 bunch spinach
1/4 cup (60 mL) roasted cashews

1 Start by making the dressing. Place all of the ingredients, except oil, in a bowl or food processor. Whisk or blend to combine. Slowly drizzle in the oil in a thin, steady stream while whisking or blending. Season to taste and transfer to a small pot. Heat the dressing gently over low heat while you prepare and steam the vegetables. Keep the dressing warm.

2 Slice the zucchini into 1/2" thick half-moon slices. Slice the carrots into diagonal 1/4" coins. Cut the pepper into 1/2" squares. Stem the spinach.

3 Set a steamer basket over a pot of boiling water. Add the carrots and cauliflower, cover and steam for 3 minutes. Add the broccoli, zucchini and pepper and steam until the vegetables are just tender.

4 To serve, toss a small amount of the warm dressing with the spinach and divide between two plates. Toss the steamed vegetables with enough dressing to liberally coat and arrange over the spinach. Garnish with chopped roasted cashews and serve extra dressing on the side.

helpfulhint ✳

Steaming vegetables is the best cooking method for preserving nutrients, so be careful not to overdo it. A stacking bamboo steamer set from Chinatown works great.

mizuna&summerplumsalad
with almonds and citrus-star anise vinaigrette

individual assets of each citrus fruit are used to produce this exciting vinaigrette. The bitter of grapefruit, acid of lemon, aromatics of lime and the sweetness of orange are combined and reduced with star anise to infuse the liquid with an exotic perfume. Whisked with fresh ginger and equal parts juice to oil, the vinaigrette is light and flavourful. In keeping with the Eastern theme, Japanese mizuna is the salad green of choice, but any slightly bitter green will work to balance the sweet and tart flavours. With a variety of summer plums to choose from, this salad is a beauty.

☯ replace honey with maple syrup or fruit sweetener (vegan).

serves 4

1. Combine juices, orange zest and star anise in a small pot and bring to a boil. Reduce heat and simmer until the liquid is reduced to measure 1/3 cup (80 mL). Cool the liquid to room temperature.

2. Strain the cooled reduction and discard the solids. Combine the liquid with honey, ginger and salt in a small bowl. Slowly whisk in the oil and season to taste.

3. Just before serving, halve each plum and remove the pits. Slice each half into 6 wedges. Toss mizuna and plums with enough vinaigrette to lightly coat. Place in an attractive bowl or on individual plates, sprinkle with lightly crushed toasted almonds and a final drizzle of vinaigrette.

vinaigrette
juice of 2 oranges
juice of 1 lime
juice of 1/2 grapefruit
juice of 1/2 lemon
1 tbsp (15 mL) orange zest
2 whole pods star anise
2 tbsp (30 mL) honey
2 tsp (10 mL) minced ginger
1/2 tsp (2.5 mL) salt
3/4 cup (180 mL) grapeseed or
    vegetable oil

salad
6 oz (180 g) mizuna
2 or 3 ripe plums
2 tbsp (30 mL) sliced almonds,
    toasted

painteddesertsalad
with maple-chipotle vinaigrette

our affinity for the desert probably stems from too much day-dreaming during wet Northwest coast winters. The earthy flavours of the Southwest seem to fulfill a deep-seated longing for red rock canyons, juniper trees and sagebrush, when everything at home is muddy and saturated. This salad is loaded with tastes that take us south of the border—smoked chiles, sage, maple, pine nuts and flame-charred sweet peppers. The smoky sweetness of the vinaigrette is enhanced with a few drops of natural hickory smoke—not a common staple in the pantry, but worth getting for this recipe (and others you'll find in the pages to follow). Candied salmon is a Northwest coast specialty of smoked, sugar-cured salmon. If it is not available, replace with regular hot-smoked salmon.

🌀 use avocado instead of salmon for a vegan salad.

serves 4

vinaigrette

(yields 3/4 cup - 180 mL)
2 garlic cloves, minced
2 tbsp (30 mL) balsamic vinegar
1 tbsp (15 mL) pure maple syrup
3/4 tsp (4 mL) Dijon mustard
2 tsp (10 mL) chipotle purée (p. 38)
1/8 tsp (.5 mL) liquid smoke
1/2 tsp (2.5 mL) salt
1/4 tsp (1.2 mL) cracked pepper
1/2 cup (120 mL) olive oil

salad

6 oz (180 g) assorted salad greens
2 red peppers, roasted (p. 50)
1/2 lb (225 g) candied salmon and/or
    2 avocados
4 oz (120 g) smoked or aged white
    cheddar cheese
2 tbsp (30 mL) pine nuts, toasted
4 sprigs of fresh sage

1 Prepare the vinaigrette by whisking together all of the ingredients, except oil, in a bowl. Slowly drizzle in the oil in a thin, steady stream while whisking. Correct seasonings to taste with more salt, pepper, chiles or syrup.

2 Seed and peel the roasted peppers and slice them into long, thin strips. Skin the salmon and remove any small bones. Slice or crumble into bite-sized pieces. Cube or grate the cheese. Stem the sage and chop the leaves coarsely.

3 To serve, toss the greens, salmon, peppers and sage with enough vinaigrette to lightly coat. Garnish with cheese, pine nuts and a swirl of vinaigrette.

quinoa**corn**salad

with cilantro, chives and lemon-lime dressing

grains are often overlooked in the salad department. This cool, south-of-the-border salad is an excellent alternative to rice in a Mexican spread. Quinoa was one of the ancient staple foods of the Inca civilization and is now being cultivated in the U.S. It has the highest protein content of all the grains and is also a very good source of calcium, iron, phosphorus, B vitamins and vitamin E. Quinoa is quick and easy to cook. The only fussy part involves an initial rinsing to rid the grain of bitterness. One of the many endearing qualities of quinoa is a cute little spiral impressed upon each individual grain when it's cooked ... you have to see it to believe it!

serves 6

1 Place quinoa in a fine mesh sieve and rinse thoroughly with cold, running water. Bring water to boil in a small pot, add the quinoa and salt and bring to a boil again. Cover and reduce heat to low for 15 minutes. Turn off the heat and keep the pot covered for an additional 5 minutes. Strain off any excess liquid and spread the quinoa out to cool on a tray while preparing the remaining ingredients.

2 Steam or lightly sauté corn until just tender and cool to room temperature. Combine all of the ingredients in a large bowl and gently toss. Season with additional salt, pepper or hot sauce to taste. Serve with fresh lime wedges.

1 cup (240 mL) quinoa
1 1/2 cups (360 mL) water
1/2 tsp (2.5 mL) salt
2 1/2 cups (600 mL) corn, fresh or
    frozen
1 small red onion, minced
2 jalapeño peppers, seeded and
    minced
1/2 red pepper, finely diced
3 tbsp (45 mL) lemon juice
3 tbsp (45 mL) lime juice
1/4 cup (60 mL) chopped cilantro
3 scallions, minced
2 tbsp (30 mL) finely minced chives
1 tsp (5 mL) salt
1/2 tsp (2.5 mL) Tabasco sauce, or
    to taste

rebarCaesarsalad

with roasted garlic, capers and lemon

our secret is finally out! Here is Audrey's celebrated egg-free Caesar recipe—a **re**bar highlight—rich with roasted garlic, capers, mustard, lemon and Parmesan. We purposefully order Caesar salads wherever we go, and still find this the best! If you don't mind slipping some seafood into your diet, this dressing tastes even better with six anchovy fillets blended into it.

serves 8

(yields 1 1/2 cups - 360 mL)
1 bulb roasted garlic (p. 158)
juice of 1 lemon
1 tbsp (15 mL) capers
1 tbsp (15 mL) caper juice
1 1/2 tsp (7.5 mL) Dijon mustard
2 garlic cloves, minced
1/4 tsp (1.2 mL) salt
1/4 tsp (1.2 mL) cracked pepper
1/3 cup (80 mL) grated Parmesan
    cheese
1 cup (240 mL) olive oil
extra Parmesan for garnish

1 Combine all of the ingredients, except oil, in a blender or food processor and blend. Add olive oil in a slow, thin stream. Correct seasoning to taste.

2 To serve, toss the dressing with washed, dried and torn romaine lettuce, fresh croutons (p. 8) and garnish with shaved Parmesan, fresh cracked pepper and lemon wedges. Enjoy!

helpful hint ✳

Use a potato peeler to make shavings from a block of Parmesan cheese. Save the rind and use it in a soup (minestrone!) for exceptional flavour. The rind can be frozen until ready to use.

romaine&bloodoranges
with fennel, Niçoise olives and Pinot Noir dressing

colour and texture combine with bold flavours to make this salad unique. Use the pale, crisp inner leaves of the lettuce head, reserving the outer leaves for the more humble Caesar salad. Blood oranges make a short-lived appearance in the winter months, but you can substitute regular oranges out of season. Garnish with delicate fronds from the fennel tops. Other scraps from the bulb would be welcome in a soup stock.

1 Combine all of the ingredients for the dressing in a bowl and whisk together to blend. Season to taste.

2 Slice fennel bulb into quarters. Remove the core from each quarter, separate the layers and finely julienne the fennel into long slivers.

3 Prepare orange slices by cutting both ends off the fruit. Stand the orange cut side down and using a sharp paring knife, remove the peel and pith by carefully slicing it away from the top down. Follow the shape of the fruit and rotate the orange as you work your way around it. Slice the peeled orange into rounds or sections, as you wish.

4 Separate the romaine leaves. Tear the larger ones and leave the smaller leaves intact. Wash and spin the lettuce and divide the leaves among serving plates. Scatter fennel, orange slices and olives evenly among serving plates and drizzle with dressing. Garnish with chopped fennel leaves and cracked black pepper.

serves 4

dressing
(yields 1 cup - 240 mL)
1/2 cup (120 mL) mayonnaise
1/2 cup (120 mL) Pinot Noir
1 tbsp (15 mL) balsamic vinegar
1/4 tsp (1.2 mL) salt
1 tsp (5 mL) honey
1/4 tsp (1.2 mL) cracked pepper

salad
1 head romaine lettuce
1 fennel bulb
2 blood oranges
1 cup (240 mL) Niçoise olives

helpfulhint ✳

Store prepared fennel in cold water until ready to serve. This will keep it crisp and prevent browning.

basilvinaigrette

fresh basil tastes great in just about everything, so it's no mystery why this is our most popular house dressing. Customers are always requesting the recipe and for years have been told to "wait for the cookbook." Finally here it is! This vinaigrette is very versatile. At the restaurant, it dresses our rustic bread salad (p. 21). At home, you can drizzle it over sliced garden tomatoes, bocconcini cheese and slivers of red onion; toss it with steamed baby potatoes, arugula and pine nuts; or use it to marinate grilled vegetables, such as eggplant, sweet peppers, zucchini and portabello mushrooms. If you have any vinaigrette left over, assemble a sandwich on a crusty Italian loaf with marinated artichoke hearts, fresh tomato, lettuce, Spanish onion and sharp fontina cheese. Wrap it up and take it on a picnic. Yum!

yields 1 1/4 cups - 300 mL

2 garlic cloves, minced
1 1/2 tbsp (22.5 mL) Dijon mustard
2 tbsp (30 mL) honey
1/4 cup (60 mL) red wine vinegar
1 tbsp (15 mL) balsamic vinegar
1 1/2 oz (45 g) fresh basil leaves
1/2 tsp (2.5 mL) salt
1 1/2 tsp (7.5 mL) cracked pepper
1 cup (240 mL) olive oil

☯ replace honey with maple syrup for a vegan vinaigrette.

1 Combine all of the ingredients, except oil, in a food processor and blend. Slowly add olive oil in a slow, thin stream until thick and creamy.

2 Season to taste and serve, or refrigerate up to 3 days.

helpfulhint ✳

To get the creamy consistency of this vinaigrette, a food processor or blender is a must. If you don't have either, whisk together the vinaigrette ingredients, minus the basil, and add torn basil leaves directly into the salad. The results are quite different from those intended, but the flavours are all present.

rusticbreadsalad

rebar style

variations on the Italian bread salad theme abound, with differences reflecting regional tastes and customs, yet the idea behind it remains a constant—a way of using up stale homemade bread. Not a glamorous purpose to be sure! Most recipes require stale bread to be soaked in water, then squeezed and tossed with the other ingredients. This approach is fine for the home cook, but to work in the restaurant we've had to bend the rules a bit, with a result that may not be entirely authentic, but is delicious in it's own right. We use basil vinaigrette to dress this salad at the restaurant, but other dressings would be great too (such as roasted tomato, garlic balsamic or Caesar dressing).

☯ substitute cucumber for the cheese for a vegan salad.

serves 4

1 Prepare the basil vinaigrette or one of the other suggested dressings. Next, make the croutons. While they are in the oven, prepare the remaining ingredients. Gently tear the lettuce and coarsely chop or tear the basil leaves.

2 When the croutons emerge from the oven, place them in a bowl and toss them with enough vinaigrette to lightly coat and set aside. In a large salad bowl, combine coarsely chopped tomatoes and olives, thinly sliced red onion, cubed bocconcini cheese, lettuce and basil. Drizzle in enough vinaigrette to lightly coat the vegetables, add the croutons, toss and serve immediately. Garnish with cracked pepper.

3/4 cup (180 mL) basil vinaigrette
4 cups (960 mL) garlic croutons (p. 8)
4 ripe tomatoes, coarsely chopped
1 cup (240 mL) Kalamata olives, pitted and halved
1 small red onion, finely sliced
2 rounds bocconcini cheese, cut into 1" chunks
1 head romaine or leaf lettuce (or a combination)
1/2 oz (15 g) fresh basil leaves

helpfulhint

To quickly remove olive pits without an olive pitter, drain olives and lay them on a cutting board. Lightly crush them with the palm of your hand. The pits will poke out and can easily be picked out.

tabbouleh**salad**

with lemon, parsley and mint ☯

potluck suppers never lack for tabbouleh salads. It's a university tradition. This rendition is classic, with fresh lemon, garlic, extra virgin olive oil, lots of parsley and a hint of fresh mint—the way we like it best.

serves 4

1 cup (240 mL) bulghur
1 1/4 cups (360 mL) boiling water
1/2 tsp (2.5 mL) salt
1/4 cup (60 mL) extra virgin olive oil
1/4 cup (60 mL) lemon juice
2 garlic cloves, minced
3/4 tsp (4 mL) salt
1/4 tsp (1.2 mL) ground cumin
1/4 tsp (1.2 mL) Tabasco sauce
1/2 tsp (2.5 mL) cracked pepper
1 (or 2) bunches Italian parsley
1/4 cup (60 mL) fresh mint leaves
1 small red onion

1   Combine bulghur and salt in a bowl and stir in the boiling water. Cover tightly with plastic wrap for 20 minutes. Uncover and fluff the grains with a fork. Let cool to room temperature.

2   Meanwhile, make the dressing by whisking together olive oil, lemon juice, garlic and seasonings. Set aside.

3   Wash stemmed parsley, shake off excess water and dry on a clean kitchen towel. Mince the parsley, mint leaves and red onion. In a serving bowl, combine cooled bulghur, prepared herbs and onion. Pour dressing over the ingredients and toss thoroughly. Let the salad rest before serving (30 minutes), or wrap and store in the refrigerator.

helpful**hint** ✳

Jazz up your tabbouleh with any, or all, of the following:

✳ 1 seeded and diced cucumber
✳ 1 can of chick peas
✳ 2 diced fresh or roasted peppers
✳ chopped olives
✳ minced green onions.

spinach&portabellosalad
with creamy feta, oregano and roasted garlic dressing

rich and creamy salad dressings should not be encouraged as part of a regular diet, but the mood for a good dose of fat can sometimes overcome even the most health-conscious of us. Of course we want you to be prepared when the urge comes, so help is on the way!

1 Squeeze the flesh from the roasted garlic bulb and blend with feta cheese until smooth. Add the remaining ingredients, reserving 1 tbsp (15 mL) oregano leaves, and stir thoroughly until well combined. Season to taste and set aside.

2 Remove portabello mushrooms from the marinade, pat dry and grill both sides until golden. Alternately, roast them on an oiled baking sheet in a 400°F oven for 15 minutes. Cool and cut 1/8" thick slices. Slice roasted pepper into long, thin strips. Finely slice red onion. Separate the radicchio leaves and tear them, and the spinach leaves into bite-size pieces.

3 In a large salad bowl, toss the vegetables and reserved oregano with enough dressing to coat evenly. Finish with cracked pepper and serve.

marinated
portabellomushrooms

4 portabello mushrooms
1/2 cup (120 mL) olive oil
1/2 tsp (2.5 mL) red chile flakes
2 garlic cloves, minced
1/4 cup (60 mL) white wine
1/4 cup (60 mL) balsamic vinegar
1 tsp (5 mL) lemon zest

Pre-heat grill or oven. Clean mushrooms and lay gill-side up in a shallow pan. Whisk together the marinade ingredients, pour over the mushrooms, cover and marinate in the refrigerator for up to 4 hours.

serves 4

dressing

1 bulb roasted garlic (p. 158)
1/3 cup (80 mL) feta cheese
1/3 cup (80 mL) crème fraîche (p. 108)
1/3 cup (80 mL) buttermilk
3 tbsp (45 mL) oregano, chopped
2 tsp (10 mL) honey
2 tbsp (30 mL) red wine vinegar
1/4 tsp (1.2 mL) salt
1/2 tsp (2.5 mL) cracked pepper

salad

1 bunch spinach, washed and stemmed
1 head radicchio
4 portabello mushrooms, marinated and grilled
2 red peppers, roasted and peeled (p. 50)
1 small red onion

tomato&bocconcini salad

with arugula, basil & roasted tomato vinaigrette

late summer is the ideal time to make this salad, when tomatoes, basil and arugula reach their peak in the garden. While vine-ripe hot house tomatoes are no match for the local field varieties, year-round availability makes it possible to enjoy this salad anytime. Substitute roasted sweet peppers and chèvre for a delicious variation.

serves 4 - 6

☯ with vine-ripe tomatoes, vegans won't miss the cheese!

vinaigrette

(yields 1 1/4 cups - 300 mL)
1 lb (450 g) ripe Roma tomatoes
1 bulb roasted garlic (p. 158)
1/2 cup (120 mL) reserved tomato juice
1/4 cup (60 mL) balsamic vinegar
1/2 tsp (2.5 mL) cracked pepper
3/4 tsp (4 mL) salt
1/2 tsp (2.5 mL) liquid smoke
1/2 cup (120 mL) olive oil

salad

1 bunch arugula
4–6 fresh ripe, organic tomatoes
2 rounds bocconcini cheese
2 tbsp (30 mL) pine nuts, toasted
2 sprigs fresh basil, stemmed

1 Begin by rubbing each tomato with olive oil. Place them on the grill of a barbecue or on a pan in a hot (400°F) oven. Roast and rotate until the skins begin to crack and blacken all over. Let cool. Peel the skin and remove the seeds while holding the tomato over a bowl to catch the juices. Reserve 1/2 cup.

2 Purée the roasted tomatoes and garlic in a food processor or blender. Add the remaining ingredients, except oil, and blend. With the motor running, pour in the oil in a slow, steady stream. Correct seasoning to taste.

3 Just before serving, stem, wash and dry the arugula leaves. Slice bocconcini into rounds or half moons. Gently tear basil leaves into small pieces and slice the tomatoes.

4 To assemble the salad, evenly divide arugula among plates and arrange tomatoes and cheese among the leaves. Drizzle with vinaigrette and scatter pine nuts, basil and cracked pepper on top. Serve immediately with extra dressing on the side.

helpful hint ✳

Chiffonade is a method of slicing fine shreds of leaf (spinach, basil) to make a pretty presentation. For basil, stack a few leaves on top of each other. Roll up from the stem end into a tight cigar. Slice crosswise very thinly with a sharp knife.

Cascade spinach salad
with hazelnuts, blue cheese and rosemary-balsamic vinaigrette

mountains of Oregon's Cascade range are Audrey's home turf. Hazelnuts and excellent blue cheeses also hail from the region; in fact, over 90% of North American hazelnuts are grown there. Audrey often reminisces about her childhood in Oregon and makes annual pilgimages to all of her favourite restaurants and neighbourhood haunts. This salad gives her a little taste of home away from home.

1 Whisk together all of the vinaigrette ingredients, except the oil, in a small bowl. Slowly drizzle in the oil while whisking, until thick.

2 Just before serving, place the spinach leaves, red onion, hazelnuts and half of the blue cheese in a large salad bowl. In a small pot, gently heat the vinaigrette until it starts to simmer. Drizzle the vinaigrette over the spinach, tossing well. Divide among salad bowls, sprinkle with remaining crumbled blue cheese, extra hazelnuts and cracked pepper. Serve immediately.

serves 4

vinaigrette
1 garlic clove, minced
1 1/2 tbsp (22.5 mL) balsamic vinegar
2 tsp (10 mL) red wine vinegar
1 tsp (5 mL) honey
1/4 tsp (1.2 mL) salt
1/4 tsp (1.2 mL) cracked pepper
1 tsp (5 mL) minced rosemary
1/3 cup (80 mL) olive oil

salad
10 oz (300 g) spinach leaves, stemmed
1/2 small red onion, julienned
1/2 cup (120 mL) crumbled blue cheese
1/4 cup (60 mL) hazelnuts, skinned and roasted (see "hint")

helpful hint ❄

To make an easy job of skinning hazelnuts, add 2 cups nuts to 4 cups boiling water with 1/4 cup baking soda. Blanch until the water turns black (3–5 min.) Rinse nuts in a colander under cold running water. The skins should slip right off. Dry in a clean kitchen towel and roast them in a 325°F oven until golden and nutty-smelling.

SouthwestCaesardressing

with asiago, chipotles and lime

kick it up a notch with this variation of our Caesar salad. The combination of flavours work so well together that you'll be hard-pressed to choose between this and the original. If you have cornbread handy, make croutons by cutting one inch cubes and baking them in the oven until they're crispy. Substitute Parmesan for asiago if it's more convenient and serve lime wedges alongside.

serves 8 - 10

(yields 1 1/2 cups - 360 mL)
1 bulb roasted garlic (p.158)
1 tbsp (15 mL) lime juice
1 tbsp (15 mL) rice wine vinegar
1 tbsp (15 mL) capers
1 1/2 tsp (7.5 mL) Dijon mustard
1 garlic clove, minced
1/4 tsp (1.2 mL) salt
1/4 tsp (1.2 mL) cracked pepper
1/3 cup (80 mL) asiago cheese
3 tbsp (45 mL) chipotle purée (p. 38)
1 cup (240 mL) olive oil

1 Squeeze out the contents from the roasted garlic bulb and combine with the other ingredients, except oil, in the bowl of a food processor. Blend until smooth. With the motor running, slowly drizzle in the oil until thick and creamy. Correct seasonings to taste.

2 Toss dressing with torn romaine lettuce and croutons. Garnish with shaved asiago and fresh lime wedges.

helpfulhint ✳

To get the most juice from a lime (or lemon), roll it on the counter several times, pressing with your palm. Cut the lime in half and push the tines of a fork into the center. Twist and squeeze the juice out over a bowl. One word of caution, the twisting motion may cause the fork to warp, so don't use your finest flatware!

saladeNiçoise

with roasted beets, new potatoes and Dijon vinaigrette

Niçoise salad sans tuna—an idea guaranteed to give Julia Child nightmares—but still an all-time favourite salad at **re**bar! Naturally, adding tuna wouldn't do any harm, but you might also want to try chilled, poached wild salmon instead. With or without the fish, this salad is a meal in itself, easy to expand for a big crowd and with something to please everybody. Start with the freshest new potatoes dug in early summer, crisp narrow beans steamed to perfection and make sure the eggs are free-range. A guaranteed hit!

☯ omit eggs and replace honey with maple syrup (vegan).

1 Prepare the vinaigrette by whisking together all of the vinaigrette ingredients, except oil, in a small bowl. Slowly drizzle in the oil while whisking. Season to taste and set aside.

2 Steam or roast whole potatoes until tender, and set them aside to cool. Steam or blanch beans until just tender; shock in ice water and pat dry in a clean kitchen towel. Peel and slice roasted beets into wedges or rounds. Halve the cherry tomatoes or slice the roasted peppers into 1/2" wide strips. Peel and quarter hard-cooked eggs.

3 Compose this salad on a large serving dish. Start by making a bed of salad greens and attractively group each component. Be creative with all these colours! Drizzle vinaigrette over all of the vegetables, reserving some to serve on the side. Scatter fresh chopped herbs, capers and cracked pepper on top. Voilà!

serves 4 - 6

vinaigrette

(yields 2/3 cup - 160 mL)
1 garlic clove, minced
1 shallot, minced
juice of 1/2 lemon
2 tbsp (30 mL) white wine vinegar
2 tsp (10 mL) grainy Dijon mustard
1 tsp (5 mL) honey
1/4 tsp (1.2 mL) salt
1/8 tsp (.5 mL) cracked pepper
1/2 cup (120 mL) extra virgin olive oil

salad

1 1/2 lb (675 g) new potatoes
1/2 lb (225 g) green and/or yellow
    beans
1 lb (450 g) beets, roasted (p. 10)
1 pint cherry tomatoes or 2 red peppers, roasted and peeled (p. 50)
4 hard-cooked free-range eggs
1 cup (240 mL) Niçoise olives
2 tbsp (30 mL) capers
4 oz (120 g) assorted salad greens
2 tbsp (30 mL) each, minced fresh
    chives and dill

Thai**3**cabbage**slaw**
with spicy red curry vinaigrette

take a detour from the comfort zone. The crisp vegetables in this slaw are dressed with a heady combination of shallots, ginger, lime and chiles that is guaranteed to get your pulse racing. The red curry paste adds a distinct Southeast Asian dimension and should be used with caution–a little goes a long way. Serve with pad Thai (p. 171), a grilled tofu steak sandwich or vegetable satay with rice.

serves 6 - 8

🌓 replace honey with sugar for a vegan dressing.

dressing

(yields 2 1/3 cups - 560 mL)

1/4 cup (60 mL) chopped shallots

2 tbsp (30 mL) chopped ginger

1 serrano chile, seeded

2 garlic cloves, minced

1/4 cup (60 mL) fresh lime juice

2 tbsp (30 mL) soy sauce

2 tbsp (30 mL) honey

3/4 tsp (4 mL) Thai red curry paste
   (we use Thai Kitchen brand)

1 tbsp (15 mL) sesame oil

1/2 cup (120 mL) peanut oil

1/4 tsp (1.2 mL) salt

salad

1/2 small head sui choy

1/2 small head green cabbage

1/2 small head purple cabbage

2 carrots, shredded

2 peppers, red and yellow

1 small red onion

1/2 bunch cilantro or Thai basil

1 Pulse shallots, ginger, garlic and chiles in the bowl of a food processor. Add the next seven ingredients and blend until smooth. Season to taste, but note that the chile heat will continue to develop as it sits.

2 Core and finely shred the cabbages. Peel carrots, thinly slice diagonal coins and then julienne each coin into thin, long matchsticks. Finely julienne the onion and sweet pepper. Mince scallions on the bias. Stem cilantro and roughly chop the leaves.

3 Toss together all of the vegetables with enough dressing to coat. Garnish with roasted peanuts and serve fresh lime wedges on the side.

vegetableslaw
with jalapeño-lime dressing, two ways

toss a bowl of crisp vegetables and shredded cabbages to make this fresh and colourful side dish that goes well with rich entrées, burgers and sandwiches. The two dressings, one creamy and the other oil-based, are equally lively with fresh lime juice and bite from the jalapeño pepper. The dill-poppy dressing is a third alternative to those searching for something a little more traditional.

serves 8

1 Combine the ingredients up to coriander in a bowl or food processor. Whisk or blend while slowly drizzling in the oil. If using buttermilk and mayonnaise, simply whisk together all of the ingredients to blend well. Adjust seasonings and set aside.

2 Core the cabbages and finely shred them. If using jicama, peel it, cut it in half and slice into thin, even rounds. Julienne slices into long, thin matchsticks. Peel carrots and slice thin, diagonal coins. Julienne each coin into long matchsticks. Seed peppers and slice into fine strips. Slice thin slivers of onion. Roughly chop the stemmed cilantro.

3 Toss all of the vegetables in a large bowl and mix in the dressing. Let the slaw sit at least 30 minutes, then toss again before serving.

dressing(s)
juice and zest of 1 lime
3 tbsp (45 mL) rice vinegar
1 tbsp (15 mL) honey
1 garlic clove, minced
1/2 tsp (2.5 mL) salt
2 jalapeño peppers, seeded and minced
1/2 tsp (2.5 mL) ground coriander
1 cup (240 mL) vegetable oil or, substitute oil with:
1/2 cup (120 mL) buttermilk plus
1/2 cup (120 mL) mayonnaise

salad
1/2 small head green cabbage
1/2 small head purple cabbage
1 small jicama (optional)
2 carrots
1 sweet red pepper
1 yellow pepper
1 medium red onion
1 bunch cilantro, stemmed
1/4 cup (60 mL) minced chives

dillpoppydressing
1/2 cup (120 mL) mayonnaise
1/2 cup (120 mL) plain yogourt
2 tbsp (30 mL) Dijon mustard
3 tbsp (45 mL) apple cider vinegar
1/2 tsp (2.5 mL) lemon zest
1 tbsp (15 mL) honey
1/4 cup (60 mL) chopped dill
1 tbsp (15 mL) poppyseeds
Combine all of the ingredients in a bowl and mix together well. Season with salt and pepper and toss with the "salad" portion of the above recipe (omit the cilantro and sweet peppers).

romaine & Gala apple salad
with spiced pecans, cheddar and creamy honey-lemon dressing

"sinful indulgence" perfectly describes this salad, but we couldn't resist including the recipe because it tastes SO good! Have it for lunch with warm corn bread.

serves 4

dressing

(yields 1 cup - 240 mL)

3 tbsp (45 mL) lemon juice

zest of 1 lemon, minced

3/4 cup (180 mL) crème fraîche (p. 108)

2 tbsp (30 mL) honey

1/2 tsp (2.5 mL) salt

salad

2 heads romaine, hearts removed and
   reserved

2 Gala apples

4 oz (120 g) aged white cheddar

1/2 cup (120 mL) spiced pecans

1 tbsp (15 mL) minced chives

1 Combine all of the dressing ingredients in a bowl and whisk thoroughly until smooth.

2 Separate leaves of the romaine hearts; gently tear the larger ones in half and keep the small ones whole. Wash the apples well in warm, soapy water; rinse and dry. Quarter and seed each apple and slice into thin wedges. Toss lettuce, apple slices and cheddar with enough dressing to evenly coat. Garnish with lightly crushed spiced pecans and minced fresh chives.

spiced pecans

1 tbsp (15 mL) butter

2 cups (480 mL) pecans

2 tbsp (30 mL) brown
   sugar

1 tsp (5 mL) chile powder

1 tsp (5 mL) coriander

1/2 tsp (2.5 mL) paprika

1/2 tsp (2.5 mL) cracked
   pepper

1/4 tsp (1.2 mL) cayenne

3 tbsp (45 mL) apple cider
   vinegar

Melt and foam butter in a skillet. Add pecans and stir to coat. Cook for 5 min. Stir in the brown sugar and let it melt; then add all of the spices and stir well to coat. Deglaze the pan with vinegar and cook until the liquid evaporates. Transfer the nuts to a parchment-lined baking pan and roast in a 300°F oven for 5–10 min.

wil**ted**spinach**salad**

with olives, feta and garlic-balsamic vinaigrette

lunch crowds at **re**bar love this salad. The vinaigrette is heated right before serving to wilt the spinach just enough to reduce the volume and soften the leaves. Tossed with creamy feta cheese, olives, fresh mint and toasted pine nuts, this salad has bold flavours, yet is light enough to be a meal in itself. Choose young bunches of smooth-leaved spinach rather than the rough and tough leaves that squeak between your teeth—these are best reserved for cooking.

serves 4

1 Thoroughly combine the first seven ingredients in a bowl. Slowly drizzle in oil, whisking all the while. Correct seasoning to taste.

2 Prepare the remaining salad ingredients. Combine spinach, olives, peppers and onions in a large salad bowl. Just before serving, heat dressing over medium heat in a small pot. When it begins to simmer, remove from the heat and drizzle over the salad while tossing with a pair of tongs. Gently mix in the fresh mint and garnish with pine nuts and feta cheese. Serve immediately.

vinaigrette

(yields 1 cup - 240 mL)

3 garlic cloves, minced

1/4 cup (60 mL) balsamic vinegar

1 tbsp (15 mL) red wine vinegar

1 1/2 tsp (7.5 mL) honey

1 1/2 tsp (7.5 mL) Dijon mustard

1/2 tsp (2.5 mL) salt

1/4 tsp (1.2 mL) cracked pepper

3/4 cup (180 mL) extra virgin olive oil

salad

1 lb (450 g) spinach leaves, washed
   and stemmed

1/4 cup (60 mL) Kalamata olives,
   pitted and chopped

1 red pepper, seeded and julienned

1 red onion, finely julienned

1/4 cup (60 mL) chopped mint

1/4 cup (60 mL) pine nuts, toasted

1/2 cup (120 mL) crumbled feta
   cheese

☯ - a vegan recipe

whole wheat pastry

☯ basic vegetable stock

caramelized onions

☯ polenta

☯ chipotle chile purée

rosemary-garlic foccacia

peanut sauce

☯ cilantro pesto

☯ three ways with tofu

☯ flour tortillas

☯ fresh-cut tomato salsa

☯ tomato-sweet basil sauce

soy-chile sauce

☯ slow roast tomatoes

☯ green curry paste

☯ roasted garlic-rosemary oil

☯ roasted red pepper sauce

☯ **re**barbecue sauce

☯ mesa red sauce

☯ tomatillo-cilantro salsa

2

basics

day in and day out, the restaurant routine involves maintaining a level of consistency and high standards of flavour on which our customers depend. One of the fundamental parts of this routine is the daily preparation of some basic items that we use in a variety of ways. "Mother" sauces such as the "mesa red" are used in many of our Southwestern-inspired dishes. "Cilantro pesto" is used in sandwiches, quesadillas, omelettes and pizzas. We rely heavily on the handful of recipes in this chapter, as will you, when preparing other dishes in the book. We're sure you'll find your own creative ways to use these basics too!

whole**wheat**pastry
for tarts and pies

bakers and cooks seem to be cut from different cloth. The precision, patience and lightness of hand required in handling pastry can often be an exercise in frustration for the knife-wielding cook accustomed to spontanaiety and high action. We've often seen assured cooks fumble and sweat over the prospect of preparing short-crust pastry when out of practise (not to mention any names!). Here is a recipe that bakers claim is "foolproof", perfect for savoury tarts.

makes one 10" tart

1 cup (240 ml) unbleached flour
6 tbsp (90 mL) whole wheat flour
1/4 tsp (1.2 mL) salt
1/4 tsp (1.2 mL) sugar
3 tbsp (45 mL) chilled unsalted butter
4 tbsp (60 mL) vegetable shortening
4 tbsp (60 mL) ice water

1 Combine the first four ingredients in a mixing bowl and stir together. Add the chilled butter and shortening. Using your fingertips, mix gingerly until the fat and flour combine to form a coarse meal. Sprinkle in the ice water and mix until the dough just holds together. Form into a ball, cover with plastic wrap and chill for 30 minutes, or until ready to use.

2 Wipe counter with a lightly damp cloth. Spread a sheet of plastic wrap over the moistened surface to cover an area slightly larger than the intended crust size. Smooth the plastic into place. Position the ball of dough in the center of the plastic and press with your palm to flatten a circle 6" across. Cover the dough with a second sheet of plastic wrap.

3 Roll out the dough in strokes radiating outwards from the center, with even pressure on the rolling pin, to a size slightly larger than the diameter of the tart pan. Gently lift the top sheet of plastic off the dough, and have a tart pan ready by your side. Lift the crust by the bottom sheet and flip the dough upside down, centered onto the pan. The dough should be overlapping all around the sides of the pan.

4 Carefully separate the plastic from the dough and gently press it against the sides. Using your thumb, push the dough all along the edge where the side meets the bottom. Fold the overhang inwards, leaving a double crust along the side and a rounded edge on top. Prick the bottom of the dough with a fork to prevent the crust from puffing up when pre-baking. Bake in the center of a pre-heated 350°F oven for 15 minutes, or until slightly golden.

basicvegetablestock
for soups and sauces ☯

rainy days mark a perfect time to make stock and soup. A steamy, fragrant kitchen warms the soul and the effort yields several days' worth of easy eating. While making soup from scratch often seems like enough of a chore in itself, don't skip the opportunity to make a stock too. This recipe can be assembled in a matter of minutes. The soup that you make with this stock will have depth, body and character unmatched by a water-based soup. Vegetable stocks are more subtle than their meat-based counterparts, therefore top-notch ingredients and attention to seasoning is essential.

yields 14 cups (3.5 L)

1   Peel and roughly chop the onions, leeks, carrots and celery. Separate the garlic bulb and smash the cloves with the flat of your knife. Quarter the apple(s).

2   Heat oil in a large stock pot and add the onions, leeks, carrots, celery, salt and bay leaves. Sauté for 5 minutes, stirring often. Add all of the remaining ingredients, including the water, and bring to a boil. Reduce heat and simmer gently for 45 minutes. Strain and cool if not using immediately. Store in the refrigerator for up to 3 days, or in the freezer for up to 2 months.

1 tbsp (15 mL) vegetable oil
1 yellow onion
2 leeks, greens only
1 garlic bulb
4 carrots
4 celery sticks
1 or 2 apples
4 bay leaves
1 tbsp (15 mL) whole black peppercorns
1 tbsp (15 mL) coriander seeds
1 tbsp (15 mL) coarse salt
few sprigs fresh thyme, parsley and/or sage
20 cups (5 L) cold water

helpfulhint ✳

Avoid these vegetables in your stock: broccoli, cabbages, cauliflower, beets, peppers. Don't use asparagus, unless you're making an asparagus soup. Just about everything else is fair game!

caramelizedonions
with balsamic vinegar and fresh herbs

creamy sweet onions patiently sautéed with butter, olive oil and seasonings add body and richness to a variety of dishes. The extended cooking yields a jam-like mixture that you can use to enrich a pot of soup, spread on sandwiches and pizzas, blend into sauces and vinaigrettes or layer in a baked vegetable gratin. Eaten straight out of the pan, it's pure candy!

yields 1 1/2 cups (360 mL)

1 tbsp (15 mL) butter
1 tbsp (15 mL) olive oil
4 yellow onions, sliced or diced
1 tsp (5 mL) salt
1/2 tbsp (7.5 mL) brown sugar
1/2 cup (120 mL) white wine
   (optional)
1/4 cup (60 mL) vegetable stock
   (p. 35), or water
2 tsp (10 mL) balsamic vinegar
1/4 tsp (1.2 mL) cracked pepper
1 tsp (5 mL) minced fresh thyme,
   sage or rosemary

❂ omit butter and use all olive oil for a vegan version.

1 Heat olive oil and butter over medium heat until the butter begins to foam. Add the onions and stir to coat. Add salt and cook for 20 minutes. Stir occasionally.

2 Sprinkle in the sugar and wine and reduce until the liquid has evaporated. Add stock, vinegar, pepper and herbs. Cook gently until the stock is reduced and the onions reach a creamy texture.

helpfulhint ✳

Everybody has a theory on how to prevent stinging, watery eyes when chopping onions, but few of them ever seem to work. You've probably heard them all ... put onions in the freezer; hold a piece of bread in your mouth; wear swimming goggles; the list goes on. Using a very sharp knife seems to be your best bet, but don't count on it. This may not be a very "helpful" hint after all!

polenta

cornmeal mush in various guises

true that polenta is little more than cooked cornmeal, so why all the fuss you ask? Doctored up with butter, a favourite cheese, fresh herbs and a delicious sauce, polenta is transformed from it's humble origins—an Italian comfort food success story! Soft cooked polenta can be mixed with a strong cheese (gorgonzola), pesto or roasted squash flesh and served as an interesting side dish. We like to spread polenta on a baking sheet until it hardens, then cut out shapes and fry them in olive oil (see the grilled polenta appetizer—p. 60). Cut triangles and layer them with roasted vegetables, cheese and tomato-basil sauce (p. 45) for a hearty casserole. Leftovers can be cubed and fried to make crispy cornmeal croutons for a Southwestern Caesar salad (p. 26). So there you have it, polenta really is so much more than the sum of its parts.

1 Heat water or stock to a boil in a heavy-bottomed saucepan; add salt. Slowly pour cornmeal into the boiling water, stirring constantly with a wooden spoon to avoid lumping. Turn the heat down to low and stir regularly for about 15 minutes, until thickened. (Be aware of spattering during cooking ... the hot polenta smarts when it splashes on your bare hand!)

2 At this point, there are two ways to go with this recipe. To serve immediately as soft polenta, stir in your chosen additions, such as gorgonzola cheese, mashed roasted garlic and fresh herbs, etc. Serve in bowls as a side dish, or top with grilled portabello mushrooms, tomato sauce and more cheese.

3 To make shapes, stir the butter and grated cheese into the hot polenta and spread it out on an oiled baking pan to measure 12" x 12". Smooth the top with a rubber spatula and let the polenta harden for a few hours, or cover and refrigerate overnight. Cut shapes (triangles, circles) to desired size. Sauté cakes in olive oil, or bake in the oven with grated cheese on top. Serve as a side dish, as part of an appetizer, or layered and baked with sauce, cheese and vegetables.

serves 4 - 6

4 cups (960 mL) water, or vegetable stock (p. 35)

1 cup (240 mL) cornmeal

1 tsp (5 mL) salt

2 tbsp (30 mL) butter

1 cup (240 mL) grated Parmigiano-Reggiano or asiago cheese

helpful hint

You can find pre-made polenta in the supermarket, packaged in a ready-to-use sausage-shaped plastic casing. These are quite good quality, come in a variety of flavours and are very handy. Slice them into rounds and follow the directions for the grilled polenta cakes (p. 60). Or spread on an oiled baking sheet and heat in the oven, top with grilled vegetables and fresh tomato sauce for an easy summer meal.

chipotlechilepurée

you'll wonder how you ever lived without it!

smoked jalapeños are commonly known as chipotle chiles. To many cooks, discovering chipotles is akin to being introduced to balsamic vinegar or fresh cilantro. You love the flavour and immediately find yourself using it in almost everything. Soon enough, loved one's chide you for your obsession and, before you know it, you've become the "cook who uses chipotles in EVERYTHING!" Indeed, chipotle chiles are addictive. If you're partial to a little heat in your food, canned chipotle chiles are extremely useful. They are packed in a red "adobo sauce" and can now be found in most well-stocked grocery stores (check the Mexican foods section). Once the can is opened, it will store in the refrigerator for at least a month.

yields 1/2 cup (120 mL)

1 x 7 oz (198 g) can chipotle chiles in
    adobo sauce

1 Purée contents of the can. Transfer to a clean glass jar and refrigerate.

helpfulhint ✳

Add chipotle purée to the following:
- ✳ beaten eggs before scrambling
- ✳ softened butter for corn on the cob
- ✳ stirred into cornbread batter
- ✳ tomato sauce, for pizza or pasta
- ✳ mayonnaise, for sandwiches
- ✳ macaroni & cheese
- ✳ mashed into hummous
- ✳ stirred into squash, bean or corn soups
- ✳ beaten into whipped cream (just kidding!!)

chipotlepicodegallo

2 lbs (900 g) Roma tomatoes, seeded and diced
4 garlic cloves, minced
1/2 small red onion, minced
2 jalapeño peppers, seeded and minced
1 tbsp (15 mL) chipotle purée (p. 38)
1 tsp (5 mL) brown sugar
juice of 1 lime
1/2 bunch fresh cilantro, stemmed and chopped
1/2 tsp (2.5 mL) salt

Combine all of the prepared ingredients in a bowl and mix well. Let stand 30 minutes before serving. Season to taste and serve.

rosemarygarlicfoccacia

addictive savoury flatbread 🌿

until recently, foccacia was an exotic Italian loaf that you may have stumbled upon in your travels or while enjoying a meal at **re**bar. We've been serving baskets of oven-fresh foccacia, loaded with fresh garlic, rosemary and cracked pepper for over a decade now, and we're still not tired of it. Indeed, some of our staff seem to subsist on a strict foccacia diet. We actually use it to help customers locate our restaurant in downtown Victoria. It's not a very big city, so when the air starts to fill with the aroma of garlic, just follow your nose and you'll end up at our doorstep! This bread is a perfect project for a beginner baker. It's as simple as making pizza dough (in fact, we use it for all of our pizza recipes).

1 In a large mixing bowl, combine the warm water, yeast and sugar. Let the mixture sit until it foams. Stir in salt and olive oil, then start adding flour, one cup at a time, beating well with a wooden spoon. When you can no longer stir, turn the dough out onto a floured surface and knead in the remaining flour. Knead the dough until smooth and elastic, sprinkling just enough flour on the counter to prevent sticking.

2 Form the dough into a ball and place in a large, lightly oiled bowl. Cover with a clean, damp cloth and set the bowl in a warm, draft-free spot. Let rise until doubled in bulk (1–1 1/2 hrs.) Punch the dough down and let it rise again until doubled.

3 Pre-heat the oven to 350°F. Place the dough on a well-oiled 12" x 16" baking sheet with 1/2" sides. Gently stretch the dough to roughly fit the dimensions of the pan. Drizzle the surface with oilve oil and spread the minced garlic over the entire area. Sprinkle chopped rosemary evenly over top, followed by coarse salt. Finish with cracked pepper. Using your fingertips, gently poke indentations over the entire surface. It should appear dimpled and rustic-looking. Let rise again for about 15 minutes, or just until it puffs up slightly.

4 Place the loaf in the center rack of the oven. Bake for 20 minutes, rotating the pan halfway through. The garlic should be lightly golden. Be careful not to overbake. Serve warm.

yields one 10" x 16" loaf

1 3/4 cups (420 mL) warm water
1 tbsp (15 mL) traditional baking yeast
1/2 tsp (2.5 mL) sugar
2 tsp (10 mL) salt
1/4 cup (60 mL) olive oil
4 cups (960 mL) unbleached flour

topping

4–6 garlic cloves, minced
4 tbsp (60 mL) olive oil
2 tsp (10 mL) coarse salt
2 tbsp (30 mL) chopped rosemary
cracked black pepper

helpfulhint ✳

Once you're comfortable with this classic combination, experiment with other delicious toppings:
✳ caramelized onions, fresh sage
✳ chopped olives, sundried tomatoes
✳ roasted garlic cloves, asiago cheese
✳ balsamic shallots (p. 156) and fresh marjoram

peanutsauce
with ginger, lime and cilantro

intense flavours in this dynamic sauce give new life to a simple bowl of steamed rice and vegetables. Toss with chilled noodles and crisp vegetables and you have an instant lunch, or use as a dipping sauce for salad rolls. Either way, use this sauce sparingly and feel free to tamper with the proportions in the recipe. More heat, less ginger and no cilantro may be more up your alley. This recipe multiplies nicely.

☯ replace honey with brown sugar for a vegan sauce.

yield 3/4 cup (180 mL)

1/4 cup (60 mL) smooth, natural
   peanut butter
2 garlic cloves, minced
1 tbsp (15 mL) minced ginger
2 tbsp (30 mL) honey
1/4 cup (60 mL) minced cilantro
   leaves
juice of 1 lime
1 tbsp (15 mL) sesame oil
1 tsp (5 mL) sambal oelek
1/4 cup (60 mL) soy sauce
2 tbsp (30 mL) rice wine vinegar

1 In the bowl of a food processor or blender, add all of the ingredients from the garlic through to the sambal oelek. Blend until smooth. Add the remaining ingredients, blend and season to taste.

2 This sauce can also be made by hand, using a bowl and whisk or wooden spoon. Blending the peanut butter with the other ingredients may require some elbow grease. To help it along, try gently heating the peanut butter to make it a little bit runny and easier to stir.

helpful hint ❋

This sauce will stiffen up considerably in the fridge. Adjust the consistency by stirring in a little warm water, stock or coconut milk. Or heat the sauce gently on the stove (or in the microwave) until it loosens up.

cilantro**pesto**

with pepitas, jalapeño peppers and asiago

twist around the elements of the classic Italian recipe and presto—a Southwestern pesto! Cilantro replaces basil, pumpkin seeds stand in for pine nuts, and asiago takes over for Parmesan cheese. At the restaurant, we use this pesto in a variety of dishes, including lasagna Rio Grande (p. 180), eggs, pasta, pizza (p. 189) and sandwiches (p. 110) ... a cilantro lover's dream come true!

☯ replace cheese with 1/4 cup (60 mL) pepitas (vegan).

1 Carefully wash the cilantro in plenty of cool water to remove clinging dirt. Shake off excess water, cut off the stem ends and lay out on paper towels to dry, or spin in a salad spinner.

2 Combine all of the ingredients, except the oil, in the bowl of a food processor or blender. Pulse several times to coarsely chop everything. Continue to pulse while slowly drizzling in the oil. Season to taste and store covered in the refrigerator for up to 3 days, or freeze up to one month.

yields 1 1/4 cups (300 mL)

2 bunches cilantro
1/2 cup (120 mL) pumpkin seeds, toasted
1/2 jalapeño pepper, chopped with seeds
2 garlic cloves
1 tbsp (15 mL) fresh lime juice
1/4 cup (60 mL) grated Parmesan or asiago cheese
1/4 tsp (1.2 mL) salt
1/4 cup (60 mL) olive oil

helpful**hint** ✳

Toasted pumpkin seeds, or pepitas, are very flavourful, healthy and simple to prepare. For small amounts, a hot skillet works best. Keep moving the seeds around in the pan to prevent burning and remove them after they begin to pop and turn golden.

threewayswithtofu ☯

despite the popularity of tofu in recent years, it's still common to hear people say that they don't know what to do with it. Here are a few ideas. Always begin by pressing the tofu, which squeezes out any excess water and makes room for a marinade to soak in. To press, place the tofu block on a plate, cover with another plate and place a weight on top, like a can of tomatoes or a brick. Leave for one hour and drain off the extra water. Now you're ready to begin!

anchochilelime marinade

1 block x-firm tofu
juice of 1 lime
zest of 1/2 lime
2 tbsp (30 mL) oil
2 garlic cloves, minced
2 tbsp (30 mL) soy sauce
2 tbsp (30 mL) ancho chile powder
1/2 tsp (2.5 mL) ground coriander
1 tsp (5 mL) chipotle purée (p. 38)

Cut tofu into slices 2" long x 1/2" wide. Combine remaining ingredients in a small pot and bring to a boil; simmer 5 minutes. Pour hot marinade over tofu slices. Cover and refrigerate overnight. Pour off the marinade and bake for 15 minutes in a 350°F oven. Baste with reserved marinade.

thaibasilsoymarinade

2 blocks firm tofu
1/4 cup (60 mL) light soy
2 tbsp (30 mL) dark soy
2/3 cup (160 mL) vegetable stock (p. 35), or water
2 tbsp (30 mL) lime juice
1 tbsp (15 mL) minced ginger
2 garlic cloves, minced
1 tsp (5 mL) sambal oelek
2 oz (60 g) palm sugar
1/4 tsp (1.2 mL) cracked pepper
1/4 cup (60 mL) Thai basil, chopped

Slice each tofu block in half so that you have two thinner slabs. Combine the remaining ingredients, except basil, in a pot and heat to a simmer. Cook 5 minutes. Add basil and pour sauce over tofu slices. Marinade for up to 8 hours. Pour off the sauce and reserve. Grill or bake tofu, using the sauce as a baste, or to season a vegetable stir-fry.

sesamebakedtofu

1 block x-firm tofu
1 tbsp (15 mL) sesame oil
2 tbsp (30 mL) soy sauce
1/4 tsp (1.2 mL) cracked pepper

Cut tofu into 1/2" cubes. Toss with remaining ingredients, spread on an oiled baking sheet and bake at 350°F for 15 minutes.

flourtortillas ☯

hand-rolled

and hot off the grill, fresh tortillas bear little resemblance to store-bought. The only shared trait is that they're round. These are simple to make (much less complicated than bread) and, most of the time you'll spend on this recipe is dedicated to resting the dough, which lets you carry on with other tasks. The resulting tortillas are tender, light and melt in your mouth.

yields 10 - 12 tortillas

1 1/2 cups (360 mL) unbleached flour
1/2 cup (120 mL) whole wheat flour
1 tsp (5 mL) white sugar
1 1/2 tsp (7.5 mL) baking powder
1 tsp (5 mL) salt
5 tbsp (75 mL) vegetable shortening
3/4 cup (180 mL) hot water

1 In a large bowl, mix together the flours, sugar, baking powder and salt. Using the tips of your fingers, add shortening by working it into the dry mix until little pea-sized balls form. Gradually add hot water while using your other hand to mix with a wooden spoon. When the dough is too stiff to mix with a spoon, reach in with your hands and gently knead for 2 minutes. Shape into a ball, place in a clean bowl and cover with plastic wrap. Let rest for at least 1 hour.

2 Next, line a baking tray or dish with parchment paper, sprinkle with flour and set aside. Uncover the dough and pinch off golf ball-sized pieces (1½ oz – 45 g). Roll the dough in your palms to form smooth spheres. Dust lightly with flour, set on parchment paper and cover loosely with plastic. Repeat with remaining dough. Set the tray aside, covered, to rest for another hour.

3 When you are ready to roll and cook, lightly sprinkle flour on the counter and set a ball of dough in the center, pressing lightly to flatten. Roll the disk out with a floured rolling pin, working from the center and rolling outwards to the edges, to form an 8" round. Repeat with remaining dough and stack tortillas between sheets of wax or parchment paper.

4 Heat a cast iron pan or non-stick skillet over medium-high heat. Brush lightly with oil and cook tortilla on the first side until you see bubbles forming underneath. Flip over and cook until lightly golden. Wrap in foil and keep in a warm oven until all of the tortillas are cooked. Serve immediately!

freshcuttomatosalsa

salsa fresca

party food at **re**bar get-togethers always includes this lively salsa. At the restaurant, we make large batches regularly to serve with huevos rancheros, almond burgers and to garnish just about anything requiring a shot of vivid colour and fresh flavour, such as black bean soup. Made with garden tomatoes in the dog days of summer, this salsa is fantastic. In the off-season, we prefer to use Roma tomatoes. You'll find even winter Romas will surprise you with late summer flashbacks once they're combined with cilantro, chiles, crisp onion and fresh lime juice.

yields 3 cups (720 mL)

6 tomatoes, finely diced
1 jalapeño pepper, minced
1/2 small red onion, minced
1/3 bunch cilantro, stemmed and finely
     chopped
juice of 1 lime
1 tsp (5 mL) brown sugar
1/2 tsp (2.5 mL) salt, or more to taste

1 Combine all of the ingredients in a bowl and stir together gently but thoroughly. Transfer into a festive bowl and serve, or cover and refrigerate for up to 2 days.

2 Alternately, use a food processor and pulse the onion, garlic and chiles until chopped. Add quartered tomatoes and remaining ingredients; pulse again to get the consistency that you like. Season to taste.

cherrytomatosalsa

1 pint cherry tomatoes, red, yellow or both
1 garlic clove, minced
3 scallions, greens only, minced
1 tbsp (15 mL) balsamic vinegar
2 tbsp (30 mL) chopped fresh basil
salt and cracked pepper to taste

Slice cherry tomatoes into quarters. Toss with remaining ingredients, season to taste and serve with eggplant rollatini (p. 59), buckwheat crêpes (p. 192), or Tuscan white bean soup (p. 139).

tomatosweetbasilsauce

divine aromas permeate the kitchen when you make this sauce. Simply sweating the onions and garlic in olive oil is enough to attract curious admirers. "What are you cooking? It smells SO good!" is the reaction of floor staff passing through the kitchen, pausing to peer into the pot. "It's only onions and garlic, just wait ...", I start to say as they hustle on. This sauce is in no hurry and a long simmer will give rewarding results. Toss with freshly cooked pasta or use as a base for pizza and lasagna. Spoon onto a bowl of gnocchi and dust with freshly grated Parmesan for an elegant, comforting meal.

1 Heat olive oil in a medium saucepan over medium heat, add onions and sauté until lightly golden, stirring often to prevent over-browning. Add the garlic, bay leaves, salt and red chile flakes. Stir and sauté gently for an additional 15 minutes. If using wine, add it now and let the liquid reduce by half.

2 Add the canned tomatoes to the onion sauté. Using a wooden spoon, break up the whole tomatoes roughly. Chop the basil leaves and add them to the pot, along with the cracked pepper. Let the sauce come to a gentle simmer, partly cover and continue simmering for at least 30 minutes.

3 At some point during simmering, taste the sauce and correct the seasonings with salt and pepper. If you find the sauce too tart, add a little bit of brown sugar. If you prefer a thicker sauce, add a few tablespoons of canned tomato paste. To thin the sauce out, add more wine or vegetable stock.

yields 6 cups (1.5 L)

2 tbsp (30 mL) extra virgin olive oil
1 small yellow onion, diced
6 garlic cloves, minced
2 bay leaves
pinch of red chile flakes
2 tsp (10 mL) salt
1/2 tsp (2.5 mL) cracked pepper
2 tbsp (30 mL) full-bodied red wine
   (optional)
1 x 28 fl.oz (796 mL) can organic
   diced tomatoes
1 x 28 fl oz (796 mL) can organic
   whole tomatoes
1 oz (30 g) fresh basil
1 tsp (5 mL) brown sugar

helpfulhint ✳

In late summer/early fall, be sure to visit a local farm market to purchase a box of vine-ripe local tomatoes. Make a big batch of this sauce (substitute 12–15 fresh tomatoes per recipe) and freeze it. Come the dead of winter, the fragrance of summer's bounty will make you swoon!

soychilesauce

a careful balance of salty, spicy and sweet flavours makes good
Asian sauces indispensable. Store-bought sauces are often too sweet and are rarely
sufficiently spicy. This sauce is extremely easy to make and will last in your fridge for up
to ten days. Use it in stir-fries, as a marinade for tofu or meats, or to drizzle on steamed
vegetables. It also makes a handy seasoning for Asian soups and noodle bowls that
require that final nudge towards perfection.

yields 2 1/4 cups (560 mL)

3 garlic cloves, minced
1/2 tsp (2.5 mL) red chile flakes
1 tbsp (15 mL) sesame oil
1 tbsp (15 mL) vegetable oil
3/4 cup (180 mL) soy sauce
3/4 cup (180 mL) vegetable stock
   (p. 35), or water
1/4 cup (60 mL) honey
2 tsp (10 mL) cornstarch, whisked
   with 1/2 cup (120 mL) water

☯ replace honey with brown sugar for a vegan sauce.

1 Gently heat the oils in a small pot until a piece of garlic sizzles.
Add the garlic and chile flakes and sauté until the garlic starts
to turn golden. Whisk in the soy sauce and stock or water
and bring the mixture to a simmer.

2 Stir in the honey and bring the sauce to a gentle boil. Slowly
whisk in the cornstarch/water slurry. Simmer 5 minutes, or until
slightly thickened and glossy. Cool and refrigerate for up to
one week.

helpfulhint ✳

Heating cooking oils until they smoke
releases free radicals which are harmful to
your health. Sesame oil has a very low
smoking point, meaning it will burn at temperatures lower than most cooking oils. For
this reason, toasted sesame oil is generally
not used for cooking, but as a flavouring or
condiment. To raise the smoking point of
sesame oil, mix with equal parts vegetable oil
and heat it over low-medium heat.

soycitrusglaze

1/2 cup (120 mL) soy sauce
juice of 1 lime or orange
1/2 tsp (2.5 mL) lime zest, or orange zest
2 tbsp (30 mL) brown sugar
1 tbsp (15 mL) minced ginger
Combine all of the ingredients in a small pot and
bring to a boil over medium heat. Reduce heat and
simmer gently for 10 minutes. Let cool. Strain and
use to drizzle on savoury vegetable pancakes (p.
65), brush on salmon, tofu or grilled vegetables.

slowroasttomatoes ☯

patience is all you need to follow this recipe. The slow-roast drying method results in a tomato that falls somewhere between fresh and sundried. Low temperatures caramelize the natural sugars and concentrate the fresh tomato essence with a subtle perfume of fresh herbs and pure olive oil. You'll discover as many uses for these as for fresh tomatoes. They're perfect as part of a winter antipasto plate with spicy Sicilian olives, white bean hummous and crostini (p. 66), arranged on a bed of peppery arugula leaves. Or toss them in a pasta with garlic-braised rapini, chick peas, a splash of fresh lemon juice and grated Parmesan. For lunch, tuck them in a sandwich with a nice sharp cheese, pickled peppers and greens.

1 Pre-heat oven to 250°F. Slice tomatoes in half and arrange, cut side up, on a parchment-lined baking tray. Brush lightly with olive oil and sprinkle with salt, pepper and chopped fresh herbs.

2 Roast tomatoes for up to 4 hours, or until they are visibly dehydrated yet still meaty. Cool and refrigerate for up to one week.

yields 1 cup (240 mL)

10 tomatoes, halved
1/4 cup (60 mL) extra virgin olive oil
1 tsp (5 mL) salt
1/4 tsp (1.2 mL) cracked pepper
2 tbsp (30 mL) minced thyme or
    rosemary

helpful**hint** ✳

If you have a barbecue or smoker, try smoking tomatoes. The fabulous smoky flavour of mesquite or alder, brings a whole new dimension to tomato soups and sauces.

greencurrypaste

for Thai coconut curries

monk's curry (p. 184) is one of our most popular menu items and this fresh curry paste is the main reason. A classic Thai combination of freshly roasted spices, green chiles, cilantro and lemongrass beats the packaged curry pastes hands down. Adding coconut milk helps to temper the heat and makes a great sauce for vegetable, seafood and chicken dishes. The paste can also be used sparingly to flavour soups.

yields 1 1/2 cups (360 mL)

1 tbsp (15 mL) whole coriander

2 tsp (10 mL) cumin seed

2 tsp (10 mL) black peppercorns

4 garlic cloves

1 oz (30 g) ginger or galangal

1/2 cup (120 mL) chopped shallots

2 jalapeño peppers, with seeds

2 lemongrass stalks

4 scallions

1/2 tsp (2.5 mL) red chile flakes

1 bunch cilantro

juice of 1 lime

1 tbsp (15 mL) salt

1/2 cup (120 mL) peanut oil

1　Toast the coriander, cumin and peppercorns in a hot, dry skillet until fragrant. Cool and grind to a fine powder.

2　Slice off the root ends and the top two-thirds of the lemongrass stalks. Peel away the outer layer of the remaining bottom pieces and discard the trimmings. Roughly chop the lemongrass. Combine all of the ingredients, including the ground spices, in a food processor. Pulse several times and stop to scrape down the sides. Purée to a smooth paste. Transfer to a clean jar and refrigerate until ready to use.

helpful hint ✳

Galangal is a root related to ginger used in Southeast Asian cooking. It's sweet, highly fragrant flavour adds a delicious twist to curries and soups. It can be bought frozen in most Chinese markets, and grated straight out of the freezer. If you live in a large city with a sizeable Chinatown, you may be lucky enough to find it fresh.

roastedgarlicrosemaryoil ☙

infused oils have many uses. Try this one tossed with pasta, brushed on grilled vegetables, drizzled over mashed potatoes or as a dip for fresh bread. We use it to garnish a roasted garlic hummous on our appetizer menu. It keeps the surface from drying out and adds great flavour. This recipe also makes a delicious base for a vinaigrette.

1 Pre-heat oven to 350°F. Place garlic cloves in a small baking dish with sides and pour the olive oil over top. Cover securely with aluminum foil and place in the oven. Roast until golden, soft and aromatic (about 20 minutes). Remove from the oven and stir in the rosemary and salt.

2 Let cool to room temperature and refrigerate for one day.

3 Leave the oil at room temperature until it liquifies and pour it through a cheesecloth-lined sieve to strain out the solids. Keep refrigerated for up to one week.

yields 1 cup (240 mL)

2 garlic bulbs, cloves separated and peeled
1 cup (240 mL) olive oil
3 tbsp (45 mL) rosemary leaves, roughly chopped
1/2 tsp (2.5 mL) salt

helpfulhint ✳

Don't waste the leftover garlic that you've roasted. Drain off the oil, mash into a paste, store in the refrigerator and use to flavour mashed potatoes, soups, sauces or dressings. Or just spread it on bread, like butter!

basiloil

1 cup (240 ml) olive oil
1/2 cup fresh basil leaves, tightly packed
1/2 tsp (2.5 ml) salt

Bring a small pot of water to a rapid boil. Submerge basil leaves for 15 seconds. Strain and plunge leaves into a bowl of ice water. After half a minute, remove the leaves with a slotted spoon and transfer to drain on a clean, dry kitchen towel. In the bowl of a food processor or blender, purée the basil leaves and salt while slowly drizzling in oil. Transfer to a glass jar and let rest for 24 hours. Line a fine mesh sieve with a layer of cheesecloth and strain the basil oil.

roasted**red**pepper~~sauce~~

jazz up your presentation with this vibrant, great tasting sauce. At the restaurant, we put it into a squeeze bottle and use it like paint to liven up plates. It also tastes great, so try it on eggs, swirl it onto soups, toss with pasta, drizzle on shrimp-corn cakes (p. 61), or use as a baste for grilled chicken. To make a yellow pepper sauce, replace red with yellow peppers, white with red onion and omit the chipotle chiles.

yields 3/4 cup (180 mL)

1 large red pepper, roasted, peeled
   and seeded (p. 50)
1 garlic clove
1/4 small red onion, chopped
1 tbsp (15 mL) fresh lime juice
1 tsp (5 mL) chipotle purée (p. 38)
1/2 tsp (2.5 mL) salt
1/2 cup (120 mL) vegetable oil

1 Thoroughly purée all ingredients, except the oil, in a food processor or blender. Gradually drizzle in the oil while the motor is running.

2 Set a fine-mesh sieve over a small bowl. Using a rubber spatula, scrape the sauce from the processor and strain it through the sieve. Use the bottom of a ladle to help push it through, applying pressure and using a circular motion. Discard the solids and refrigerate the purée up to 3 days.

helpful**hint** ✳

When using cheesecloth to strain a liquid, wet it first, squeeze it out and then line your sieve. This will help prevent the cloth from slipping during straining.

roasted**peppers**

4 sweet peppers (or chiles)
There are 3 ways to roast peppers, depending on your equipment—a barbecue, gas stove or regular oven, in order of desirability. On the flame of a barbecue or gas stove, roast the peppers whole until the skins are charred and blistered, using a set of tongs to turn the pepper over to expose all surfaces. Transfer peppers to a bowl and cover with plastic wrap for 10 minutes. Remove wrap, cool slightly and peel away the seared skin. To oven roast, pre-heat oven to 400°F. Halve and seed the peppers. Place them cut-side down on an oiled or parchment-lined baking sheet and roast until the skins puff up and blister (about 15 minutes). Proceed as with flame-roasted peppers.

rebarbecue**sauce** ☯

baste grilled foods, dip or season with this sweet and fiery sauce. Stir it into hot beans, use as a dip for roasted yams or potatoes (p. 157), or whisk into soups and sauces that are begging for some sweet heat. Multiply the recipe and give away bottles to friends and relatives. Take some along to your next barbecue party. It makes a great baste for chicken, ribs and veggie burgers too!

yields 2 cups (480 mL)

1. Combine vinegar and whole spices in a small pot and bring to a boil. Reduce heat and simmer until the liquid is reduced by half (15 minutes). Strain out the solids and cool.

2. Meanwhile, heat oil in a skillet and sauté the onion until golden, adding garlic halfway through. Sprinkle sugar into the pan and when it melts, add all of the remaining ingredients, including the vinegar. Bring mixture to a simmer and cook for 20 minutes, or until the sauce is thick and glossy. Season to taste.

3. Cool and purée the sauce until smooth. Refrigerate for up to 3 weeks.

1 cup (240 mL) apple cider vinegar
1 tsp (5 mL) coriander seeds
1 tsp (5 mL) mustard seeds
1 1/2 tsp (7.5 mL) whole cloves
4 allspice berries
4 cardamom pods
2 tbsp (30 mL) vegetable oil
1 medium yellow onion, diced
2 garlic cloves, minced
1/3 cup (80 mL) brown sugar, firmly
   packed
2 tbsp (30 mL) molasses
2 tbsp (30 mL) soy sauce
2 tbsp (30 mL) chipotle purée (p. 38),
   or more to taste
1 x 5 1/2 oz (196 mL) can tomato paste
1 bottle dark beer

helpful**hint** ✳

Store whole spices in 250 mL jelly Mason jars kept in a dark cupboard. You can see what is inside them and it's easy to scoop out what you need with a measuring spoon.

mesa**red**sauce

a mother sauce ☯

authentic Mexican flavour makes this sauce invaluable to our Southwestern fetish at **re**bar. This "mother" sauce is ideal with huevos, quesadillas, enchiladas, Mexican poached eggs and so much more. We spent several years pursuing the perfect sauce, and eventually discovered that masa harina was the missing link—it thickens the sauce while imparting an unmistakeable essence of the South.

yields 4 cups (960 mL)

2 tbsp (30 mL) vegetable oil
1/2 yellow onion, diced
6 garlic cloves, minced
4 tbsp (60 mL) masa harina
4 tbsp (60 mL) ancho chile powder
1/2 tsp (2.5 mL) ground cumin
1/4 tsp (1.2 mL) cayenne powder
1 tsp (5 mL) salt
1/2 tsp (2.5 mL) cracked pepper
1 tbsp (15 mL) minced oregano
4 cups (960 mL) vegetable stock
   (p. 35) or water, heated
2 tbsp (30 mL) tomato paste
1 tsp (5 mL) brown sugar

1 Heat vegetable oil in a saucepan over medium-high heat. Add onions and sauté until translucent. Add garlic and cook 3 minutes. Sprinkle in the masa harina and stir constantly as it cooks and turns golden.

2 Add the spices and oregano and stir for another 2 minutes. Slowly whisk in the warm vegetable stock and bring to a boil. Reduce to a simmer and whisk in the tomato paste and sugar.

3 Simmer partially covered for 30 minutes, stirring regularly. Season to taste.

helpful**hint** ✳

Be on the lookout for ancho and a range of pure chile powders at your nearest Mexican market. The generic supermarket variety is loaded with salt and other ingredients that mask the clean chile taste. The difference will not go unnoticed, particularly if you love Southwestern cuisine as much as we do!

tomatillocilantrosalsa
salsa verde 😊

green husked tomatillos are often mistaken as kin to the tomato. They are in fact related to the gooseberry, which would be immediately evident if you took a bite of a raw tomatillo (sour!). This recipe uses canned tomatillos because they are easy to find and convenient to use. Perhaps better known as salsa verde, this tangy emerald sauce is a great finishing touch for any Mexican dish. At **re**bar we spoon it on enchiladas, quesadillas, poached eggs, fajitas, Southwestern lasagna and even as a dip for nachos.

1. Heat oil in a small skillet over medium-high heat. Add onion and sauté until translucent. Add garlic, salt and chiles and sauté until the garlic is lightly golden. Remove from heat and let the mixture cool.

2. Prepare the remaining ingredients and combine them in the bowl of a food processor along with the cooled onion mixture. Pulse to desired consistency. Season to taste and serve within 3 days.

yields 2 cups (480 mL)

2 tbsp (30 mL) vegetable oil
1/2 small yellow onion, minced
2 garlic cloves, minced
1/4 tsp (1.2 mL) salt
3 jalapeño peppers, seeded and chopped
24 oz (680 g) can tomatillos, drained
2 tbsp (30 mL) chopped cilantro
1 tbsp (15 mL) fresh lime juice
1 tsp (5 mL) sugar
1 tsp (5 mL) salt

helpful hint ✻

If you are fortunate enough to come across fresh tomatillos at the market, you can use them for this recipe, and get the best results. Remove the husks, give them a light rub down with oil and broil them on a tray until they are slightly charred and collapsed. Proceed with the recipe.

 – a vegan recipe

bruschetta romesco
 eggplant and tofu satay
Chimayo chile popcorn
eggplant rollatini
grilled polenta cakes
shrimp-corn cakes
 oven-baked spring rolls
 shiitake-tofu potstickers
mango-shrimp salad rolls
savoury vegetable pancakes
 white bean hummous
arugula, chèvre & fig pizzette
baked chiles rellenos
the **re**bar appetizer

3

starters

part of the fun of having friends over for dinner is drawing out the evening with food and drink—serving multi-course meals that progress from salads through to dessert. This offers plenty of room for kitchen play, either all on your own, or by collective effort. The recipes in this chapter are a handful of popular starters seen on our menus over the years. However there's really no need to relegate these dishes to the starter course. "Oven baked spring rolls" and "mango-shrimp salad rolls" make great appetizers to introduce an Asian meal, but they are just as well suited to feeding crowds of hungry people at a party or buffet table. Other dishes, such as the "savoury vegetable pancakes" and "eggplant-tofu satay" can double as a main course with the addition of side dishes. Some of the others would make an ideal light lunch. It's up to you!

bruschetta**romesco**
with roasted eggplant and gorgonzola cheese

kick off a dinner party or a wine tasting with these rich and tasty bruschetta. Romesco is a pesto-like sauce, thickened with nuts and fried bread, originating in the Catalan region of Spain. It goes particularly well with roasted eggplant and the assertive bite of gorgonzola. This sauce has other great uses too. We feature it in an omelette in the brunch section, and it's also great as a dip for vegetables, a sandwich spread or tossed with pasta.

serves 10 - 12 @ 2 each

◔ omit the gorgonzola cheese for a vegan dish.

romesco sauce

1 slice sourdough bread, crust removed
2 tbsp (30 mL) olive oil
2 red peppers, roasted (p. 50)
2 tbsp (30 mL) sliced almonds, toasted
2 tbsp (30 mL) pine nuts, toasted
2 garlic cloves, peeled
1/2 tsp (2.5 mL) paprika
1/4 tsp (1.2 mL) cayenne
1 tbsp (15 mL) balsamic or red wine
    vinegar
1/2 cup (120 mL) extra virgin olive oil
1/2 bunch Italian parsley, chopped
1/4 cup (60 mL) chopped mint
1/2 tsp (2.5 mL) cracked pepper
1/2 tsp (2.5 mL) salt

bruschetta

1 medium globe eggplant
3 tbsp (45 mL) olive oil
1/2 tsp (2.5 mL) salt
1/4 tsp (1.2 mL) cracked pepper
1 tbsp (15 mL) balsamic vinegar
1 cup (240 mL) gorgonzola cheese,
    crumbled
2 baguettes, sourdough or multigrain

1 Begin by preparing the romesco sauce. Cut the bread into cubes. Heat olive oil in a skillet and add the bread cubes. Sauté until the bread is golden and crispy.

2 In the bowl of a food processor, combine the toasted bread, roasted peppers, almonds, pine nuts, garlic, paprika and cayenne powder. Pulse to combine. Add the remaining ingredients and pulse again to mix, being careful not to purée the sauce entirely (it should have some texture). Season the sauce to taste and set aside while you prepare the other ingredients, or refrigerate up to 3 days.

3 Heat the oven to 350°F. Cut the eggplant into 1/2"– 3/4" cubes. Toss with olive oil, salt and pepper and spread on a parchment-lined baking sheet. Bake until soft and golden (15 minutes). Toss eggplant with balsamic vinegar when it emerges from the oven. Meanwhile, cut the baguette into 1/2" thick slices. Brush with olive oil, arrange on a baking tray and toast in the oven for 5 minutes.

4 To serve, spread a generous amount of romesco sauce on each of the toasts, arrange eggplant cubes and crumble cheese over top. The recipe can be prepared to this point up to 2 hours in advance. Arrange on a baking sheet and pop in the oven for 5 minutes, or until the cheese is melted. Serve hot.

eggplant and tofu satay
with lemon-miso glaze ☯

memorable dining experiences in Seattle, specifically at the fabulous Wild Ginger, inspired this dish. A meal there invariably begins with a much-needed drink and a choice of satay appetizers to ward off thirst and hunger pangs brought on by so much shopping! This recipe is for those long stretches of time when we're too busy for a weekend frolic across the border. Serve these with a sake martini, or as a main course with shiitake-brown rice pilaf (p. 149) and wok-fried Asian greens.

1 Prepare the glaze by whisking together the first eight ingredients in a small bowl. Set aside for 1 hour, then strain through a sieve to remove the solids. Next, cut pressed tofu into 1-inch cubes. Arrange them in a single layer in a shallow dish with sides. Pour half of the glaze over the tofu, toss to coat and marinate in the fridge for at least 1 hour, preferably overnight.

2 Slice eggplants into 1/2" thick coins and pour remaining glaze over the eggplant. Toss to coat and let marinate for 30 min.

3 To assemble, pre-heat the grill or oven to 375°F. Thread 4 cubes of tofu per skewer, leaving a bit of space between each cube. Thread 4 or 5 eggplant coins on remaining skewers. Reserve glaze for basting. If oven-baking, arrange the skewers on an oiled baking sheet and bake for 20 minutes, or until the eggplant and tofu are golden and cooked through. Halfway through baking, turn the skewers over and baste. Serve hot and use leftover glaze for dipping.

serves 4

1 tbsp (15 mL) minced lemon zest

2 tbsp (30 mL) miso, genmai or shiro

3 tbsp (45 mL) fresh lemon juice

1/2 cup (120 mL) soy sauce

2 tsp (10 mL) sesame oil

4 tbsp (60 mL) brown sugar

2 tsp (10 mL) minced ginger

1 tbsp (15 mL) wasabi powder

1 block extra firm tofu, pressed and drained (p. 42)

2 Japanese eggplant

8 bamboo skewers

helpful hint ✳

Soak bamboo skewers in cool water for 30 minutes before using. This will prevent them from splintering and burning when exposed to the high temperatures of the grill or oven.

Chimayochilepopcorn

with garlic-sage butter

bowls of popcorn at the dinner table are not exactly customary but they actually make a great appetizer before a casual meal—it's not filling, so it won't spoil your dinner. Of course plain ol' popcorn just won't do, but this spicy, garlicky version, with a hint of sage and enriched with butter and nutritional yeast is enough to get the tastebuds going and crying for more. It's a perfect snack food too—wash it down with an icy brew.

serves 4 - 6

1/2 cup (120 mL) popcorn
1/4 cup (60 mL) butter
2 garlic cloves, minced
2 tsp (10 mL) Chimayo chile powder
2 tsp (10 mL) dried sage leaves,
   crumbled
1/8 tsp (.5 mL) cayenne
1/2 tsp (2.5 mL) salt, or more to taste
2 tbsp (30 mL) "Red Star" nutritional
   yeast (optional)

1 Pop popcorn in an hot-air popper or on the stovetop. Meanwhile heat butter over very low heat in a small saucepan. Add garlic and simmer the butter and garlic very slowly for a couple of minutes. Add the chile powder, sage and cayenne and continue to simmer for another minute. By now your popcorn should be popped and warm.

2 Slowly drizzle in the melted butter mix into the popcorn while stirring with the other hand. Scrape any remaining mix into the popcorn with a rubber spatula. Add salt and yeast, if using, and stir everything up thoroughly, so that all of the kernels are well coated. Season to taste and serve right away!

eggplantrollatini
with ricotta, mint and arugula

versatile eggplants are a mainstay of the vegetarian diet, due to their bulk and ability to assume many guises. In this recipe, eggplant "planks" are roasted, cooled and filled. As an appetizer, serve rollatini drizzled with balsamic syrup (p. 60) and fresh basil oil (p. 49). For an outdoor summer lunch, garnish rollatini with cherry tomato-basil salsa (p. 44) and serve with cool tabbouleh salad (p. 22). Warmed in the oven, they make a unique entrée served with tomato-basil sauce (p. 45), cracked wheat pilaf (p. 159) and braised rapini with lemon and garlic. Wow, what more could you ask from just one recipe?!

yields 8 - 10 rolls

1 Pre-heat the oven to 375°F. Slice away the stem ends from the eggplants. Cut each lengthwise into 1/4" to 1/3" thick slices. You should end up with at least six long "planks" from each eggplant. Brush both sides of each slice with olive oil and place on an oiled or parchment-lined baking sheet. Season with salt and pepper and roast for 20 minutes, or until the eggplants are tender. Remove from the oven and cool.

2 While the eggplant bakes, combine the cheeses, mint, salt and pepper and mix well. Set aside. Slice each roasted pepper into six long strips. Wash, stem and dry the arugula leaves.

3 To assemble, place an eggplant plank in front of you, with the narrow end closest to you. Place a pepper strip along the narrow bottom. Spread 2 tbsp (30 mL) cheese mix over the pepper strip. Next, lay two arugula leaves over the cheese, in opposite directions so that the stems face inward and the leafy ends hang over the outside edges. Carefully lift the end of the eggplant up and over the filling and roll it up away from you. Poke a toothpick through the roll to keep it together and place seam side down on a serving tray. Repeat with remaining ingredients. Store in the refrigerator and bring to room temperature before serving.

2 large eggplant (choose longer, over the shorter, squat eggplant)
4 tbsp (60 mL) olive oil
1 cup (240 mL) ricotta cheese
1 cup (240 mL) crumbled feta cheese
1/3 cup (80 mL) chopped mint
1/2 tsp (2.5 mL) salt
1/4 tsp (1.2 mL) cracked pepper
2 red peppers, roasted (p. 50)
24 arugula sprigs

helpfulhint ✳

Summer and early fall are prime eggplant seasons. Choose vegetables that are very firm and have glossy skins. Eggplant slices are great for the barbecue. Brush with olive oil, balsamic vinegar, salt and pepper. Serve as a side dish with meats, as a vegetarian main course or in salads and sandwiches.

grilledpolentacakes

with Parmesan cheese, fresh thyme and chanterelle mushrooms

autumn on the West Coast signals a fungus foraging frenzy as an array of exotic wild mushrooms pop out of the forest floor. At the restaurant, we get daily calls from harvestors selling their pick. Chanterelle mushrooms are common and relatively affordable, so we buy them for weekend menu specials during the season. Here is a lovely starter—sophisticated, impressive and simple to prepare. We like to serve it with slow-roast tomatoes (p. 47) and roasted shallots (p. 156) drizzled with balsamic syrup.

serves 4 - 6

1 recipe polenta (p. 37)
1 1/2 lb (675 g) chanterelle mushrooms
2 garlic cloves, minced
2 tbsp (30 mL) thyme leaves
3 tbsp (45 mL) olive oil
1 tbsp (15 mL) balsamic vinegar
salt and cracked pepper to taste

1 After following directions for making plain polenta, stir in the butter and Parmesan cheese while the polenta is hot. Proceed with directions for making polenta cakes. (We suggest you cut the polenta into 3" squares.)

2 Clean the mushrooms by wiping off any surface dirt with a cloth or mushroom brush. Remove the ends of the stems and slice the larger mushrooms in half.

3 To serve, pre-heat oven to 300°F. Heat 1 tbsp (15 mL) olive oil in a skillet and sauté the polenta cakes on both sides until golden. Transfer to a baking tray, sprinkle with remaining Parmesan cheese and transfer to the oven to melt the cheese. Meanwhile, heat the remaining olive oil and add the mushrooms. Season with salt and sauté for 5 minutes. Add the garlic and half of the thyme; sauté until the mushrooms are tender and browned. Add balsamic vinegar to deglaze the pan. Season the mushrooms with cracked pepper. Serve hot over polenta cakes, sprinkled with reserved thyme leaves.

balsamicsyrup

1/2 cup (120 mL) balsamic vinegar

Pour vinegar into a small pot and bring to a boil over medium heat. Reduce heat and let the vinegar simmer until the liquid is reduced to a thick and syrupy consistency. Drizzle sparingly for garnish.

shrimpcorncakes
with pumpkin seed crust

Darren is our kitchen manager and veteran line-cook who commands his post with precision, speed and energy to spare. When he came to work for us over 5 years ago, he was somewhat ambivalent about our meatless menu and we teased him endlessly about his post-shift fast food restaurant trips. He has since sworn off his fast food ways, and these cakes have become one of his favourite dishes. Tender hand-peeled shrimp combine with corn and bold seasonings to contrast the crispy pumpkin seed crust. Serve with mango salsa (p. 98) and roasted pepper sauce (p. 50) for an impressive starter, or serve with honey-lime baked yams (p. 152) and vegetable slaw (p. 29) for a full-course meal.

serves 4 - 6

1 Combine the jalapeños and cream in a small pot and bring to a boil. Reduce heat to low and simmer until the cream is reduced to 1/4 cup (60 mL). Cool to room temperature.

2 Meanwhile, heat oil in a skillet over medium-high heat and sauté the onion, garlic and pepper until softened. Add corn and salt and cook just long enough to heat the corn through. Transfer to a bowl and cool.

3 Add the scallions, shrimp, dill, pepper and Tabasco to the cooled sauté. Add the jalapeño-cream reduction and mix it in thoroughly. Season the mixture to taste. Stir in the beaten eggs, cover with plastic wrap and refrigerate for one hour.

4 Toast the breadcrumbs on a baking tray in a 350°F oven for 5 minutes to dry them out slightly. Combine the ground pumpkin seeds and breadcrumbs in a bowl. Remove 1 3/4 cups (420 mL) and stir it into the cake mixture. Form one small cake to see if the mixture holds together. Add an extra 1/2 cup (120 mL) crumbs if necessary. Form 3 oz (90 g) handfuls of the mix into 2 1/2" round cakes and coat them in the remaining crumb mixture. Cover and refrigerate the cakes for up to an hour if you like, or cook them immediately.

5 Heat a skillet over medium-high heat and pan-fry the cakes in oil or clarified butter until golden on both sides and heated through. Handle and flip the cakes gently as they can be rather fragile. Serve hot.

2 jalapeño peppers, minced
1 cup (240 mL) whipping cream
1 tbsp (15 mL) vegetable oil
1 small red onion, finely diced
2 garlic cloves, minced
1 small red pepper, finely diced
1/2 tsp (2.5 mL) salt
1 1/2 cups (360 mL) corn, fresh or frozen
6 scallions, minced
1 lb (450 g) fresh shrimp
1 tsp (5 mL) dried dillweed
1/4 tsp (1.2 mL) cracked pepper
3/4 tsp (4 mL) Tabasco sauce
2 eggs, beaten
1 1/2 cups (360 mL) pumpkin seeds, toasted and finely ground
1 1/2 cups (360 mL) fresh sourdough breadcrumbs

ovenbakedspringrolls
with mango-ginger dipping sauce ☯

hot and crispy spring rolls are always a sell-out on our menu. People love the fact that they're baked rather than deep-fried. We serve them with an Asian noodle salad as part of a main course, but here we suggest you start by making small appetizer rolls that are easier to handle. These make great party food when served with mango-ginger dipping sauce!

yields 20 – 25 rolls

mango-ginger dipping sauce

1 cup (240 mL) prepared mango
   chutney, such as Major Grey's
1 fresh mango (optional)
juice of 2 limes
zest of 1 lime
1 tbsp (15 mL) minced ginger
1/2 cup (120 mL) rice wine vinegar

spring rolls

1 block extra firm tofu, pressed (p. 42)
2 tbsp (30 mL) soy sauce
2 tsp (10 mL) sesame oil
10 dried shiitake mushrooms
1 tbsp (15 mL) peanut or vegetable oil
1 bunch scallions, minced
1 lemongrass stalk, trimmed to the
   bottom 4" and finely minced
2 tbsp (30 mL) minced ginger
6 garlic cloves, minced
2 tsp (10 mL) salt
1/2 tsp (2.5 mL) red chile flakes
6 cups (1.5 L) finely shredded sui choy
8 oz (240 g) bean sprouts
2 cups (480 mL) shredded carrot
1 package 8" x 8" frozen spring roll
   pastry, thawed

1 Make the dipping sauce by thoroughly blending all of the sauce ingredients in a blender or food processor. You can store the sauce up to 1 week in the refrigerator.

2 Slice the tofu block in half width-wise to make two small blocks. Slice each of these into 1/4" thick rectangles. Arrange slices on a baking tray and drizzle with soy sauce and sesame oil. Turn the pieces over to coat and leave them to marinate for 1 hour. Bake in a 350°F oven until puffy and golden (about 12 minutes). Cool and slice the tofu into thin shreds. Set aside. Cover the dried mushrooms with boiling water and soak for 1 hour. Strain, remove stems and slice the mushrooms thinly. Set aside.

3 Heat the oil in a wok or skillet and add the scallions, lemongrass, ginger, garlic, salt and chile flakes. Sauté and stir constantly to prevent sticking until the garlic is golden. Transfer to a large bowl and cool. Mix in the prepared vegetables and sliced shiitakes, cover and refrigerate for at least one hour, or overnight. Just before baking, squeeze the excess moisture from the vegetables one handful at a time and transfer to another bowl. Toss with baked tofu strips and prepare to roll!

4 Pre-heat the oven to 400°F. Separate the spring roll wrappers and keep them underneath a barely damp cloth. On a clean, dry work surface, place a wrapper directly in front of you in a diamond shape. Place a small handful of filling in a line along the lower half of the wrapper. Lift the bottom tip up over the filling, fold in the sides and firmly roll into a cigar. Brush with oil and place seam side down on a parchment-lined baking tray. Repeat with the remaining filling. Bake spring rolls for 8 minutes. Turn them over and bake another 5 minutes, or until they are golden and crispy. Serve hot.

shiitake tofu potstickers

with scallions, ginger and cilantro ☯

wonton wrappers filled and steam-fried are best known as potstickers. Contact with hot oil makes them stick to the pot, resulting in a crispy wonton with a savoury, steamy filling. We serve these as a starter, accompanied by a dipping sauce (our favourite is the dressing used for the Szechuan noodle salad on p. 11). They are also delicious as a main course, nesting atop a large bowl of fragrant jasmine rice and wok-fried bok choy.

serves 4 - 6

1. Place mushrooms in a bowl and cover with boiling water. Put a small plate on top to keep the mushrooms submerged, and soak for 1 hour. Drain, cool and finely chop. Set aside.

2. Drain pressed tofu and crumble. Heat oils in a skillet and sauté the garlic, ginger, chile flakes and scallions until golden. Add crumbled tofu, pepper and soy sauce and sauté until the mixture is dry and heated through. Cool and stir in minced cilantro.

3. Whisk cornstarch and water in a small bowl. Take a wonton wrapper and hold it in the palm of your hand. Place a teaspoonful of filling in the center of the wonton. Lightly brush some cornstarch water along the edge of the wonton with your finger. Press the edges together to form a half moon, making sure the filling remains packaged within and all the edges are well-sealed. If you like, crimp the edges slightly for an attractive dumpling. Repeat with remaining filling. To this point, the wontons can be prepared and frozen for up to 1 month.

4. To cook, heat oil in a heavy skillet until a drop of water bounces and sizzles. Working with up to 8 potstickers at a time, place them in the hot oil and fry for several minutes until golden. Turn over, carefully add a few tablespoons of water to the pan and immediately cover with a lid. (Be extra careful! Oil will sputter when you add the water, so have a lid ready and stand back!). Fry a few more minutes to heat through and crispen. Drain on a paper towel and repeat with remaining potstickers. Serve immediately.

1 oz (30 g) dried shiitake mushrooms
1/2 block firm tofu, pressed (p. 42)
1 tbsp (15 mL) vegetable oil
1 tbsp (15 mL) sesame oil
1 tbsp (15 mL) minced ginger
3 garlic cloves, minced
4 scallions, finely minced
1/4 tsp (1.2 mL) red chile flakes
1/4 tsp (1.2 mL) salt
1/4 tsp (1.2 mL) cracked pepper
2 tbsp (30 mL) soy sauce
2 tbsp (30 mL) minced cilantro
30 round wonton wrappers
1 tbsp (15 mL) cornstarch
4 tbsp (60 mL) water

helpful hint ✳

If fat intake is a concern, these dumplings can also be steamed. Line a steamer with Chinese cabbage leaves. Arrange the dumplings on top of the cabbage, cover and steam for 5 min. until heated through.

mango**shrimp**sala**drolls**

with jicama, Thai basil and chile-lime dipping sauce

handling
delicate rice paper requires some degree of patience and practise. We like to make bite-sized rolls for precisely this reason. The small wafer-like, easy-to-shatter rounds are much easier to handle than their larger counterparts. So, forge ahead without fear! Salad rolls are ideal warm weather fare with clean, fresh flavours in every bite. They make a tasty light lunch or opener to an Asian-inspired feast.

yields 20 - 25 rolls

1 lb (450 g) fresh hand-peeled shrimp
1 mango
1/2 jicama
4 cups pea shoots
few sprigs of Thai basil
1 x 14 oz (400 g) pkg rice paper
    wrappers (8 1/2" diameter)

helpful**hint** ✳

If Thai basil is unavailable, substitute with regular basil, cilantro or mint. Pea shoots can be replaced with sunflower sprouts, butter lettuce or watercress.

☯ replace shrimp with baked Thai basil-soy tofu (p. 42) strips.

1 Peel the mango and cut long, thin slices from around the pit. Julienne the jicama and store in cool water. Stem the basil and tear the leaves into small pieces. Set all of the ingredients aside in separate bowls lined up on your kitchen counter.

2 To roll, place a clean, dry kitchen towel on your work space. Fill a large bowl with very hot water and set it beside you. Submerge a rice paper round into the hot water and let it soak until soft and pliable (the hotter the water, the shorter the required soaking time). Gently lift the wrap out of the water and lay it out on the towel. Place a small horizontal mound of sprouts in the center of the lower half of the wrapper. Top with a few jicama batons and a slice of mango. Arrange shrimp on top and sprinkle with basil leaves.

3 Fold the sides of the wrapper inward over the filling. Lift the lower edge of the wrapper up and over and roll up away from you to form a log-shaped package. Place the salad roll on a large plate and cover with a dampened kitchen towel. Repeat with remaining ingredients, keeping all the rolls under the damp towel. Serve immediately or seal with plastic wrap and refrigerate up to 2 hours. Serve with chile-lime dip.

chile**lime**dip

1/4 cup (60 mL) lime juice
1/4 cup (60 mL) fish sauce
1/2 cup (120 mL) water
3 tbsp (45 mL) brown sugar
1 tbsp (15 mL) sambal oelek
Whisk together all of the ingredients in a small bowl and serve.

savoury**vegetable**pancakes
with shiitake mushrooms and snow peas

delicate vegetable pancakes make a charming starter course or light meal. These feature vibrant wok-fried vegetables, tangled and bound with just the right amount of egg and flour to give them form. Accompany with miso soup (p. 122) and tofu-watercress salad (p. 3) for a nicely balanced, light meal.

serves 6 - 8

1 Soak dried mushrooms in boiling water to cover for at least 30 minutes. Place a small plate on top to ensure that the mushrooms remain submerged. Strain and reserve 1 cup (240 mL) of soaking liquid. Trim the stems, slice the mushrooms thinly and set aside.

2 Finely julienne all of the vegetables and toss them together in a large bowl with the sliced mushrooms.

3 Heat the oils over high heat in a large wok or frying pan. When the oil is hot, add half of the vegetables and fry, stirring constantly for about 1 minute. Add half of the garlic, ginger, red chile flakes and soy sauce and continue to stir-fry for another 2 minutes. The carrots should be just barely done. Turn the vegetables out to cool on a large tray and repeat with the remaining vegetables (wipe out your wok first!) Strain off any excess liquid from the cooled vegetables. Season with cracked pepper and minced cilantro. Transfer the vegetables to a large bowl and set aside.

4 Just before serving, beat the egg in a mixing bowl. Blend in flour and enough of the reserved mushroom-soaking liquid to get the consistency of a thick pancake batter. Combine the batter with the vegetables and mix thoroughly.

5 Heat vegetable oil in a skillet or griddle (a water droplet should bounce and sizzle). Scoop a heaping tablespoon of the mix into the pan and spread it out to make a round, thin pancake about 3" in diameter. Repeat with remaining batter. Cook until golden on both sides. Keep cakes warm in a low oven until ready to serve. Serve drizzled with soy-citrus glaze and a light sprinkle of sesame seeds.

1 oz (30 g) dried shiitake mushrooms
2 medium carrots
4 oz (120 g) snow peas
1 red pepper
1 bunch scallions, minced
2 cups (480 mL) shredded sui choy
1 tbsp (15 mL) minced ginger
1/4 tsp (1.2 mL) red chile flakes
2 tbsp (30 mL) soy sauce
1/2 tsp (2.5 mL) cracked pepper
1 tbsp (5 mL) sesame oil
1 tbsp (15 mL) vegetable oil
2 tbsp (30 mL) minced cilantro
1 egg, at room temperature
3/4 cup (180 mL) unbleached flour
2 tbsp (30 mL) vegetable oil
1 recipe soy-citrus glaze (p. 46)

helpful**hint** ✳

A simple method for cutting carrots in a thin julienne is the Chinese cut. Slice carrots into thin coins on a sharp angle. Slice each coin into strips, adjusting the thickness of the strips to your liking.

whitebeanhummous

with roasted garlic, sage and pine nuts ☯

creamy white cannellini beans make a smooth base for this hummous, rich with roasted garlic, sage, pine nuts and extra virgin olive oil. Use rosemary if sage is unavailable. Spread on crostini and top with chopped fresh tomatoes, or cherry tomato salsa (p. 44). Wrap in a warm pita pocket with chopped olives, tomatoes, cucumbers and greens for a knock-out sandwich, or use as a dip for oven-baked pita bread crisps.

yields 4 cups (960 mL)

2 x 15 oz (425 g) cans cannellini or
    white kidney beans, drained and
    rinsed
2 garlic bulbs, roasted (p. 158)
juice of 1 large lemon
5 tbsp (75 mL) minced fresh sage
1/4 cup (60 mL) pine nuts, toasted
1 1/2 tsp (7.5 mL) salt
1/3 cup (80 mL) extra virgin olive oil

1. Squeeze or scoop the roasted garlic flesh from the skins. Mash all of the ingredients together in a bowl, or pulse in a food processor. Add stock or water to thin and season to taste.

2. Refrigerate for up to 3 days. Serve at room temperature drizzled with extra virgin olive oil and cracked pepper on top.

helpfulhint ✳

Make hummous "from scratch" by soaking 2 cups (480 mL) dried cannellini beans overnight. Drain, rinse and cover with cold water in a medium pot. Add a bay leaf, a couple of smashed garlic cloves and sprig of sage or rosemary. Bring to boil and simmer until the beans are very tender. Add 1 tsp (5 mL) salt 15 minutes before they come off the stove. Strain and reserve cooking liquid to use for thinning.

garliccrostini

1 baguette, plain, wholegrain or sourdough
1/4 cup (60 mL) extra virgin olive oil
2 garlic cloves

Pre-heat oven to 350°F. Slice baguette 1/2" thick on the bias. Arrange on a baking tray and brush with oil. Bake until golden (5-10 minutes.) Cut garlic cloves in half and rub the cut side of the clove on the toasted bread. Serve in cloth-lined basket.

arugulachèvre&figpizzette
with sundried tomatoes, caramelized onions and rosemary

friends are often a valuable source of inspiration for recipes and food combinations. This delicious pizza comes from Wanda's friend Basia in Toronto. Though they haven't lived in the same city for almost 20 years, annual get-togethers find them connecting instantly, as only strong childhood bonds can do. Bas is a fine cook in her own right and after enjoying this pizza on several visits, we tried variations of it on the **re**bar crowd to much applause. It's rich, so small servings make ideal meal starters with wine.

1 Follow directions for preparing the foccacia through the first rising. While the dough is rising, prepare toppings. Soak the sundried tomatoes in boiling water for 30 minutes. Strain and reserve the water. Heat butter and olive oil in a skillet and add the onion and salt. Sauté until the onion is lightly golden, then add the sugar and cracked pepper. Continue to cook, adding balsamic vinegar and the reserved dried tomato water to keep the onions from sticking. After 30 minutes, the onions should have a nice, jam-like texture. Remove and set aside. Stem the arugula leaves and chop them coarsely. Slice the figs.

2 Pre-heat the oven to 500°F. Divide the dough into four equal pieces, cover with a cloth and let rest for 30 minutes. On a floured surface, roll each ball out 1/8" thick. On an oiled baking sheet or a pizza peel, dress the pizzas, starting with a layer of caramelized onions, followed by arugula, sundried tomatoes and figs. Crumble chèvre over top and sprinkle with rosemary.

3 Slide the pizzas into the oven, reduce heat to 400°F and bake for 10-15 minutes, or until the crusts are golden and the toppings bubbly. Transfer the pizzas to a cutting board and slice each round into quarters. Crack pepper over top and serve immediately.

serves 8 @ 2 slices each

1/2 recipe rosemary-garlic foccacia (p. 39)
5 oz (150 g) sundried tomatoes (not oil-packed)
2 tbsp (30 mL) olive oil
1 tbsp (15 mL) butter
2 yellow onions, chopped
1/2 tsp (2.5 mL) salt
1 tsp (5 mL) brown sugar
1 tbsp (15 mL) balsamic vinegar
6 oz (180 g) arugula leaves
2 tbsp (30 mL) minced rosemary
8 dried Calimyra figs
4 oz (120 g) chèvre
cracked pepper to taste

helpfulhint ✳

For crispy, thin crusts, place a baking stone on the bottom of your oven before pre-heating. If you don't own a baking stone, bake the pizza on a baking sheet placed on the bottom shelf of the oven.

baked chiles rellenos
with yam and corn tamal

stuffed chiles are cross-bred with another of our favourite Southwestern dishes—tamales—in this lower-fat alternative to the commonly deep-fried, cheese-filled chiles rellenos. Baking, rather than steaming the masa dough makes the filling crispy-crunchy on the outside, tender and cakey within. For a unique appetizer, serve one chile per person napped in a pool of mesa red sauce (p. 52), or serve as part of a main course with green rice (p. 153) and tomatillo-cilantro salsa (p. 53).

yields 8 chiles rellenos

1 1/3 cups (320 mL) masa harina
1/2 cup (120 mL) hot water
6-8 chiles, Anaheim, Poblano or Pasilla
2 tsp (10 mL) vegetable oil
1 medium yam, peeled and diced
1 cup (240 mL) corn, fresh or frozen
2 jalapeño peppers, seeded and minced
2 tbsp (30 mL) butter, softened
2 tbsp (30 mL) vegetable shortening
1/2 tsp (2.5 mL) salt
1/2 tsp (2.5 mL) baking powder
1/4 cup (60 mL) warm water
1 cup (240 mL) grated Jack cheese
2 tsp (10 mL) ancho chile powder
1/2 x recipe mesa red sauce (p. 52)

1 Combine masa harina and water in a mixing bowl and mix at medium speed for 5 minutes. Cover with plastic wrap and let the dough rest for one hour. Meanwhile, prepare the vegetables.

2 Pre-heat oven to 400°F. Place whole chiles on a parchment-lined baking sheet. Cut a slit along the length of each pepper and roast for 15-20 minutes, until the skins blister. Transfer the chiles to a bowl and cover with plastic wrap for 10 minutes. Remove wrap, cool and gently peel away the skin from the flesh, being very careful to keep the chile as intact as possible. If possible, leave the stem attached for an attractive presentation. Gently rinse out the seeds with running tap water and set aside to dry.

3 Reduce oven heat to 350°F. Heat oil in a skillet, add diced yams and sauté 5 minutes. Add corn and jalapeños, season with a pinch of salt and sauté until the vegetables are tender. Transfer the vegetables to a bowl and set aside to cool.

4 Returning to the masa dough, mix in butter and shortening one tablespoonful at a time until well blended. In a separate small bowl, combine the salt, baking powder, warm water and stir to dissolve. Mix into the masa dough until well combined, then stir in the vegetables, grated cheese and chile powder. Season the mixture to taste and fill each chile until generously plump. Place chiles on a lined baking sheet and bake 20 minutes, until the filling is golden brown and heated through. To serve, heat the mesa sauce, spoon 1/4 cup (60 mL) sauce on each plate and place a chile relleno on top. Garnish with chopped cilantro, scallions or chives.

the**rebar**appetizer

with tomato-ginger chutney, roasted garlic and Cambozola cheese

year after year, this **re**bar favourite retains its' popularity. We've tried to sneak it off the menu several times, hoping to introduce something new. Customers were on to us immediately and inevitably someone would come all the way from San Francisco raving about "that delicious appetizer" they ordered on their previous visit and were "SO looking forward to having again!" Well, we've since learned that some things are better left unchanged, even at the expense of innovation. The robust tomato-ginger chutney also makes a great condiment for a mild curry, or with hummous (p. 112) and crisp pappadum chips, all washed down with a cold beer.

serves 4

1. Pre-heat oven to 325°F. Arrange tomato halves, cut side up, on a baking tray. Lightly brush with oil and sprinkle with salt and pepper and roast for 45 minutes. Cool. Meanwhile, cover the sundried tomatoes with boiling water and soak for 10 minutes. Strain and reserve the tomato water.

2. Heat oil in a skillet over medium heat. Add onion and sauté for 5 minutes. Add minced garlic, ginger, cumin, chile flakes and cinnamon sticks. Sauté 5 minutes; remove from heat, remove cinnamon sticks and set aside to cool.

3. Place roasted tomatoes, soaked tomatoes, onion mixture and all remaining ingredients into the bowl of a food processor. Pulse to combine, trying to maintain some texture. Thin with reserved sundried tomato water if necessary. Season to taste and let sit for 30 minutes before serving. Store in the refrigerator for up to 1 week.

tomato-ginger chutney

(yields 1 1/2 cups – 360 mL)

4 Roma tomatoes, halved
1/2 cup (120 mL) sundried tomatoes
   (not oil packed)
1/2 medium yellow onion, chopped
1 tbsp (15 mL) vegetable oil
2 garlic cloves, minced
1 tbsp (15 mL) minced ginger
1 tsp (5 mL) cumin seed, toasted and
   ground
1/2 tsp (2.5 mL) red chile flakes
1 cinnamon stick, broken in two
2 tbsp (30 mL) honey
2 tbsp (30 mL) balsamic vinegar
1/4 tsp (1.2 mL) salt

4 whole garlic bulbs, roasted (p. 158)
6 oz (180 g) Cambozola cheese
1 recipe garlic crostini (p. 66)

to**serve**:

Everything but the crostini can be made well ahead of time. Allow one bulb of garlic per person and re-heat them in a microwave for 45 seconds just before serving. Serve the chutney, garlic and cheese (at room temperature) arranged on a platter decorated with fresh baby salad greens. Serve hot crostini in a cloth-lined basket alongside.

☺ – a vegan recipe

4

brunch

weekend mornings at the restaurant can best be summed up with one word—mayhem! Where do all these people come from? And why aren't they at home, fixing up a simple bowl of cereal for themselves? Seems that going out for brunch is all the rage. Three-generation family gatherings, gangs of friends who look like they've danced ALL night, intimate lovers, and running club jocks crowd the tables hungry for a morning feast. Orders for 3-egg omelettes with potatoes, toast, coffee and juice, and giant platefuls of pancakes slathered in butter pour in non-stop from morning until mid-afternoon. Our staff is pushed to the max but we're grateful for the enthusiastic response. Here are pages of recipes that should keep you and your family happy when you don't have time to go out for breakfast or brunch. Be sure to use free-range eggs which are now widely available ... and they really do taste better!

appleandspinachtart
with blue cheese and sweet onion-thyme confit

savoury and sweet strike a nice balance in this tart. Spinach and apples provide a sweet mellow background for the heady blue cheese. A small portion of rich onion confit served alongside is a simple detail to indulge those at the brunch table, though the tart passes all tests served on its own.

serves 8

1 pre-baked whole wheat tart shell
   (p. 34)
1 tbsp (15 mL) butter
1 tbsp (15 mL) olive oil
1 cup (240 mL) chopped leeks
1/2 tsp (2.5 mL) salt
1/4 tsp (1.2 mL) cracked pepper
1 bunch spinach, stemmed,
   washed and wilted
3 eggs
1 cup (240 mL) light cream
1 cup (240 mL) crumbled blue
   cheese
3 apples, a combination of red
   and green
1 egg white, lightly beaten

1 Heat butter and olive oil in a pan over medium-high heat. Add the leeks and a pinch of salt and sauté until the leeks are soft. Set aside to cool. Wilt the spinach, squeeze out excess water and chop. Next, lightly beat the eggs in a bowl. Add cream, salt and pepper and whisk together.

2 To assemble the tart, evenly distribute crumbled blue cheese over the bottom of the pre-baked tart shell. Follow with the leeks and the spinach. Pour the egg mixture over top.

3 Quarter and core the apples. Thinly slice each quarter into 8 thin wedges. Starting at the outer edge of the tart, overlap apple slices, skin sides facing out, in a circle around the edge. Spiral the overlapping slices towards the center of the tart to cover the entire surface. Beat the egg white in a small bowl and brush over the apples. Place the tart on a baking tray and bake at 350°F for 20-25 minutes, or until the egg is set and the crust has browned. Let the tart rest for at least 15 minutes before removing from the pan. Cut into wedges and serve.

helpfulhint ✳

Leeks are notorious for hiding garden dirt in between their layers. For a thorough cleaning, chop the leeks first, place them in a colander and rinse well with cold water.

onionthymeconfit

2 tbsp (30 mL) butter
2 large yellow onions,
   thinly sliced
1/2 tsp (2.5 mL) salt
1 tsp (5 mL) brown sugar
1 tsp (5 mL) minced
   thyme
1 tbsp (15 mL) balsamic
   vinegar

Melt butter in a skillet; add onions, salt and sauté 10 min. Stir in the remaining ingredients and continue to cook for 20 min., until the onions are golden, sweet and broken down.

poached eggs & latkes

with lox, watercress and dill hollandaise sauce

crispy potato latkes are a great platform for poached eggs. Slip a slice of lox in between, along with a few sprigs of fresh and tangy watercress, and a brunch sensation is in the making! The lemon-dill hollandaise sauce is icing on the cake.

1 To make latkes, grate potatoes using a food processor or box grater, using the largest holes to get long, thick strands. Grate the onions onto the potatoes and mix them together. Scoop out a handful, and holding over a small bowl, squeeze out as much excess moisture as you can. Transfer to yet another bowl and repeat with the remaining potato/onion mix.

2 Add the remaining ingredients (except cooking oil) to the potatoes. Strain off the excess liquid from the first bowl and on the bottom you will find a layer of potato starch. Scoop this out and add it to the mixture. Stir everything together.

3 Heat a large cast-iron pan or non-stick skillet over medium-high heat. Pour in about 1/8" oil and heat until a piece of potato sizzles on contact. Scoop about 1/4 cup (60 mL) of the mixture into your hands and form a small cake about 1/2" thick. Fry latkes in hot oil, until golden brown on both sides, gently pressing down on the cakes with the back of a spatula. Flip only once to reduce oil absorption and add more oil as needed, making sure it gets hot before adding the latke mix. Drain on paper towels and keep warm in a low oven while you poach the eggs.

4 To serve, place 2 latkes on a plate and top with a few watercress sprigs and a slice of lox. Top with poached eggs and spoon hollandaise sauce over top. Garnish with cracked pepper and fresh dill sprigs.

serves 4

latkes

2 lbs (900 g) Yukon Gold or russet potatoes (4 large)
2 medium yellow onions
1 large egg, lightly beaten
1/4 cup (60 mL) unbleached flour
1 tsp (5 mL) salt
1/2 tsp (2.5 mL) cracked pepper
vegetable or peanut oil, for cooking

poached eggs

8 eggs
8 slices lox
small bunch of watercress

dill hollandaise

2 large egg yolks
2 tbsp (30 mL) lemon juice
1/2 tsp (2.5 mL) minced lemon zest
1/2 cup (120 mL) melted butter
2 tbsp (30 mL) minced fresh dill

Place egg yolks, lemon juice and zest in a blender. With the motor running, add the melted butter very slowly. Transfer to a bowl, season with salt, cracked pepper and dill. Whisk in a tablespoon or two of hot water to thin, if necessary.

buttermilk**corn**cakes
with blueberries

corn and blueberries are the highlight of this **re**bar breakfast favourite. These pancakes have a delicate texture that makes each bite melt away in your mouth, so don't be alarmed by the high liquid content of the batter. Naturally, this superior hotcake is worthy of no less than a swath of sweet butter and the best pure Canadian maple syrup.

serves 2 - 3

2/3 cup (160 mL) fine cornmeal

1/2 cup (120 mL) unbleached flour

2 tbsp (30 mL) stone-ground cornmeal

1/2 tsp (2.5 mL) salt

1 tbsp (15 mL) brown sugar

2 tsp (10 mL) baking powder

1/4 tsp (1.2 mL) baking soda

1 egg, at room temperature

1/4 cup (1.2 mL) plain yogourt

1 1/2 cups (360 mL) buttermilk

1 tbsp (30 mL) melted butter, or oil

1 cup (240 mL) blueberries, fresh or
    frozen

extra butter or oil for cooking

1. Measure the dry ingredients and stir them together in a bowl. In a separate bowl, lightly beat the eggs and stir in the remaining ingredients, except the blueberries. Combine the wet and dry mixes, gently stir them together, being careful not to overmix. Let the batter rest for at least 5 minutes.

2. Heat a griddle at medium-high heat (350°F). Add just enough butter or oil to lightly coat the surface. When a droplet of water sizzles in the pan, use a ladle to drop batter into 4" diameter circles, or use a 1/3 cup (80 mL) measuring cup. As the first side of the cakes cook, evenly distribute whole blueberries onto the uncooked surface. When small bubbles appear on the surface and the edges start to dry, flip the cakes over and continue to cook for a few minutes until the other side is golden and the berries begin to release their juice. Serve immediately ... have your plates warm and coffee ready!

helpful**hint** ❄

For a secure supply of blueberries year-round, buy a flat when they are in season and freeze them. Line a baking tray with wax paper, spread a single layer of fresh berries on top and pop them into the freezer until solid. Remove and store in sealed freezer bags.

Greek tofu scramble
with spinach, olives and fresh herbs

slip tofu into your diet with this versatile dish, which is great for lunch or a light dinner too. At the restaurant we serve it with warm whole wheat pita bread and hummous on the side. Experiment with a range of proportions of tofu, egg and cheese to suit your tastes. For the strict vegan, this is a delicious all-tofu dish. There are plenty of wonderful bold flavours here to make all renditions superb.

☯ use half a tofu block and omit the cheese and eggs (vegan).

serves one

1 Drain the tofu, crumble into a small bowl and set aside. Heat olive oil in a non-stick pan over medium heat. Add onion and sauté until soft. Add the crumbled tofu, garlic, a pinch of salt and pepper and sauté for another couple of minutes.

2 Add the egg (if using), tomato, olives, spinach and fresh herbs and stir until the egg is set and the spinach wilted. Mix in the feta cheese and lemon juice. Turn onto a warm plate, crack pepper on top and serve.

1/3 block firm tofu, plain or herb
1 tbsp (15 mL) olive oil
2 tbsp (30 mL) diced red onion
1 garlic clove, minced
1/2 tomato, diced
4 Kalamata olives, pitted and chopped
1 egg, lightly beaten
8 spinach leaves, stemmed and
    roughly chopped
2 tbsp (30 mL) minced oregano or
    Italian parsley
2 tsp (10 mL) fresh lemon juice
2 tbsp (30 mL) crumbled feta cheese
salt and cracked pepper to taste

helpfulhint ✳

Make a vegan curried tofu scramble with scallions, red pepper, diced and seeded tomato, curry powder, chopped cilantro. Serve with warm chapathi, Bombay hummous (p. 112) and tomato-ginger chutney (p. 69).

wholewheathotcakes
with wheatgerm and buttermilk

reliable recipes like this one have elevated our whole wheat hotcakes to "house hotcake" status at **re**bar. Hundreds of happy diners have enjoyed these wholesome cakes, delicious on their own or jazzed up in countless ways. Serve them with butter and maple syrup when you want a no-fuss, hearty and healthy hotcake breakfast.

serves 2 - 3

1 egg
1 1/2 cups (360 mL) buttermilk
1 tbsp (15 mL) melted butter or
    vegetable oil
1/2 tsp (2.5 mL) vanilla
1/2 cup (120 mL) whole wheat flour
1/2 cup (120 mL) unbleached flour
4 tbsp (60 mL) wheat germ
1 tsp (5 mL) baking powder
3/4 tsp (4 mL) baking soda
1/4 tsp (1.2 mL) salt

1 In a small bowl, lightly whisk together the egg, buttermilk, vanilla and melted butter. In another bowl, sift the flours together and stir in the remaining dry ingredients. Add the wet mix to the dry mix and gently stir them together, taking care not to overmix. Let the batter rest for a few minutes while your griddle heats up to 350°F.

2 Lightly grease the griddle with butter or vegetable oil. Using a ladle, or 1/3 cup (80 mL) measuring cup, drop batter into 4" circles. When bubbles begin to appear on the uncooked surface and the edges begin to dry out, flip the cakes over and cook until golden brown. Serve immediately.

helpfulhint ✳

Wheatgerm is the part of the wheat kernel extracted during milling. It is high in protein, fiber, Vitamin E, folic acid, riboflavin, niacin, zinc, thiamine, iron, magnesium and potassium. Because it is vulnerable to rancidity, purchase only vacuum packed, refrigerated wheatgerm. Buy the raw, unprocessed form and always check the packing date and freshness label. Store refrigerated in an airtight container.

jazzuphotcakeswith:

- ✳ raspberries, orange zest
- ✳ grated fresh apple, ground cardamom
- ✳ banana slices, nutmeg and pecans
- ✳ pumpkin purée, cinnamon, freshly grated ginger
- ✳ fresh peach slices, nutmeg, flax seed meal
- ✳ blackberries, lemon zest

brownbasmatipudding
with coconut, cardamom and ginger ☯

rice pudding is a universal comfort food. In Thailand it's made with black sticky rice and palm sugar. In Persia, with honey and rosewater. In Mexico, with lime zest and cinnamon. This Indian-inspired variation uses brown basmati instead of the traditional white, and a combination of rice and coconut milk, making it a healthy vegan breakfast option. Our basic recipe will help get you started, leaving you plenty of room to experiment with your favourite spices, sweeteners and toppings.

1 Rinse the basmati rice and place in a heavy-bottomed pot. Add water, soy milk, salt, ginger, cardamom and cinnamon. Bring to a boil, reduce heat to low and cover for 45 minutes.

2 Stir in the sugar and coconut milk and simmer the rice without a lid over low heat. Cook until the liquid evaporates and the pudding thickens (about 30 minutes). Remove the ginger slices, cardamom pods and cinnamon stick. Serve hot, warm, or at room temperature.

serves 4

1 cup (240 mL) brown basmati rice
2 cups (480 mL) water
1 cup (240 mL) soy, or rice milk
1/2 tsp (2.5 mL) salt
1-inch piece of ginger, peeled and
    thinly sliced
6 cardamom pods, crushed
3-inch long cinnamon stick
2 oz (60 g) palm, or brown sugar
1 can "lite" coconut milk

helpfulhint ❊

Some of our favourite rice pudding toppings include:
❊ diced fresh mango and papaya
❊ banana slices
❊ unsweetened applesauce
❊ fresh blueberries and toasted almonds
❊ chopped dried apricots, figs, cranberries

overnight grain & seed
an as-you-sleep breakfast cereal

comforting
hot cereals are an ideal way to begin the day, but often the most healthful unrefined grains take too long to cook. Here is a recipe that solves that problem, but requires a little forethought. Assemble this cereal before going to bed at night and reap great rewards in the morning. You'll wake up to a comforting, nutty aroma. At first you'll be puzzled by its origin. Perhaps you'll even rise, get dressed, and as you stumble down the hall toward the kitchen, it will suddenly hit you that a healthy breakfast is ready, hot and waiting in the oven!

yields 4 generous breakfasts for 2

1 cup (240 mL) oat groats
1/2 cup (120 mL) barley groats
1/2 cup (120 mL) rye berries
1/2 cup (120 mL) whole almonds
1/4 cup (60 mL) sunflower seeds
1/4 cup (60 mL) pumpkin seeds

1 Mix the dry ingredients together and store sealed until ready to use.

2 Before going to bed on the night before you want to serve the cereal, scoop 1 cup (240 mL) of the grain/seed mix into a small (6–8 cup) casserole dish with a lid. Mix in 4 cups (960 mL) water and a pinch of salt. Bake overnight, covered, at 200°F.

3 In the morning, stir up the cereal and serve warm with milk, soy or rice milk and brown sugar or maple syrup.

helpfulhint ✳

For a very different (but also delicious) way of serving this cereal, grind the grain/seed mix to a fairly fine grind. Bring water to a boil in a saucepan and pour the cereal in slowly as you stir, to prevent lumping. Cover, reduce heat to low and cook for 20–30 minutes until thick and creamy. Serve.

squash&smokedcheddartart

with sage and roasted garlic custard

experienced cooks can usually predict whether or not a recipe will be a success based on the list of ingredients. Knowing how different flavours combine is one of the many payoffs of spending years in the kitchen. The creation of this recipe is a great example of that process in action. While drawing up a list of brunch ideas for the book over coffee one day, we started to draw up a list of ingredients for a tart that we had never made. That same day we began a recipe-testing session by making this tart, which turned out fabulous, just as we had imagined, so here it is ...

serves 8

1 pre-baked whole wheat tart shell
  (p. 34)
1 small butternut squash
1 tbsp (15 mL) butter
2 shallots, minced
1/2 tsp (2.5 mL) salt
3 eggs
1 cup (240 mL) heavy cream
1/2 cup (120 mL) light cream
2 garlic bulbs, roasted (p. 158) and
  mashed
1 1/2 tbsp (22.5 mL) minced sage
1/4 tsp (1.2 mL) cracked pepper
1 1/4 cups (300 mL) grated smoked
  or aged white cheddar

1 Cut the squash where the long neck and the bulbous part meet (the neck is easier to work with.) Peel the neck, halve it lengthwise and cut 1/8" thick half-moon slices. You should have about 2 cups (480 mL). If you come up short, peel and seed the other half of the squash and cut enough slices to make up the difference. Toss the squash with just enough oil to coat and a pinch of salt. Line a small baking sheet with parchment paper or foil and spread the squash slices on it. Roast in a 375°F oven until tender (about 15 minutes).

2 While the squash is roasting, heat butter in a small pan and sauté the shallots with 1/4 tsp (1.2 mL) salt until crisp and golden. Set aside.

3 Lightly whisk the eggs in a small bowl. Add the cream, mashed garlic, pepper, and 1/4 tsp (1.2 mL) salt; whisk to combine.

4 To assemble the tart, sprinkle grated cheese over the surface of the pre-baked shell. Evenly distribute the shallots and sage over the cheese. Arrange the squash slices in a single layer and pour the custard over top. Bake for 20-30 minutes, or until the custard is set and the top is lightly browned. Cool thoroughly. Slice and serve.

sweetcheeseblintz

with summer berry compote

"extravagant" is the best word to describe this brunch specialty. Certain occasions merit a little morning luxury, and this recipe is bound to make the fortunate souls at your table feel special. Serve with compote or fresh berries and maple syrup.

serves 4 - 6

crêpes

3 eggs

1 cup (240 mL) milk

1/2 cup (120 mL) water

1/2 tsp (2.5 mL) vanilla

1 1/2 cups (360 mL) unbleached flour

1 tsp (5 mL) sugar

1/4 tsp (1.2 mL) salt

3 tbsp (45 mL) melted butter

sweet cheese filling

3 cups (720 mL) dry curd farmer's
   cheese

1 1/2 cups (360 mL) softened cream
   cheese

1 tsp (5 mL) vanilla

1/4 cup (60 mL) honey

zest of 1 lemon, minced

juice of 1 lemon

1 Whisk together the eggs, milk, water and vanilla. In a separate bowl, combine the flour, sugar and salt. Whisk the dry mix into the wet mix to form a smooth batter. Stir in melted butter until well combined.

2 Heat an 8" non-stick skillet or crêpe pan over medium-high heat. Brush the pan with a light coat of melted butter and heat until a bead of water bounces off the pan. Ladle 2 oz (60 g) of batter onto the pan, tilting it so that a thin film of batter coats the entire surface. When bubbles appear on the underside of the crêpe and the edges begin to dry, flip the crêpe over and cook the other side briefly until lightly golden. Repeat with remaining batter, stacking the crêpes on a plate.

3 Prepare the filling by mixing together all of the ingredients. To assemble the blintz, place a crêpe in front of you and put 1/3 cup (80 mL) filling in the center. Fold in all of the sides to form a square package. Repeat with remaining crêpes and filling.

4 To serve, heat a skillet or griddle over medium heat. Melt the butter and pan-fry the blintz until golden on both sides. Serve hot, topped with berry compote and a sprinkle of icing sugar.

helpfulhint ✳

The crêpes for this recipe can be prepared several days before serving. Seal and refrigerate for two days or freeze up to one month.

summerberrycompote

juice of 1 lemon

1 tbsp (15 mL) water

4 cups (960 mL) fresh berries

zest of 1/2 lemon, minced

1/2 tsp (2.5 mL) cornstarch

1 tbsp (15 mL) maple syrup

1/8 tsp (.5 mL) cinnamon

Combine all of the ingredients in a pot and cook over medium heat until hot and slightly thickened. Serve hot or cold.

lemonricottacakes
with fresh strawberries

special mornings, such as a partner's birthday or Mother's Day, are the perfect time to make these hotcakes The ricotta cheese makes a smooth, rich batter which is brightened up with lemon zest and juice. Top with fresh sliced strawberries, as suggested, or any variety of berry that is at its' peak.

1 Combine the flour, baking soda, baking powder, salt and sugar in a bowl and stir together. In a separate bowl, whisk together the remaining ingredients, except the egg whites. Add the wet mix to the dry mix and gently fold them together. Beat the egg whites until stiff peaks form and fold them into the batter.

2 Heat a griddle and melt the butter. Use a 1/3 cup (80 mL) measure to drop batter onto the pan. When small bubbles appear on the surface of the cakes and the edges begin to dry, flip them over and cook until golden. Serve immediately.

serves 3 - 4

1 3/4 cups (420 mL) unbleached flour

2 tsp (10 mL) baking powder

1 tsp (5 mL) baking soda

1/2 tsp (2.5 mL) salt

2 tbsp (30 mL) sugar

juice of 2 lemons

zest of 1 lemon, minced

1 1/2 cups (360 mL) whole milk

1 1/2 cups (360 mL) ricotta cheese

2 tbsp (30 mL) melted butter

2 eggs, yolks and whites separated

1 tbsp (15 mL) butter, for cooking

helpfulhint ✳

When adding melted butter to a batter, slightly cool the butter first and then whisk it in slowly. This prevents clumping that may occur if the butter is hot enough to cook the egg in the batter.

eggs**Kurosawa**

with tofu, brown rice and soy-chile sauce

film is a popular topic of conversation in the **re**bar kitchen. Countless hours spent on our feet makes movie-going a cherished diversion for the restaurant-working crowd. This dish is dedicated to the late great director Akira Kurosawa for his contribution to our favorite art form. The Japanese connection to the recipe is obvious, but by no means traditional. Nevertheless, this is the darling of our breakfast menu—healthy, filling and a welcome departure from standard breakfast fare.

serves 2

2 cups (480 mL) cooked short grain
    brown rice
1 tbsp (15 mL) vegetable oil
1/2 block firm tofu, cut into 1/2" cubes
1/4 cup (60 mL) soy-chile sauce (p. 46)
2 scallions, thinly sliced
4 eggs, lightly beaten
2 tsp (10 mL) oil or butter
1/4 sheet nori seaweed, thinly sliced
1 tsp (5 mL) toasted sesame seeds

1 Heat oil in a non-stick pan over medium-high heat. Add tofu cubes and sauté until lightly browned. Add soy-chile sauce and simmer the tofu in the sauce for 2 minutes. Add the scallions and keep warm over low heat.

2 Meanwhile, beat the eggs in a bowl. Heat oil or butter in a small skillet and scramble the eggs until light and fluffy.

3 To serve, divide hot rice among two shallow bowls. Top each with scrambled eggs, tofu and sauce. Sprinkle with sesame seeds and nori slivers. Serve with chopsticks.

helpful**hint** ✳

Store unused portions of tofu in the refrigerator, covered with cool tap water. Change the water regularly and it will last up to a week or more.

veganfrenchtoast
with coconut milk and banana ☯

brunch is all about the decadent food that we feel we deserve to indulge in on the weekends, so it's easy to feel sorry for vegans at this time. With this in mind, we hit the drawing board to consider how we could get away without eggs, cream and butter and essentially still have "french toast". Here is a recipe that Senz, one of our dear ex-cooks, conjured up, much to the delight of vegans and non-vegans alike!

serves 4

1 Place all ingredients (except bread!) into a blender and blend until smooth. Pour into a large shallow bowl and set aside.

2 Slice bread into 8 thick slices. Heat a griddle or pan and brush with oil. Submerge bread slices in the batter, lift out with a pair of tongs and place on the hot pan. Cook until golden brown, flip and cook on the reverse side. Serve immediately with your favourite toppings.

1 banana
1 cup (240 mL) plain rice or soy milk
1 cup (240 mL) coconut milk
1 tsp (5 mL) vanilla
1/4 tsp (1.2 mL) freshly grated nutmeg
1/4 tsp (1.2 mL) cinnamon
1 1/2 tsp (7.5 mL) arrowroot powder, or cornstarch
1/4 tsp (1.2 mL) salt
1 loaf multigrain bread

yummyfrenchtoast toppings

* organic apple butter
* summer berry compote (p. 80)
* cinnamon-brandy pears (p. 90)
* peanut butter and maple syrup
* lemon-vanilla flavoured soy yogourt with raspberry coulis (p. 209)

helpfulhint ❋

The sugars in this recipe may cause the french toast to stick to the pan. Minimize this pesky problem by pre-heating the pan well and making sure the oil is hot before loading on the battered bread.

huevosrancheros
rebar style

many restaurants serve huevos rancheros, but we think ours is one of the best. The key is using fresh house-made salsas, flavourful refried beans, free-range eggs and good quality tortillas. Of course, you may not have all of these ingredients at home, but if you take the time to make a fresh salsa, it's well worth the effort. There are also many fine commercial salsas and refried beans that will give good results, especailly with a little doctoring. Toss chopped cilantro and scallions into your scrambled eggs and spice up a can of beans with sautéed onion, cumin, coriander and chopped tomato. Plain or fancy, this is a guaranteed breakfast hit. Lunch or dinner? Why not?!

☯ replace eggs with scrambled tofu and use vegan cheese.

serves 2

smoky pinto beans

1 x 14 fl oz liq (398 mL) can pinto
   beans
1 tsp (5 mL) chipotle purée (p. 38)
1 tbsp (15 mL) vegetable oil
1 tsp (5 mL) balsamic vinegar
1 tsp (5 mL) brown sugar
1/4 tsp (1.2 mL) salt

huevos rancheros

4 eggs
1 tbsp (15 mL) butter or oil
1 cup (240 mL) smoky pinto beans
2 whole wheat tortillas
4 tbsp (60 mL) mesa red sauce (p. 52),
   or other spicy red sauce
1/2 cup (120 mL) grated Jack cheese
1/2 cup (120 mL) fresh-cut salsa (p. 44)

1 Prepare the smoky pinto beans by draining the canned beans and tossing them with all of the remaining ingredients. Heat them in a small pot over low heat, or in the microwave. Keep warm while assembling the rest of the dish, or refrigerate and reheat when ready to use.

2 Lightly beat eggs in a small bowl with a pinch of salt and pepper. You will need to heat two pans, a small one for scrambling the eggs and a second one large enough to accomodate the circumference of a tortilla.

3 Heat oil or butter in the small pan and quickly scramble the eggs. Cover and set aside. Brush the larger pan with a light coat of oil and cover with a tortilla. Spoon on some chile sauce and spread it around to cover the entire surface. Sprinkle with grated cheese. Spoon 1/2 cup (120 mL) beans over the lower section of the tortilla. Top the beans with scrambled eggs and salsa. When the tortilla browns and the cheese melts, fold the top half of the tortilla over the lower half and transfer to a plate. Keep warm in a low oven while you prepare the second tortilla. Serve immediately with extra salsa and your favourite hot sauces on the side.

orange**yogourt**hotcakes
with fresh raspberries

years of **re**bar breakfasts have become synonymous with one person—Andy, our notorious breakfast chef, who manned the early morning stoves until 1998 and was integral to the early development of the restaurant. Andy could make us laugh like no other with his quick wit and countless songs, jokes and stories. Working a shift with Andy took the edge off the hectic early morning hours. So this recipe is dedicated to Andy Impett, who was always very proud of his breakfasts. This tender hotcake was one of his favourites to make and serve and while passing them off to servers he would exclaim "Chest out, serve with pride!" His voice still echoes through the **re**bar kitchen and makes us giggle.

serves 2 - 3

1 In a large bowl, combine the dry ingredients. In a separate bowl, lightly whisk the eggs. Add the liquid ingredients to the eggs and stir well to combine. Add the wet mix to the dry mix and gently fold them together. Let the batter rest for a few minutes as your griddle heats up to 350°F.

2 Brush the griddle with a light coat of oil or butter and use a 1/3 cup (80 mL) measure to ladle the batter onto the pan. Cook until small bubbles appear on the uncooked surface and the edges begin to dry. Flip the cakes over and cook a few minutes more. Serve immediately with fresh raspberries and maple syrup.

1 1/2 cups (360 mL) unbleached flour
1 1/2 tsp (7.5 mL) baking soda
3/4 tsp (4 mL) baking powder
1 tbsp (15 mL) brown sugar
1/4 tsp (1.2 mL) salt
2 eggs
1 1/2 cups (360 mL) plain yogourt
1/2 cup (120 mL) milk
zest of 1 orange, minced
1/2 cup (120 mL) fresh orange juice
1 tbsp (15 mL) butter, or oil for cooking

helpful**hint** ✳

When using the zest of a citrus fruit, we recommend that you buy organic fruit. If they're not available, wash the fruit well in hot, soapy water before zesting. Rinse, dry and proceed.

migasfortwo
tortilla-egg scramble with cilantro and cheddar

eggs are so incredibly versatile that we're never surprised to discover yet another great way to serve them. In this dish, strips of corn tortilla are briefly fried in a pan preceding the addition of beaten eggs. Scrambling them together results in an ethereal fusion of masa harina and egg. Add some onion, chiles, fresh cilantro and/or grated cheddar cheese and ... we'll be right over!

serves 2

2 good quality corn tortillas
4 free-range eggs
1 tsp (5 mL) chipotle purée (p. 38)
2 tbsp (30 mL) light cream or milk
1/4 tsp (1.2 mL) salt
1/4 tsp (1.2 mL) cracked pepper
1 tbsp (15 mL) butter
1/2 red pepper, diced
4 scallions, minced
1 oz (30 g) aged white cheddar, grated
2 tbsp (30 mL) chopped cilantro

1 Stack tortillas on top of each other and cut in half. Stack halves and slice into 1/4" thick strips. Set aside. In a small bowl, beat together the eggs, chipotle purée, cream or milk, salt and pepper.

2 Heat a skillet over medium-high heat and melt the butter. Add the peppers and sauté 2 minutes. Add tortilla strips and sauté for 1 minute. Add scallions and eggs and scramble until the eggs are just set. Stir in the grated cheddar and cilantro. Divide among 2 plates and serve immediately!

helpfulhint ✳

Be cautious when working with hot chile peppers. The heat will absorb into your skin and cause your hands, and any part of you that you touch, to burn. To avoid this rather unpleasant sensation, wear surgical gloves, or coat your hands in a layer of olive oil. Once the chiles are minced, wash your hands thoroughly with soap and water.

cranberryhazelnutgranola
with coconut, seeds and maple syrup ☯

wool socks and Birkenstocks may be a West Coast trademark, but make no mistake, this is no hippie-dippy granola recipe! This is what you get when granola heads uptown. Wear your best silk pajamas, grab a Sunday New York Times, and dip in with your silver spoon!

1 In a large bowl, combine the first eight ingredients. In a smaller bowl, whisk together the oil, water, honey and vanilla. Combine the wet and dry mixes and stir thoroughly.

2 Spread the mixture out onto two baking sheets (or do it in two batches). Bake at 250°F for 20-30 minutes. Stir the mixture every 10 minutes to ensure even baking and remove from the oven when golden brown. Cool and stir in the dried fruit. Seal and store for up to 1 month.

yields 8 cups (2 L)

3 cups (720 mL) large flake oats
1 1/2 cups (360 mL) barley flakes
1/2 cup (120 mL) oat bran
1 cup (240 mL) unsweetened coconut
1/2 tsp (2.5 mL) salt
1 cup (240 mL) hazelnuts, coarsely
    chopped
1/2 cup (120 mL) pumpkin seeds
1/2 cup (120 mL) sunflower seeds
1/2 cup (120 mL) vegetable oil
1/4 cup (60 mL) water
2/3 cup (160 mL) maple syrup (or
    honey, or a combination)
1 tsp (5 mL) vanilla
1 cup (240 mL) dried cranberries
1/2 cup (120 mL) dried blueberries

helpfulhint ✳

Other seed/nut/fruit combinations
✳ almonds, wheatgerm, dried cherries
✳ pecans, flax seeds, dried mango
✳ walnuts, dried apricots and figs

redpotato**home**fries

chile-dusted and herby ☯

dining out for breakfast or brunch remains a luxury to most, but we still manage to pack the house on weekends. Somehow a restaurant breakfast seems incomplete without potato home-fries. Why not treat yourself at home once in a while? Here are two simple and tasty options prepared in the oven. Serves 2–4.

chile**dusted**homefries

1.5 lb (675 g) red potatoes
　(about 4 medium)
2 tbsp (30 mL) vegetable
　oil
1/2 tsp (2.5 mL) salt
1/2 tsp (2.5 mL) ancho
　chile powder
1/4 tsp (1.2 mL) cayenne
1/4 tsp (1.2 mL) chipotle
　chile powder

Pre-heat the oven to 400°F. Quarter the potatoes lengthwise and chop into 1-inch square pieces. Toss with oil, sprinkle with seasonings and toss well. Spread the potatoes out on a large baking sheet lined with parchement or foil. Roast for 30 minutes, or until golden brown and soft in the middle. Halfway through roasting, stir up the potatoes with a spatula. Serve hot.

herby**home**fries

1.5 lb (675 g) red potatoes
　(about 4 medium)
juice of 1/2 lemon
2 garlic cloves, minced
1/2 tsp (2.5 mL) salt
1/4 tsp (1.2 mL) cracked
　pepper
2 tbsp (30 mL) minced
　fresh herbs (parsley, dill,
　oregano, chives, etc ...)

Pre-heat the oven to 400°F. Quarter the potatoes lengthwise and chop into 1-inch square pieces. Toss with lemon, oil, garlic, salt and pepper. Spread out on a large lined baking sheet Roast for 30 minutes, or until golden brown and soft in the middle. Halfway through roasting, stir up the potatoes with a spatula. Toss with chopped fresh herbs when they come out of the oven and serve.

Briebagelmelt

with honey and almonds

amber liquid honey, creamy melted Brie cheese and crunchy toasted almonds make this dish a real knife and fork affair. This a breakfast for well-behaved kids, or rather naughty adults. Serve with a fresh fruit salad.

serves 1

1 bagel, split in half
1 1/2 oz (45 g) Brie cheese
honey, to taste
1 tbsp (15 mL) sliced almonds, toasted

1 Lightly toast the bagel. Arrange thin Brie slices to cover the toasted bagel halves. Place them on a baking tray, cheese side up, and broil until the Brie starts to melt (keep an eye on them!)

2 Carefully remove the bagels, transfer to a plate and drizzle liquid honey over the cheese. Sprinkle with toasted almonds and serve.

bagelmeltcombos

* apple slices, aged cheddar, walnuts
* cilantro pesto (p. 41), sweet pepper rings, Vidalia onion, Jack cheese
* pear slices, roquefort, arugula, rosemary
* basil pesto, beefsteak tomato slice, chèvre, pine nuts

helpfulhint ❋

Bagels freeze beautifully, so if you don't happen to live near a great bagel bakery (like our favourite—Mount Royal Bagels in Victoria), buy several dozen at once, pack them into heavy-duty freezer bags and put them in your deep freeze.

buckwheat**hotcakes**
with cranberry-hazelnut butter

earthy buckwheat hotcakes make a great breakfast on cold, rainy (or snowy) mornings. As buckwheat has a tendency to make a dense batter, we've included a side recipe for sautéed pears, which can be stirred directly into the batter for a tenderizing effect. They're lovely served as a topping too. The cranberry butter is pure whimsy, adding sparkle to the natural grey tones of the buckwheat.

serves 2 - 3

1/2 cup (120 mL) buckwheat flour

1/2 cup (60 mL) unbleached flour

1/4 cup (60 mL) whole wheat flour

1 tsp (5 mL) baking powder

1/2 tsp (2.5 mL) baking soda

1/2 tsp (2.5 mL) salt

2 eggs

1 1/2 cups (360 mL) buttermilk

2 tbsp (30 mL) fancy molasses

cranberry-hazelnut butter

1/3 cup butter

1/4 cup (60 mL) chopped fresh or
    frozen (thawed) cranberries

2 tbsp (30 mL) toasted, skinned and
    chopped hazelnuts

1 Sift together the flours, baking powder, soda and salt. In a separate bowl, lightly whisk the eggs. Stir in the buttermilk and molasses. Combine the wet and dry ingredients and gently mix.

2 Cook hotcakes on a hot, buttered griddle, using 1/3 cup (80 mL) batter per hotcake. Serve immediately with cranberry-hazelnut butter and maple syrup.

cinnamonbrandypears

2 tbsp (30 mL) unsalted butter

2 pears, quartered, cored and sliced

1 tbsp (15 mL) brown sugar

1/2 tsp (2.5 mL) cinnamon

4 tbsp (60 mL) brandy

Set a skillet over medium heat and as it warms, prepare the fruit. Melt butter in the pan and add the pear slices. Stir to coat the fruit and sauté for 2 min. Sprinkle in the sugar and cinnamon and sauté for a few more minutes. Add brandy to deglaze the pan. When the pan is dry remove from the heat. Cool the pears for 10 minutes before stirring them into the hotcake batter, or serve on top.

helpful**hint** ✳

Buckwheat is a fruit, not a grain. As such, it is wheat-free and gluten-free, making it a great alternative to those suffering from celiac disease and other less severe wheat allergies.

omelettes

for all seasons

this selection of seasonal omelettes will keep two people happy throughout the year. Each recipe yields enough filling for 2 three-egg omelettes. Whisk a splash of cream into the eggs and season lightly with salt and pepper. Serve omelettes with red potato home-fries (p. 88), latkes (p. 73) or a favourite salad for a full meal.

spring
asparagus, chives
Gruyère

12 thin asparagus spears
2 tbsp (30 mL) minced chives
2/3 cup (160 mL) grated Gruyère cheese

Steam or blanch asparagus until just tender. Place 6 spears in each omelette, with tips poking out both ends. Sprinkle with chives and Gruyère and heat through to melt the cheese.

summer
zucchini, cherry tomato salsa,
Parmesan

1 medium zucchini
1/2 cup (120 mL) cherry tomato salsa (p. 44)
1/2 cup (120 mL) grated Parmesan

Cut zucchini in 1/4" thick half-moon slices. Sauté in a splash of olive oil until tender. Season with salt and pepper. Divide sautéed zucchini, salsa and cheese among omelettes and heat through.

autumn
spinach, romesco sauce,
feta cheese

1/2 bunch spinach, washed, stemmed, wilted
3 tbsp (45 mL) romesco sauce (p. 56)
2 tbsp (30 mL) crumbled feta cheese

Squeeze out excess moisture from wilted spinach. Divide spinach, sauce and feta among omelettes and cook until the cheese melts.

winter
portabello mushrooms,
onion confit, Cambozola

2 portabello mushrooms
4 tbsp (60 mL) onion-thyme confit (p. 72)
3 oz (90 g) Cambozola cheese

Brush mushrooms with olive oil and season with salt and pepper. Roast in a 375°F oven for 12 min. Cool and slice. Divide mushroom slices, confit and Cambozola among omelettes and melt the cheese.

parfaitAruba!

with banana, strawberries and mango coulis

layers of yogurt, fresh fruit, granola and fruit coulis look festive and enticing in an old-fashioned parfait glass, which is how we serve this dish at the restaurant. It appears to be something decadent but is, in fact, a healthy breakfast or snack anytime of the day. Kids might be fooled into thinking they're getting a treat, and you'll just be happy knowing they're getting something healthy too.

☯ use soy yogourt for a vegan parfait.

serves 2

1 cup (240 mL) plain yogourt
1/2 tsp (2.5 mL) vanilla
2 tbsp (30 mL) pure maple syrup
1/2 tsp (2.5 mL) lemon zest (optional)
2/3 cup (160 mL) cranberry-hazelnut
    granola (p. 87)
1 banana
8 strawberries
2 tbsp (30 mL) toasted coconut

1 Stir together the yogourt, vanilla and lemon zest, if using. Slice banana and strawberries.

2 To assemble, alternately layer yogourt, fruit, coulis and granola, repeating twice and ending with granola. Sprinkle with toasted coconut and serve.

mangocoulis

1/2 ripe mango, peeled
1 tbsp (15 mL) fresh lime juice
1 tbsp (15 mL) water
1 tsp (5 mL) honey
Purée the ingredients in a food processor until very smooth. Serve immediately or refrigerate up to 2 days.

Christine's summer strata

with spinach, basil and roasted garlic custard

baby G is our nickname for Christine Nagasawa, our brunch chef. Christine is a kitchen powerhouse, the backbone that keeps the rigourous kitchen pace going from day to day. Valuable employees like Chris don't come around very often and her hard work and commitment is greatly appreciated by everyone. Her brunch specials, like this popular strata, pack the house weekend after weekend. Serve this summery version with thick slices of vine-ripe tomatoes, and be sure to experiment with different vegetable, herb and cheese combinations in the cooler seasons.

serves 8 – 12

1 Prepare all of the ingredients for the filling. Soak the sundried tomatoes until soft, strain and chop coarsely.

2 To make the custard, whisk the eggs in a large bowl. Whisk in the milk, cream, mashed roasted garlic, salt and pepper. Stir in the bread cubes, cover and let stand for 1 hour. Stir occasionally to ensure that all of the bread is evenly soaked. Stir in the remaining ingredients, reserving half of the grated cheese.

3 Heat the oven to 350°F. Butter or oil a 9" x 13" baking dish and scoop the bread pudding mixture into it. Sprinkle with the reserved cheese and bake until crusty, golden brown and just set in the middle (about 45 minutes). Let stand for several minutes, cut into squares and serve.

filling

1 x 1 lb (450 g) sourdough loaf, cut into 3/4" cubes

2 bunches of spinach, wilted, squeezed and chopped

1 x recipe caramelized onions (p. 36)

1/2 cup (120 mL) sundried tomatoes (not oil-packed)

1/2 cup (120 mL) chopped basil

1/2 cup (120 mL) chopped Italian parsley

1 1/2 cups (360 mL) grated fontina cheese

custard

6 eggs

2 cups (480 mL) milk

1 cup (240 mL) light cream

2 bulbs roasted garlic (p. 158), mashed

2 tsp (10 mL) salt

1/2 tsp (2.5 mL) cracked pepper

smokedsalmonscramble

with green onions, fresh dill and cream cheese

impress visiting relatives with this special scramble (they think we West-Coasters eat smoked salmon every day). This is a perfect father's day dish, never failing to draw comments like "you really DO know how to cook, dear"! Serve with toasted poppy seed bagels. To really steal the show, knock off a batch of potato latkes (p. 73), set out a bowl of sour cream and feast away. Enough calories here to last you the day!

serves 4

8 eggs
1/4 cup (60 mL) milk or light cream
1/4 tsp (1.2 mL) salt
1 tbsp (15 mL) butter
4 oz (120 g) hot smoked salmon,
    crumbled
1/2 bunch scallions, minced
2 tbsp (30 mL) chopped dill
3 tbsp (45 mL) cream cheese
cracked pepper to taste

1 Whisk together eggs, cream and salt. Set aside. Crumble or slice salmon into bite-size pieces.

2 Heat a non-stick skillet over medium heat and add butter. Once the butter has melted, add salmon and green onions and sauté for 1 minute. Add the egg mix and gently scramble until the eggs are half set. Add the cream cheese in small pieces and continue to scramble until the eggs are set and the cream cheese blended in. Stir in minced dill and divide among 4 warm plates. Pass around the pepper mill and enjoy!

helpfulhint ❄

Lower the fat content of scrambled eggs by replacing the milk or cream with carbonated water. Makes fluffy eggs!

birchermeusli
with apples, berries and seeds

oatmeal people take heart! This traditional Swiss breakfast is a refreshing change to porridge, particularly in warmer weather. Rolled oats are soaked in water overnight, then mixed with grated apple, maple syrup, toasted seeds and fresh berries in the morning. No waiting and no pot to scrub! Once you've tried our recipe, experiment with different ingredients and methods. Toast the oats before soaking for a rich, nutty taste. Soak the oats in apple juice rather than water. Use pear instead of apple or applesauce. Try banana, mango or papaya. Replace maple syrup with honey, fruit syrup, or no sweetener at all. We like pumpkin and sunflower seeds, but nuts such as almonds and hazelnuts are also great. As for berries, choose the best of the season.

☯ replace yogourt with soy milk or yogourt, or rice milk (vegan).

serves 2

1 In the evening before serving bircher meusli, place oats in a bowl and cover with water by 1-inch. Cover and leave it to rest on the kitchen counter overnight.

2 In the morning, briefly toast nuts and seeds in a heated skillet (this can be done the night before.) Peel the apples and grate them into the bowl with the soaked oats. Add lemon juice and all of the remaining ingredients. Stir thoroughly, divide among 2 bowls and serve!

1 cup (240 mL) large flake rolled oats, preferably organic
2 apples
juice of 1/2 lemon
2 tbsp (30 mL) maple syrup, or more to taste
1 cup (240 mL) plain yogourt
2 tbsp (30 mL) pumpkin seeds
2 tbsp (30 mL) sunflower seeds
2 tbsp (30 mL) sliced almonds
1 cup (240 mL) fresh berries

helpful hint ✳

Bircher meusli is a great low-fat alternative to breakfast granola on backpacking or camping trips. Replace fresh fruit with dried apples and raisins, for instance, and soak them overnight with the oats.

☯ – a vegan recipe

☯ Anaheim black bean burger

tempeh Reuben sandwich

botanical burger

☯ calypso roti

yam and pepita quesadilla

panini alla Pugliese

☯ **re**bar sushi roll

vegetable clubhouse

☯ falafel burger

the **re**bar club

roasted veggie quesadilla

cheddar-chutney grilled cheese

Southwest grilled cheese

☯ sensitive new age sloppy Joe

Bombay roll up

papaya salsa quesadilla

mushroom-pecan burger

☯ steamed vegetable wraps

5

lunch

few people eat lunch at home these days, which is why lunch is such a popular time of day at the restaurant. Nevertheless, we put this chapter together to inspire great lunch ideas for weekends, holidays and for those at home. All of these recipes are ideal for dinner too. Healthy, stick-to-the-ribs burgers can be made ahead and frozen, ready for quick weekday meals. Quesadillas are fast and can double as appetizers. Sandwiches and wraps are particularly substantial with a soup or salad on the side.

Anaheim black bean burger
with mango salsa ☯

ten years on **re**bar's "most popular items" list means our almond burger is a signature dish with staying power. It is a blow to the kitchen staff, who work hard to maintain a creative menu, yet we still overhear the inevitable, "Oh we love **re**bar, they make that deeelicious almond burger!" Regardless of it's popularity, we've decided to keep the recipe secret. Instead we offer alternative burger recipes, all carefully chosen as serious rivals in the bid to give the almond burger a break. This burger for instance, is low-fat, high-protein category and very tasty—extra points for being vegan!

yields 6 burgers

2 x 19 fl oz (540 mL) cans black
    beans
1/2 cup (120 mL) cooked brown rice
1 1/2 tbsp (22.5 mL) vegetable oil
1 small red onion, diced
3 garlic cloves, minced
1 tsp (5 mL) pure chile powder
1/2 tsp (2.5 mL) each cumin and
    coriander seed, toasted and
    ground
1/8 tsp (.5 mL) cayenne pepper
1 tsp (5 mL) salt
2 tsp (10 mL) chipotle purée (p. 38)
1 small can Anaheim chiles, drained;
    or 4 Anaheim chiles, roasted,
    seeded and peeled (p. 50)
1/4 cup (60 mL) masa harina
1/4 cup (60 mL) toasted pumpkin
    seeds, finely ground
3/4 cup (180 mL) fresh bread crumbs

1 Heat oil in a small skillet, add onion and sauté until translucent. Add garlic and spices and continue sautéing and stirring for 5 minutes. Set aside to cool.

2 In the bowl of a food processor, add 2 cups (480 mL) beans, rice, Anaheim chiles and the cooled onion/spice mix. Pulse to coarsely grind the mix. Turn into a large bowl and add the masa harina, pumpkin seeds and breadcrumbs. Mix together thoroughly. Add the reserved whole black beans and mix in well. Season with salt and pepper to taste.

3 Divide the mixture into 6 equal portions and form them into patties. Dredge with a light coating of masa harina and fry in a lightly oiled pan until browned on both sides. Serve hot on sourdough buns with the suggested salsa, butter lettuce, avocado, sweet pepper and red onion slices.

mango salsa

2 mangoes, finely diced
1/4 red pepper, finely diced
1/4 red onion, finely diced
1 serrano chile, minced
1 tbsp (15 mL) lime juice
1 tbsp (15 mL) chopped
    cilantro

Combine all of the prepared ingredients in a bowl, mix them together and season with salt. Serve immediately.

tempehReuben
with Swiss cheese, beets and sauerkraut

classic flavours of a Reuben sandwich get the vegetarian treatment in this recipe, which recalls memories of big deli sandwiches, juicy kosher pickles and tangy coleslaw. The tempeh marinade is infused with whole cloves, red wine and black peppercorns to simulate the corned beef flavour. We sneak in a layer of freshly grated beets to balance the richness of the cheese (looks pretty too!) Serve with a creamy dill-poppyseed slaw (p. 29), potato chips and dill pickles on the side.

☯ omit the cheese and use tofu may for a vegan sandwich.

1 Cut each tempeh rectangle in half width-wise and then slice each of these into two thinner slabs. Marinate the tempeh at least one day before serving. Combine the ingredients for the Russian dressing and refrigerate until ready to use.

2 To cook tempeh, strain off marinade and gently fry in a lightly oiled non-stick skillet until golden brown on both sides. Keep warm while preparing the rest of the sandwich ingredients.

3 On half of the bread slices, spread a generous swath of Russian dressing. Top with a layer of sauerkraut, grated beets and a slice of grilled tempeh. Top with grated cheese and place under the broiler until the cheese melts. Spread Dijon mustard on the top bread slice, cover and serve.

serves 4

8 slices rye bread
1/2 cup (120 mL) sauerkraut, squeezed
1 large beet, peeled and grated
4 tbsp (60 mL) Dijon mustard
8 slices Swiss cheese
2 kosher pickles, sliced
2 pkg tempeh, marinated

Russian dressing

1/2 cup (120 mL) mayonnaise
4 tbsp (60 mL) hot horseradish
2 tbsp (30 mL) **re**barbecue sauce
(p. 51), or ketchup

marinatedtempeh

1/2 oz (15 g) dried shiitake mushrooms, soaked
in 1/2 cup (120 mL) boiling water
1 tsp (5 mL) dried oregano, lightly toasted
2 garlic cloves, minced
1/3 cup (80 mL) soy sauce
2 tbsp (30 mL) vegetable or olive oil
1/3 cup (80 mL) red wine vinegar
1/3 cup (80 mL) red wine
1 tsp (5 mL) whole cloves
1/2 tsp (2.5 mL) cracked pepper
Combine ingredients in a small pot and bring to a boil. Reduce heat and simmer 10 minutes. Pour over tempeh slices, cover and refrigerate for one day.

helpfulhint ✳

To make this a vegan sandwich, use eggless mayonnaise and substitute vegan cheese for the Swiss cheese, or omit the cheese altogether.

botanicalburger
with lime-tarragon mayonnaise

shocking pink beets in this recipe yield a burger patty with an uncanny resemblance to ground beef; however, you can rest assured that this burger is kind to animals, low-fat and high in protein. The lime-tarragon mayonnaise highlights the fresh garden flavours. Thick-cut tomato slices, sweet onion rings and leafy greens, as always, make great burger toppings. If you can get your hands on a bottle of green tomato salsa or homemade preserve, load that on too!

☯ omit mayonnaise or use tofu mayo for a vegan burger.

yields 8 - 10 burgers

2 tbsp (30 mL) olive oil

1 yellow onion, minced

3 garlic cloves, minced

1 cup (240 mL) grated carrot

1 cup (240 mL) grated turnip

1 cup (240 mL) grated beets

1 cup (240 mL) grated zucchini,
    water squeezed out

2 tsp (10 mL) salt

1 tsp (5 mL) dried dill weed

1 tsp (5 mL) cracked pepper

1 cup (240 mL) mashed potatoes

1 cup (240 mL) cooked brown rice

1/2 cup (120 mL) hazelnuts, roasted

2 tbsp (30 mL) soy sauce

2 tbsp (30 mL) nutritional yeast

2 tbsp (30 mL) minced tarragon

2 tbsp (30 mL) minced parsley

fresh breadcrumbs (optional)

1 Heat oil in a wide-bottomed pan and sauté onion until translucent. Add garlic, grated vegetables, dill, salt and pepper. Stir thoroughly and cook for 10 minutes over medium-high heat, stirring regularly. Transfer to a large bowl and cool.

2 Place cooled vegetables, rice and hazelnuts in a food processor and pulse until coarsely combined. Transfer to a large bowl and mix in all of the remaining ingredients. Season to taste. Take a handful of the mix and test to see if it holds together. If not, add breadcrumbs, 1/2 cup (120 mL) at a time, until the mixture firms. Shape into 5 oz (150 g) patties and sauté in olive oil until browned on both sides.

3 While the patties fry, stir together the mayonnaise ingredients and assemble your favourite burger condiments. Enjoy!

limetarragon mayonnaise

1 cup (240 mL) regular, homemade or eggless
    mayonnaise

zest of 1 lime

2 tbsp (30 mL) minced tarragon

Combine all of the ingredients in a small bowl and stir thoroughly. Serve or refrigerate for up to 3 days.

calypsoroti

with black bean hummous, grilled peppers and mango mojo 🌀

West Indian food typically combines fruity tropical flavours with the intense heat of fresh chiles. The habañero and scotch bonnet peppers are deemed the "hottest of the hot" and are a favourite among serious chile-heads. Experience the bite of the habañero in the fruity mango mojo—a punchy sauce that livens up the crisp fresh cabbage, sweet grilled peppers and smooth and silky black bean hummous, all wrapped in a warm whole wheat roti. Guaranteed to get your tastebuds dancing!

serves 4

1 Prepare the black bean hummous and mango mojo up to one day in advance. Combine all of the hummous ingredients in a food processor and pulse to combine. Purée to desired consistency and season to taste.

2 To serve, wrap roti in foil and place in a 300°F oven. Meanwhile, halve, seed and julienne the red peppers. Heat vegetable oil in a skillet and sauté the peppers with a pinch of salt for 5 minutes. Set aside.

3 Next, remove roti from the oven. Spoon a line of hummous down the centre of each roti. Top with grilled peppers, shredded cabbage and drizzle with mango mojo. Sprinkle with toasted pumpkin seeds, roll up and serve.

4 roti, chapathi, or whole wheat
   tortillas
2 sweet red peppers
1 tbsp (15 mL) vegetable oil
2 cups (480 mL) shredded cabbage
4 tbsp (60 mL) toasted pumpkin seeds

black bean hummous

1 x 19 fl oz (540 mL) can black beans,
   or 2 cups (480 mL) cooked
1/2 cup (120 mL) pumpkin seeds,
   toasted
1–2 garlic cloves
juice of 1/2 lime
2 tsp (10 mL) chipotle purée (p. 38)
1/4 tsp (2.5 mL) salt
1/2 tsp (2.5 mL) ground cumin
1/2 tsp (2.5 mL) ground coriander
2 tbsp (30 mL) chopped cilantro
2 tbsp (30 mL) flax seed oil (optional)

mangomojo

1 ripe mango
juice of 2 limes
2 garlic cloves
1/2 habañero chile
1 tsp (5 mL) salt
2 tbsp (30 mL)
   chopped cilantro

Purée all of the ingredients in a food processor, or blender, until smooth. Season to taste and serve.

helpfulhint ✳

Black bean hummous makes a great dip for thick-cut tortilla chips and a delicious spread for sandwiches and crackers.

yamandpepitaquesadilla
with honey-chipotle sauce and Jack cheese

over the years we've served our fair share of quesadillas. We've also come up with a rather stunning array of filling combinations, some of which would definitely classify as oddball. (The stir-fried vegetable quesadilla with hot Chinese mustard and housemade plum-ginger sauce springs to mind!) Here is a recipe that has become a favourite, and is now a permament menu item, replacing the weekly special quesadillas. While the pressure to create a new filling each week is off, it's possible that we just may have disappointed some of our more "adventurous" customers!

serves 4

2 large yams
1 tsp (5 mL) vegetable oil
1/4 tsp (1.2 mL) salt
1 bunch scallions, chopped
1/4 cup (60 mL) toasted pumpkin seeds
2 cups (480 mL) grated Monterrey Jack cheese
4 whole wheat tortillas
1/3 cup (80 mL) honey-chipotle sauce

☯ replace Jack cheese with vegan cheese.

1 Pre-heat oven to 375°F. Peel the yams and quarter them lengthwise. Slice each quarter into 1/2" thick pieces. In a small bowl, toss the yams with oil and salt. Spread them out on a parchment-lined or lightly oiled baking sheet and roast until tender and golden (about 20 minutes).

2 To assemble the quesadillas, heat a large skillet over medium-high heat. Brush lightly with oil and cover with a tortilla. Spread a thin layer of honey-chipotle sauce over the surface, sprinkle with a quarter of the grated cheese, scallions and pepitas. Spoon a quarter of the roasted yams over the bottom half of the tortilla. Heat through until the cheese melts and the tortilla crispens. Fold the top half over the bottom, slide onto a baking sheet and keep warm in a low oven while preparing the remaining quesadillas.

honeychipotlesauce
4 tbsp (60 mL) tomato paste
1 tbsp (15 mL) chipotle purée (p. 38)
1 tsp (5 mL) lime juice
1 tbsp (15 mL) honey
2 tbsp (30 mL) water
Combine all of the ingredients in a small bowl and whisk until well blended. Refrigerate up to 2 weeks.

paniniallaPugliese

with fontina, arugula and sundried tomato pesto

Italians in the sunny southern Puglia region are serious about sundried tomatoes. This luscious sandwich puts them (the tomatoes, not the Italians) to good use in a pesto made with fresh oregano, mint, garlic and pine nuts. Sandwiched between thick slices of rustic Italian bread, this vivid blend is nicely balanced with a sharp fontina cheese and nutty arugula leaves. The combination is particularly good made in a panini sandwich press, but is also great pan-grilled. Leftover pesto can be frozen and is delicious tossed with pasta or used as pizza sauce (p. 200).

serves 4

1 Start by making the pesto, which can be done up to 2 days in advance. Soak sundried tomatoes in boiling water for 15 minutes. Strain and reserve about 1/2 cup (120 mL) soaking water for thinning the consistency of the pesto. Cool. Combine all ingredients in a food processor and pulse until blended. Season to taste and refrigerate if not using immediately.

2 To serve, heat a griddle and brush with olive oil. Spread a thick layer of pesto on half of the bread slices and place the bare sides on the hot oiled griddle. Add a layer of cheese and a pile of arugula leaves. Top with a bread slice and repeat with remaining ingredients. Cook both sides until cheese is melted and the bread is golden. Add more olive oil to the pan if necessary.

8 slices hearty Italian bread
olive oil
2 cups (480 mL) grated fontina cheese
4 oz (120 g) arugula
1 red onion, thinly sliced rounds

sundried tomato pesto

1/2 cup (120 mL) sundried tomatoes
   (not oil-packed)
2 garlic cloves
2 tbsp (30 mL) pine nuts, toasted
1/4 cup (60 mL) grated Parmesan
1/4 tsp (1.2 mL) red chile flakes
2 tsp (10 mL) capers
1 tbsp (15 mL) balsamic vinegar
2 tbsp (30 mL) chopped oregano
4 tbsp (60 mL) chopped mint or basil
3 tbsp (45 mL) extra virgin olive oil
1/4 tsp (1.2 mL) salt
cracked pepper to taste

stackitupwith:

❊ marinated & grilled portabellini mushrooms (p. 23)
❊ grilled zucchini brushed with balsamic vinegar
❊ roasted eggplant rounds
❊ marinated artichoke hearts
❊ thick fresh yellow tomato slices
❊ white bean hummous

rebar**sushi**roll

with brown rice and wasabi mayonnaise ☯

purists will undoubtedly be aghast at this rather blatant mock-up of sushi; nevertheless, we must confess to really enjoying this dish AND it's wildly popular with our lunch crowd. This strange fusion was born out of necessity, at once pacifying our love of sushi while surrendering to the frantic pace of a typical **re**bar lunch. Serve this unexpectedly filling and delicious lunch with a small bowl of miso soup to help wash it down.

serves 6

2 cups (480 mL) short grain brown rice

1/4 cup (60 mL) rice wine vinegar

1 tbsp (15 mL) sugar

2 tsp (10 mL) salt

6 whole wheat (or spinach) flour tortillas

6 sheets nori seaweed

2 carrots

1/2 cucumber, seeded

1/2 red pepper, seeded

2 tbsp (30 mL) toasted sesame seeds

1/2 cup (120 mL) pickled ginger

wasabi mayonnaise

1/3 cup (80 mL) tofu mayonnaise

1 tsp (5 mL) sesame oil

1 tbsp (15 mL) wasabi powder

1 Cook rice according to package directions. In a small bowl, combine rice wine vinegar, sugar and salt. When the rice is cooked, turn it out into a large bowl and thoroughly mix in the vinegar solution. Cover with a clean kitchen towel and set aside while you prepare the remaining ingredients.

2 Peel carrots and shave long strips using a potato peeler. Slice the cucumber and red pepper into long, thin strips. Stir together the wasabi mayonnaise ingredients and set aside.

3 To assemble, have all of the prepared ingredients laid out before you. The rice should still be a little bit warm but not hot. Heat tortillas briefly in a hot skillet, turning them over when small bubbles appear underneath. On a clean, dry surface, lay down a tortilla and spread a thin layer of rice over the surface with moistened fingers, leaving a 1/2" border around the edge. Cover with a sheet of nori. Spread 1 tbsp (15 mL) wasabi mayonnaise in a line across the lower part of the nori. Lay out a line of carrot shavings, cucumber, red pepper strips and pickled ginger, reaching from one end of the tortilla to the other. Sprinkle with sesame seeds. Lift the bottom of the tortilla and roll up and over the filling. Keeping a tight grip, continue rolling into a solid cylinder. Set aside and repeat with remaining ingredients.

4 To serve, use a serrated knife to gently slice the roll diagonally into three sections. Arrange on a plate and serve with tamari or soy-chile sauce (p. 46) for dipping.

helpful**hint** ❈

Other great filling combinations:

❈ avocado, arugula, steamed asparagus

❈ smoked salmon, watercress, cucumber

❈ grilled shiitake mushrooms, steamed spinach and snow peas

vegetableclubhouse
with basil-lemon aïoli

stack up this juicy collection of roasted, balsamic-glazed eggplant slices, rich portabello mushrooms and sweet peppers, and forget any tired old notions of a clubhouse sandwich. The summery flavours of fresh basil and lemon will also help purge any stale memories. Use a good quality sourdough bread for double-decker layering and pass around a bowl of extra aïoli for dipping corners.

serves 4

1 Pre-heat oven to 350°F. Arrange eggplant slices and whole, stemmed portabello mushrooms on an oiled baking sheet. Brush with olive oil and sprinkle lightly with salt and cracked pepper. Roast for 10–15 minutes, until tender and golden. Remove from the oven and brush with balsamic vinegar. Cool and slice mushrooms into 1/4" thick strips. Slice roasted pepper halves into 1/2" thick strips.

2 Toast bread slices. Generously spread aïoli on one side of each slice. Layer eggplant and mushroom slices on top of 4 of the toasts. Place another toast on top, aïoli side up. Layer arugula leaves, red pepper, red onion and tomato slices on top and cover with the final toast, aïoli side down. Slice each sandwich into quarters, secure with toothpicks and serve.

- 1 eggplant, sliced into 1/2" thick rounds
- 4 portabello mushrooms
- 4 tbsp (60 mL) olive oil
- 4 tbsp (60 mL) balsamic vinegar
- 2 red peppers, roasted and peeled (p. 50)
- 1 red onion, sliced into thin rounds
- 2 tomatoes, sliced
- arugula, spinach or lettuce leaves
- 12 slices sourdough bread
- basil-lemon aïoli

basillemonaïoli

- 1 whole egg
- 1 egg yolk
- 1 tbsp (15 mL) fresh lemon juice
- 2 garlic cloves
- 1/2 oz (15 g) basil leaves
- 1 cup (240 mL) olive oil
- zest of 1 lemon
- 1/2 tsp (2.5 mL) salt

In a blender or food processor add the egg and yolk. Blend for 15 seconds. Add lemon juice, garlic and basil leaves and blend for another 15 seconds. While the motor is running, slowly drizzle in the oil, starting drop by drop and working up to a thin, steady stream. Stop the engine when you run out of oil and the mixture is thick. Blend in lemon zest and salt. Refrigerate up to 2 days.

helpfulhint ❋

For those uncomfortable with eating raw egg, commercial mayonnaise, available with or without egg, can substitute for the aïoli. Replace egg, egg yolk and olive oil with 1 cup (240 mL) mayonnaise; stir in the remaining ingredients.

falafelburger
with taratour sauce ☯

exotic flavours of the Middle East dominate in this burger. A base of chick peas, onions and roasted bulghur is boldly seasoned with toasted cumin, coriander, garlic and fresh herbs. Unlike traditional deep-fried falafel, this burger is lightly sautéed in olive oil. Creamy taratour sauce, rich with sesame and lemon, adds great flavour. Top with cucumber, tomato and red onion slices and serve with tabbouleh salad (p. 22).

yields 10 burgers

1/2 cup (120 mL) bulghur
2 tbsp (30 mL) olive oil
1 red onion, finely minced
8 garlic cloves, minced
1 tsp (5 mL) ground cumin
2 tsp (10 mL) ground coriander
1/2 tsp (2.5 mL) turmeric
1/4 tsp (1.2 mL) ground fennel seed
1 1/2 tsp (7.5 mL) salt
1/4 tsp (1.2 mL) cayenne
1 tsp (5 mL) red chile flakes
2 cups (480 mL) fresh bread crumbs
6 cups (1.4 L) canned chick peas
1/4 cup (60 mL) tahini
1/2 bunch parsley chopped

1 Spread bulghur out on a baking sheet and roast for 5 minutes, or until golden brown. Cool and grind thoroughly in a spice or coffee grinder. Set aside.

2 Heat olive oil in a skillet. Add onion and 1/2 tsp (2.5 mL) salt and cook until translucent. Add garlic and spices and sauté 5 more minutes.

3 If you have a food processor, combine all of the ingredients and pulse them together to blend in 2 or more batches. Otherwise, mash the chick peas in a large bowl and mix ingredients in thoroughly (use your clean hands!) Season to taste, cover with plastic wrap and refrigerate for 1 hour, or overnight.

4 Before serving, stir together ingredients for taratour sauce and prepare other favourite toppings. Shape the burger mixture into patties. Sauté in olive oil until golden brown. Serve on wholegrain or sesame seed buns.

helpfulhint ✳

Another great condiment for this burger is a quick and easy cucumber-mint salsa. Simply dice equal parts seeded cucumber and tomato and add minced red onion, mint, garlic, lemon juice, a splash of extra virgin olive oil and salt and pepper to taste.

taratoursauce

1/4 cup (60 mL) tahini
1/4 cup (60 mL) water
1 tbsp (15 mL) flax seed or olive oil
juice of 1 small lemon
1 tbsp (15 mL) shiro (light) miso
1 garlic clove, minced
1 1/2 tsp (7.5 mL) honey
1 tsp (5 mL) chipotle purée (p. 38)
Combine all of the ingredients in a small bowl. Season to taste and serve.

therebarclub

with lox, shrimp, chipotle mayonnaise and avocado

Victoria is a beautiful, if small, city and the winter months are a painful reminder of the fragility of the restaurant business in such a location. Thanks to our loyal local clientele we always manage to squeak through these difficult times. To help matters, we pad our menu with the occasional dish that includes smoked salmon or shrimp, hoping to entice customers that may otherwise never enter a "vegetarian" restaurant. This works for us so we make no apologies. This clubhouse sandwich is always a sell-out with lunch-time business crowds and evening movie buffs.

serves 4

1 — Begin by stirring together the mayonnaise ingredients. Thinly slice the red onion and sweet red pepper.

2 — To assemble sandwiches, lightly toast bread. Spread mayonnaise over one side of each slice. Arrange two slices of lox over one toast and top with a quarter of the shrimp. Top with another toast. Cover with avocado slices, red onion and pepper rings. Lay lettuce leaves to cover and top with the final toast, mayonnaise side facing down. Quarter, secure with toothpicks and repeat with remaining ingredients.

1 loaf (12 slices) sourdough bread
1/2 cup (120 mL) chipotle mayonnaise
1 large avocado
8 slices lox
6 oz (180 g) hand-peeled shrimp
1 small red onion
1 sweet red pepper
lettuce leaves

chipotle mayonnaise

1/2 cup (120 mL) mayonnaise
2 tbsp (30 mL) chipotle purée (p. 38)
2 tbsp (30 mL) chopped cilantro
2 garlic cloves, minced

helpfulhint ✳

For easy avocado pit removal, hold the avocado half with the pit in one hand, and a large knife in the other. Carefully but forcefully strike the pit with the knife blade until it's securely lodged in the pit and twist until it comes out.

roasted veggie quesadilla
with basil, fontina cheese and smoked chiles

squeeze this quesadilla into any category ... lunch, appetizer, brunch, or even dinner. The rich roasted vegetables lend a fabulous backdrop for the bright fresh flavours of basil, lemon zest and chipotle chiles.

serves 6

3 Japanese eggplant

4 Roma tomatoes, seeded and
    cut into 6 wedges

1 red onion, chopped

4 oz (120 g) oyster or button
    mushrooms, roughly chopped

1 red bell pepper, seeded and
    chopped

2 tbsp (30 mL) olive oil

1/2 tsp (2.5 mL) salt

1 tsp (5 mL) chipotle purée (p. 38)

1/2 oz (15 g) chopped basil

1 tsp (5 mL) minced lemon zest

1/2 tsp (2.5 mL) cracked pepper

1 1/2 cups (360 mL) grated fontina
    cheese

6 whole wheat tortillas

1 Pre-heat oven to 400°F. Halve the eggplant lengthwise and cut 1/8" thick slices. In a large bowl, toss the prepared eggplant, tomatoes, onion, mushrooms and pepper with the olive oil and salt. Spread the vegetables out on a large baking sheet and roast until the vegetables are soft and turning golden (about 15 minutes). Transfer the vegetables back into the bowl and cool. Stir in chipotle purée, basil, lemon zest and cracked pepper.

2 Just before serving, heat a large skillet over medium-high heat. Cover with one of the tortillas and sprinkle shredded cheese over the surface. Top with the vegetable mixture, spreading it out over the lower half of the tortilla. Heat through until the cheese is melted and the tortilla is golden and crispy. Fold the top half of the tortilla over the bottom half, slide onto a baking sheet and keep warm in a low oven while you prepare the remaining quesadillas. Slice each quesadilla into 3 wedges and serve hot.

helpful hint ❊

Quesadillas are ideal party appetizers. Make a variety of fillings, cut into small triangles and keep warm in a low oven. Serve with crème fraîche seasoned with minced cilantro, a few drops of your favourite hot sauce, salt and pepper.

crème fraîche

1 cup (240 mL) whipping cream

1/4 cup (60 mL) buttermilk

Stir together the cream and buttermilk. Cover loosely with plastic wrap and let sit at room temperature for 24 hrs. Unwrap, stir and refrigerate. Will keep up to one week.

cheddarchutneygrilledcheese
with green apple and watercress

grown-up grilled cheese sandwiches are always popular with our business lunch crowd. In this favourite, sharp cheddar and creamy, sweet onion chutney are just the right match for the crisp sour apple, bitter leaves of watercress and the bite of Dijon mustard. Use a hearty multigrain loaf with nuts and seeds for best results. Serve with pickled beets and roasted yam soup (p. 121) for a well-rounded lunch.

serves 4

1 Have the chutney prepared and cooled before proceeding with the sandwich assembly.

2 Butter one side of each bread slice. On the unbuttered side of half of the slices, spread Dijon mustard and layer with chutney, apple slices, cheddar and watercress. Top with remaining bread slices, buttered side up.

3 Heat a griddle and cook sandwiches on both sides until the cheese is melted and the bread is crispy and golden. Slice each sandwich in half diagonally, pierce each with a toothpick and serve hot.

8 slices multigrain bread
2 tbsp (30 mL) butter
12 slices aged white cheddar cheese
4 tbsp (60 mL) Dijon mustard
1 Granny Smith apple, quartered and thinly sliced
1 bunch watercress, washed and stemmed
1/2 cup (120 mL) onion chutney

onionchutney

2 tbsp (30 mL) butter
2 yellow onions, sliced or diced
1/2 tsp (2.5 mL) salt
1/2 tsp (2.5 mL) red chile flakes
1 tsp (5 mL) ground coriander
1 tsp (5 mL) brown sugar
4 tbsp (60 mL) apple cider vinegar
1/4 tsp (1.2 mL) cracked pepper

Heat butter in a pan over medium heat and add onions. Sauté until translucent. Add salt, chile flakes and coriander and continue to cook for 15 minutes. Add remaining ingredients and cook until the onions are very soft and creamy.

Southwest grilled cheese

with cilantro pesto and asiago cheese

pack all of our favourite ingredients in between two slices of bread and you get this sensational sandwich. Cilantro, pumpkin seeds, chipotle chiles, asiago cheese—it's all here, in one brilliant bite after another. This sandwich is rich and rather spicy, but the crisp sweet peppers, red onion and lettuce lift it up and soften the blow. We use a lovely honey-cornmeal bread from our sister bakery "Cascadia" to create the perfect package, but almost any loaf will stand up to this daring sandwich.

serves 4

8 bread slices

butter for spreading

4 tbsp (60 mL) cilantro pesto (p. 41)

4 tbsp (60 mL) honey-chipotle sauce
    (p. 102)

1 1/2 cups (360 mL) grated asiago
    cheese

1 red onion, sliced in thin rings

1 red pepper, sliced in rings

4 lettuce leaves

1 Prepare cilantro pesto and honey-chipotle sauce; or refer to the "helpful hint".

2 To assemble the sandwich, slice red onion and pepper in thin rings. Spread butter on one side of each bread slice. Spread cilantro pesto on the unbuttered side of half of the slices. Layer cheese, red pepper, onion rings and lettuce over the pesto. Spread a thin layer of honey-chipotle sauce on the unbuttered side of the remaining bread slices and top the sandwich, buttered side up.

3 Heat a griddle and fry the sandwiches until the cheese is melted and the bread is crispy and golden on both sides. Slice each sandwich in half diagonally and pierce a toothpick through each half. Serve right away and enjoy!

helpfulhint ✳

If you don't have time to make cilantro pesto, you can still enjoy this great sandwich by substituting fresh cilantro leaves for the pesto. No time for honey-chipotle sauce? Replace with chipotle purée (p. 38) or a commercial chipotle hot sauce spread in a very thin layer.

sensitive new age sloppy Joe
with sweet & spicy tofu and pinto beans ☯

childhood food memories are fun to revisit, but pose interesting challenges if you've become a vegetarian in adulthood. We couldn't resist the temptation to update this campy classic. Obviously presentation is not an issue here, but bold flavours are, so be generous with seasoning. This dish also makes a delicious chili-like sauce that is great with brown rice (a protein powerhouse!), or accompanied with fresh cornbread (p. 155) and a crunchy vegetable slaw (p. 29).

serves 8

1. Pre-heat oven to 350°F. Drain water from the pressed tofu and crumble it coarsely. Toss with 1 tbsp (15 mL) oil and a pinch of salt. Spread on a small parchment-lined baking tray and bake the tofu until firm and light golden brown (about 15 minutes).

2. Heat 2 tbsp (30 mL) oil in a wide-bottomed pot. Sauté onion with 1 tsp (5 mL) salt until translucent. Add garlic, jalapeños, red pepper, cumin, chile powder and allspice; sauté for 5 minutes. Add the remaining ingredients and bring to a simmer. Cover partially and simmer for 30 minutes. Add the tofu and heat through.

3. To serve, heat Kaiser buns in a warm oven. Split and generously ladle the mixture over the bottom half of the bun. Replace the top and serve, making sure that each serving is sufficiently sloppy!

1 block firm tofu, pressed
3 tbsp (45 mL) vegetable oil
1 yellow onion, diced
8 garlic cloves, minced
2 tsp (10 mL) salt
3 jalapeño peppers, minced
1 red pepper, diced
1 tsp (5 mL) ground cumin
1 tsp (5 mL) ancho chile powder
1/2 tsp (2.5 mL) ground allspice
2 x 540 mL (19 fl oz) cans pinto beans, or 3 cups cooked
1 cup (240 mL) reserved bean liquid
3 tbsp (45 mL) molasses
2 tsp (10 mL) chipotle purée (p. 38)
2 tbsp (30 mL) apple cider vinegar
1/4 tsp (1.2 mL) liquid smoke
1/2 x 5 1/2 oz (196 mL) can tomato paste
4 Roma tomatoes, chopped
1 tbsp (15 mL) chopped oregano
8 whole wheat Kaiser buns

Bombay**roll**up

with chick pea-cashew hummous and cucumber raita

the wrap and roll craze did not pass unnoticed in the **re**bar kitchen.

Dare we say that we were doing it long before there was a craze? Regardless, customers seem to enjoy gobbling them up at lunchtime, so over the years we've had our
share of wild and wonderful combinations. From lavash bread to rice paper, we hold no
loyalty to the tortilla when it comes to wrapping. Chapathi, particularly when fresh and
hot off the grill, are the perfect foil for countless exciting fillings. Here is one favourite.

☯ leave out the raita for a vegan dish.

serves 4

4 chapathi or whole wheat tortillas
2 cups (480 mL) grated carrot
2 cups (480 mL) shredded lettuce
1/2 English cucumber, sliced
1/2 cup (120 mL) roasted tomato-
    ginger chutney (p. 69)

Bombay hummous

1/4 cup (60 mL) canola oil
1-inch piece of ginger, peeled and
    thinly sliced
1 x 19 fl oz (540 mL) can chick peas
1/4 cup (60 mL) cashews, roasted
juice of 1 lime
2 garlic cloves
1 tsp (5 mL) salt
1 tsp (5 mL) ground cumin
1 tsp (5 mL) ground coriander
1/2 tsp (2.5 mL) cracked pepper
1/4 tsp (1.2 mL) cayenne
pinch turmeric
pinch cinnamon
2 tbsp (30 mL) chopped cilantro
2 tbsp (30 mL) chopped mint

1 Begin by making the hummous. Gently heat the oil and ginger
in a small saucepan. Let the ginger sizzle, but not brown.
After 10 minutes, remove from heat and set aside to cool.

2 Combine all of the ingredients in a food processor, including
the ginger and oil, and pulse to blend. Blend to a rough purée
and season to taste.

3 To serve, wrap a stack of chapathi in foil and place in a 300°F
oven for 15–20 minutes. Spread 1/2 cup (120 mL) hummous
and 2 tbsp (30 mL) chutney down the center of each
chapathi. Arrange shredded vegetables on top and roll up.
Serve with raita on the side.

cucumber raita

1 cup (240 mL) plain yogourt
1/2 cucumber, peeled, seeded and grated
juice of 1/2 lime
1/2 tsp (2.5 mL) ground cumin
1/2 tsp (2.5 mL) salt
Place the yogourt in a cheesecloth-lined sieve set
over a bowl and strain in the refrigerator for 4 hrs.
Combine strained yogourt with the remaining ingredients and mix well. Let sit 1 hour before serving.

papaya**salsa**quesadilla
with avocado and Brie cheese

tropical fruit imported to Canada is often disappointing to those lucky enough to have tasted the real thing. In making fruit salsas however, adding ginger, chiles, cilantro and lime juice breathes new life into mangoes, papaya and pineapple. For the perfect outdoor summer lunch, accompany this lively quesadilla with a light salad of cucumbers, yellow cherry tomatoes and sweet red onions dressed with honey-ginger dressing (p. 9) and an icy bowl of green gazpacho (p. 124).

1 Before serving, prepare salsa by gently mixing all of the ingredients in a bowl. Set aside.

2 Heat a griddle or non-stick skillet and brush lightly with oil. Place a tortilla on the hot pan and when bubbles begin to appear underneath, flip it over. On the bottom half of the tortilla, distribute small pieces of Brie. Spread one quarter of the salsa on the cheese and top with one quarter of the avocado slices. Fold the top half of the tortilla over the filling and heat until the tortilla crisps and cheese melts. Keep warm in a low oven while preparing the remaining quesadillas. Slice each into 3 triangles and serve with crème fraîche (p. 108).

serves 4

4 whole wheat tortillas
4 oz (120 g) Brie cheese
1 avocado, thinly sliced

papaya salsa

(yields 3 cups - 720 mL)
1 large ripe papaya, peeled and diced
1 lime, juiced
1 serrano chile, seeded and minced
1 tbsp (15 mL) minced ginger
1 tbsp (15 mL) minced cilantro
2 tbsp (30 mL) minced red onion
2 tsp (10 mL) honey
1/8 tsp (.5 mL) salt

helpful**hint** ✳

Add chopped strawberries to the papaya salsa for a special summery presentation. If papayas are unavailable, mangoes are an excellent substitute. Add fresh hand-peeled shrimp for a delicious twist.

mushroompecanburger

with grilled onions and horseradish mayonnaise

robust mushroom flavour and the nutty crunch of roasted pecans are an irresistible combination in this popular burger. Serve with dill-poppyseed slaw (p. 29) and cowpokes (p. 157) for a deluxe hungry-person's meal.

🌓 leave out the mayo, or substitute with tofu mayo (vegan).

yields 10 - 12 burgers

2 tbsp (30 mL) vegetable oil
1 red onion, diced
1 tsp (5 mL) salt
4 garlic cloves, minced
2 tbsp (30 mL) thyme leaves
1/2 tsp (2.5 mL) red chile flakes
6 cups (1.5 L) sliced button mush-
    rooms
2 tbsp (30 mL) balsamic vinegar
1 1/2 cups (360 mL) cooked brown rice
1 1/2 cups (360 mL) grated carrot
1 cup (240 mL) pecans, roasted and
    finely ground
2 cups (480 mL) fresh breadcrumbs
1/2 tsp (2.5 mL) cracked pepper
1/4 tsp (1.2 mL) Tabasco sauce
2 tbsp (30 mL) soy sauce

grilled onions

2 Spanish onions
2 tbsp (30 mL) olive oil
1/2 tsp (2.5 mL) salt
cracked pepper to taste

1 In a large skillet, heat oil over medium heat and sauté onion. Turn up the heat and add the garlic, mushrooms, salt, thyme and chile flakes. Stir and sauté until the mushrooms have released their juices and the pan begins to dry out. Deglaze the pan with balsamic vinegar. Let the liquid evaporate, turn the mushrooms out into a large bowl and let cool.

2 Add the brown rice and grated carrot to the mushrooms. In a food processor, pulse the mixture in two or more batches until well combined but still coarse in texture. Return to the bowl and add all of the remaining ingredients. Mix thoroughly and season to taste. Refrigerate for 1 hour, or overnight. Shape into patties and sauté until golden brown on both sides.

3 Before serving, prepare the grilled onions by heating oil in a large skillet and adding the onions and salt. Fry until golden and season with cracked pepper. Prepare the horseradish mayonnaise. Serve hot burgers on your favourite buns with lettuce or sprouts, sliced tomato, pickle, Dijon mustard, ketchup or **re**barbecue sauce (p. 51). Top with grilled onions.

horseradish mayonnaise

1 cup (240 mL) regular, homemade or eggless
    mayonnaise
4 tbsp (60 mL) prepared hot horseradish

Stir mayonnaise and horseradish until well combined.

steamed**vegetable**wraps
with ponzu sauce

fresh hand-rolled tortillas are a must-have for this recipe. The tender home-made tortilla is the perfect wrap for lightly steamed vegetables and lively ponzu sauce. Ponzu is also delicious sprinkled on steamed vegetables or poached fish and rice, or as a light dressing for cool soba noodles tossed with toasted sesame seeds, long ribbons of cucumber and crumbled nori seaweed on top. So healthy!

serves 4 - 6

1 Prepare the tortillas to the final stage just before cooking them off. Then prepare the vegetables. Snap the tough ends from the asparagus. If the stalks are thick, cut them in half length-wise. Trim the beans. Peel carrots. Cut carrots and zucchini along their length to make batons about 1/4" thick. Halve, seed and slice the pepper into 1/4" thick strips.

2 Heat up a griddle to cook the tortillas and set up a steamer basket over boiling water to steam the vegetables. Start steaming the beans, since they will take the longest to cook, then add carrots and eventually the remaining vegetables. Cook until the vegetables are just tender and still have a bit of crunch. Meanwhile, cook off the tortillas, one by one, and transfer them to a plate, covered with a clean cloth and placed in a 200°F oven.

3 To serve, toss steamed vegetables with enough ponzu sauce to lightly coat. Wrap a small bundle of mixed vegetables in a warm tortilla, sprinkle with sesame seeds and serve, with remaining ponzu on the side for dipping.

1 x recipe flour tortillas (p. 43)
1/2 bundle asparagus
8 oz (240 g) green beans
2 large carrots
1 medium zucchini
1 large red pepper
2 tsp (10 mL) toasted sesame seeds
ponzu sauce

ponzu**sauce**

(yields 1 1/4 cups - 300 mL)
2 tbsp (30 mL) fresh lemon juice
2 tbsp (30 mL) fresh lime juice
2 tbsp (30 mL) fresh orange juice
2 tbsp (30 mL) rice wine vinegar
1/4 cup (60 mL) mirin
1/2 cup (120 mL) soy sauce or tamari
1 tsp (5 mL) sesame oil

Stir together all of the ingredients in a bowl. Let stand one hour, allowing the flavours to mingle, then serve or refrigerate for up to one week.

@ – a vegan recipe

soup

you can spot a good cook by tasting a pot of his/her homemade soup. At the restaurant, the soup cook reigns as queen (or king) of the kitchen—a wonderful position to be in because a great pot of soup will summon hundreds of compliments in a day! Everyone at **re**bar, staff and customers, gobble up more soup than any other item on our menu.

Making a fresh vegetable stock is the first critical step, so don't skip this task! Making a vegetable stock is entirely different from preparing a meat, fish or chicken stock (there's no greasy mess or carcass to deal with). Vegetables simply require a quick cleaning, a rough chopping and less than an hour of gentle simmering. In the end, your soup will have more flavour, greater body and more food value. Naturally, the depth of flavour from a vegetable stock cannot match that of a good meat stock. For this reason, quality ingredients and attention to proper seasoning with spices and fresh herbs are essential.

carrotlemongrass
with coriander, ginger and coconut ☯

restore body and soul with this lively purée loaded with sweet organic carrots and a generous dose of fresh lemongrass and ginger. This soup is invigorating when spirits are low and you feel a cold coming on. To reduce fat intake, omit the coconut milk and add stock to thin. Chopped cilantro and a swirl of plain yogourt are ideal garnishes.

serves 6 - 8

8 cups (2 L) Asian (p. 127) or vegetable
    stock (p. 35)
6 kaffir lime leaves, fresh or frozen
2 tbsp (30 mL) vegetable oil
1 yellow onion, diced
1 tbsp (15 mL) coarse salt
3 lemongrass stalks
5 garlic cloves, minced
3 tbsp (45 mL) minced ginger
1/2 tsp (2.5 mL) Thai red curry paste
    (we use Thai Kitchen brand)
1 tbsp (15 mL) coriander seeds, ground
2 lbs (900 g) carrots, roughly chopped
1 x 398 mL can coconut milk
2 tsp (10 mL) sambal oelek
1 tsp (5 mL) minced lemon zest
juice of 1 lemon
chopped cilantro leaves
plain yogourt (optional)

1 Begin by heating the stock while you prepare the soup ingredients. Add the lime leaves and keep warm. Prepare lemongrass by cutting the stalk 4" from the root end. Discard the top and peel the outer layer from the bottom piece. Using a large, broad-bladed knife, smash the lemongrass. To do this safely, lay the blade flat on the stalk (sharp end facing away from you) and bang the blade with your fist. The lemongrass should lightly crush under the impact. Mince and set aside. Prepare the remaining ingredients.

2 Heat oil in a heavy-bottomed soup pot over medium heat. Add onion and 1 tsp (5 mL) salt. Cook the onions until translucent. Add minced garlic, ginger, lemongrass, curry paste and coriander; sauté and stir for 5 minutes. Stir in the chopped carrots and remaining 2 tsp (10 mL) salt. Sauté for several minutes, then pour in the hot stock. Bring to a boil and simmer until the carrots are soft (about 15 minutes).

3 Remove the lime leaves and purée the soup with a hand blender or food processor until smooth. Whisk in coconut milk and sambal oelek and simmer gently for 15 minutes. Just before serving, add the lemon zest, juice and season to taste with salt or more sambal. Garnish each bowl with freshly chopped cilantro leaves and a spoonful of yogourt, if you like.

helpfulhint ✳

When preparing vegetables for a puréed soup, save time and effort by chopping them roughly and quickly. Shape and size don't matter, because they will eventually be puréed.

smoky green split pea
with sage and roasted garlic ☯

who says you need a ham bone to make a good hearty green pea soup?
Earthy sage and mellow roasted garlic give fabulous flavour, but the secret is a dash of
liquid smoke! A small hit of chipotle chiles accents the smokiness and adds a bite.
Garnish with garlic croutons (p. 8) or crispy fried sage leaves.

serves 8 - 10

1 Heat the stock and keep it warm while you prepare the
soup. Drain the peas and rinse well in cold water. Heat oil in
a large soup pot and sauté onion until translucent. Add bay
leaves, half the sage, chile flakes, salt, carrots, celery and
minced garlic. Stir and sauté for 10 minutes. Add the green
split peas and warm stock. Bring to a boil, reduce heat and
simmer until the peas are soft and falling apart. Remove the
bay leaves.

2 Squeeze the flesh from the roasted garlic bulbs and add it to
the soup pot with the remaining sage, black pepper, liquid
smoke and chipotle purée. With a hand blender or food
processor, purée the soup until smooth, adding more stock
if it's too thick. Before serving, reheat the soup gently and
season to taste with more chipotles, pepper or salt.

2 cups (480 mL) green split peas,
   soaked overnight
8 cups (2 L) vegetable stock (p. 35)
1 large yellow onion, diced
1 tbsp (15 mL) vegetable oil
4 bay leaves
1/4 tsp (1.2 mL) red chile flakes
2 tsp (10 mL) salt
2 carrots, finely diced
3 celery sticks, finely diced
2 garlic cloves, minced
1/2 cup (120 mL) minced sage
2 garlic bulbs, roasted (p. 158)
1 tsp (5 mL) cracked pepper
3/4 tsp (4 mL) liquid smoke
1 tsp (5 mL) chipotle purée (p. 38)

helpful hint ✳

Before soaking beans or legumes,
spread them out on a tray and sort
through to find and remove any stones.

tomatocream
with fresh tarragon

velvety smooth tomato cream soup can be made with canned tomatoes, fresh tomatoes, or a combination, depending on the season. Tarragon is a natural partner for tomatoes but different fresh herbs, such as fresh basil, mint or lovage would also be lovely. Garnish with shavings of Parmesan cheese.

serves 10

6 cups (720 mL) vegetable stock (p. 35)
2 tbsp (30 mL) olive oil, or butter
1 yellow onion, diced
2 tsp (10 mL) salt
6 garlic cloves, minced
4 bay leaves
1/4 tsp (1.2 mL) red chile flakes
1/2 cup (120 mL) chopped tarragon
2 x 28 oz liq (796 mL) cans whole
   tomatoes, drained OR
8 cups (2 L) ripe tomatoes, peeled,
   seeded and chopped
1 cup (240 mL) heavy cream
cracked pepper to taste

1 Heat vegetable stock and keep it warm while preparing the soup. Heat olive oil in a soup pot over medium heat. Sauté the onions with 1 tsp (5 mL) salt until soft and translucent. Stir in the garlic, bay, chiles and half of the chopped tarragon; sauté 5 more minutes.

2 Coarsely chop the canned or fresh tomatoes. Add to the soup pot with the remaining salt and cook for 10 minutes. Add stock to cover and bring to a boil. Reduce heat and simmer for 15 minutes.

3 Purée the soup until smooth, whisk in the cream and remaining tarragon and reheat to a simmer. Before serving, season with salt and freshly cracked pepper.

helpfulhint ✳

Peeling and seeding tomatoes is an extra step required for a smooth textured soup or sauce. Slice an "x" at the base of each tomato, just enough to break the skin, and blanch in boiling, salted water until you see the skin beginning to peel away (1 minute or so). Remove with a slotted spoon, cool, seed and chop.

roasted**yam**and**garlic**
with smoked chiles and lime ☯

sweet potatoes and yams can be used interchangeably in this recipe, though the yams have the deep orange colour that makes this soup look so warm and inviting. Sweet and smoky is the theme—our favourite!

serves 6

1. Pre-heat oven to 375°F. Using a fork, poke a few holes in each yam. Place on a baking tray and roast until soft and collapsed (about 45 minutes). You can roast the garlic bulbs at the same time. When the yams are tender, cool slightly and remove skins. Squeeze flesh from the roasted garlic bulbs.

2. Halve and seed peppers. Place peppers and whole tomatoes on an oiled baking tray and roast until the skins begin to puff and brown (about 15 minutes). Transfer to a bowl and cover with plastic wrap for 10 minutes. Peel away the skins and set aside.

3. Heat vegetable oil in large soup pot. Add onions and sauté until translucent. Add garlic, spices and herbs and cook until the garlic is golden. Stir in the peeled, roasted vegetables, the stock and chipotle chiles. Bring to a boil, reduce heat and simmer for 20 minutes.

4. Purée the soup until smooth. Whisk in maple syrup, lime juice and season to taste with salt, pepper and more chipotles, if desired. Serve hot.

6 cups (1 1/2 L) vegetable stock (p. 35)
3 large yams
2 garlic bulbs, roasted (p. 158)
4 tomatoes
2 red peppers
2 tbsp (30 mL) vegetable oil
1 medium yellow onion, diced
2 tsp (10 mL) salt
3 garlic cloves, minced
2 tbsp (30 mL) minced sage
2 tbsp (30 mL) minced oregano
2 tsp (10 mL) coriander seeds, toasted
  and ground
1 tsp (5 mL) ancho chile powder
pinch allspice
2 tsp (10 mL) chipotle purée (p. 38)
1 tbsp (15 mL) maple syrup
juice of 1 lime
salt and pepper to taste.

helpful**hint** ✳

Great garnishes for this soup:
✳ roughly chopped roasted pecans
✳ spiced pecans (p. 30)
✳ fried whole sage leaves
✳ flame-roasted pepper salsa (p. 195)
✳ fried blue & yellow corn tortilla squares

genmai**miso**
with soba, tofu & hijiki ☯

nourish and warm yourself head to toe with this steaming broth enriched with buckwheat noodles, shiitake mushrooms, seaweed and tofu. Unlike traditional miso soup, this is a meal in a bowl and has been a staple on our menu since day one. Genmai is a brown rice miso with a rich, pungent flavour. Another good choice is barley miso, which is great on it's own or combined with other miso, such as aka (red) or shiro (white) miso. Experiment to discover your favourite combinations.

serves 2

3 1/2 cups (840 mL) water

2 tbsp (30 mL) hijiki seaweed

3 tbsp (45 mL) soy-chile sauce (p. 46), OR 2 tbsp (30 mL) soy sauce and 1 tbsp (15 mL) mirin

1/2 block firm tofu, 1/2" cubes

4 tbsp (60 mL) genmai miso

1 cup (240 mL) cooked soba noodles

2 oz (60 g) spinach leaves

3 scallions, minced

2 tsp (10 mL) sesame seeds, toasted

1 Heat water to a simmer; add the hijiki and soy-chile sauce. Cover and remove from heat. Allow the hijiki to soak for 20 minutes.

2 Return the pot to the burner and reheat to a simmer. Add the tofu and simmer 5 minutes. Whisk in the miso and add the remaining ingredients. Heat through gently without letting the broth come to a boil. Sprinkle toasted sesame seeds over top and serve.

helpful**hint** ✳

Miso is a fermented soybean paste available in many varieties that vary in flavour and texture. Miso has many healthful properties, including a high protein content, an amino acid pattern similar to meat and it is a live food containing lactobacillus, which aids in digestion and nutrient absorption. Cooking destroys the beneficial microorganisms in miso, so avoid boiling by stirring it into soups in the last moments before serving.

Greekredlentil

with lemon, rosemary and feta cheese

SOUP cooks at **re**bar face the daunting daily pre-dawn task of concocting a fresh, vegetarian soup five days a week, 52 weeks a year. Harbans is one of our veteran chefs who spent three years in our kitchen before moving to Cascadia, and she was soup cook supreme at both locations. This is a favourite of her repertoire—still popular with customers, and our soup cooks looking for a reliably delicious, easy to prepare and healthy soup of the day. Serve with warm whole wheat pita bread.

❂ omit the feta cheese for a vegan soup.

serves 8

1 Rinse lentils thoroughly in a colander under cold running water. Set aside to drain. Heat oil in a soup pot over medium-high heat and sauté onion with 1 tsp (5 mL) salt until translucent. Add garlic, carrot, pepper, chiles, herbs, bay leaves and remaining salt. Stir well and sauté until the carrots are just tender. Add rinsed lentils and stock and bring to a boil. Reduce heat to a simmer and cook, partially covered, until the lentils are soft and falling apart. If you like, the soup can be puréed or left as is. If you choose to purée, remove the bay leaves first.

2 Season the soup with lemon zest, lemon juice and more salt and pepper to taste. Before serving, stir together the feta cheese, rosemary and pepper. Sprinkle over hot bowls of soup and enjoy!

2 cups (480 mL) red lentils
2 tbsp (30 mL) olive oil
1 large yellow onion, diced
2 tsp (10 mL) salt
8 garlic cloves, minced
2 carrots, diced
1 tsp (5 mL) cracked pepper
1/4 tsp (1.2 mL) red chile flakes
1 tbsp (15 mL) minced rosemary
2 tbsp (30 mL) minced oregano
2 bay leaves
8 cups (2 L) vegetable stock (p. 35)
zest of 1/2 lemon
juice of 2 lemons
1 cup (240 mL) crumbled feta cheese
2 tsp (10 mL) minced rosemary
cracked pepper to taste

helpfulhint ✳

Try replacing rosemary with fresh mint for a delicious twist. Use at least double the amount of fresh mint.

greengazpacho
with tomatillos, cucumber, fresh herbs and lime crema

icy cool gazpacho in bright emerald hues is a real attention-getter and a jazzy alternative to classic tomato gazpacho. Bring this along to a summer potluck ... no cooking involved! Prepare a lively mix of finely diced red pepper, scallions, cucumber and basil to sprinkle over top and serve with a bowl of organic blue corn tortillas on the side.

☯ leave out the lime crema for a vegan soup.

serves 8 - 10

1/2 lb (225 g) tomatillos
1/2 lb (225 g) zucchini
1/2 lb (225 g) cucumber
1 green pepper
1 bunch scallions
4 garlic cloves
2 jalapeño peppers, with seeds
1/2 cup (120 mL) olive oil
1/4 cup (60 mL) rice wine vinegar
1/4 cup (60 mL) each chopped basil,
    parsley, cilantro
juice of 3 limes
1 tsp (5 mL) salt
1/2 tsp (2.5 mL) cracked pepper
1 cup (240 mL) sour cream
zest of 1 lime

1. Remove husks from the tomatillos and give them a rinse. Roughly chop the tomatillos, zucchini, cucumber, pepper, garlic, scallions and jalapeños. Place the chopped vegetables in a large bowl and toss with olive oil and vinegar. Cover and refrigerate overnight.

2. In a food processor or blender, pulse marinated vegetables with herbs and half of the lime juice. Add water to get desired consistency. Season with salt, pepper, more lime juice and sugar to counter acidity. Chill thoroughly for at least 2 hours before serving. Stir together sour cream and lime zest and serve on top.

helpfulhint ✳

Thin and chill the gazpacho at the same time by adding a tray of ice cubes to the soup about 2 hours before serving.

Thaisweetcorn

with coconut, Thai basil and lemongrass

summer is your only opportunity to make this soup, so don't miss out. Fresh sweet corn on the cob is the heart and soul of this recipe. Stripped ears are used to make a delicate stock and the resulting fresh corn infusion combines beautifully with lemongrass, basil and coconut milk. Serve with salad rolls (p. 64) for an exotic lunch.

1 To prepare stock, remove corn kernels from the cob and reserve (you will need about 4 cups – 960 mL.) Roughly chop onion, lemongrass and garlic. Place cobs and stock ingredients in a stock pot and bring to a boil. Reduce heat and simmer 45 minutes. Strain and keep warm.

2 Heat oil in a soup pot over medium heat; add onion and sauté until translucent. Add shallots, garlic, lemongrass, ginger, lime leaves and 1 tsp (5 mL) salt. Gently sauté until golden and softened, adding a bit of stock to prevent sticking if necessary.

3 Add the reserved corn kernels, remaining salt and stock to cover. Bring to a boil, reduce heat and simmer until the corn is tender. Remove the lime leaves. Using a hand blender or a food processor, purée the soup and return it to the pot along with the coconut milk, sambal and more stock. Simmer the soup for 15 minutes.

4 Before serving, add basil leaves and season to taste with salt, white pepper and lime juice.

serves 8 - 10

corn - lemongrass stock

8 ears fresh corn
8 cups (2 L) water
2 lemongrass stalks
6 kaffir lime leaves, fresh or frozen
1 yellow onion
1 garlic bulb
1 tsp (5 mL) salt

soup

1 tbsp (15 mL) vegetable oil
1 small yellow onion, diced
1 cup (240 mL) minced shallots
6 garlic cloves, minced
1 lemongrass stalk, trimmed and
    minced
4 tbsp (60 mL) minced ginger
6 kaffir lime leaves
2 tsp (10 mL) salt
1 x 398 mL can "lite" coconut milk
2 tsp (10 mL) sambal oelek
1/4 cup (60 mL) chopped Thai basil
ground white pepper, to taste
juice of 1 lime

tomatillocornchowder
with Anaheim chiles and zucchini

chunky chowder is always a hit and this version is a light alternative to its traditionally thick and rich counterpart. Cream is optional, so enjoy this soup with or without. Use sweet summer corn and small firm garden zucchini for best results. Add the stripped cobs to the soup stock to boost the fresh corn flavour. Vibrant yellow zucchini blossoms can be chopped and sprinkled on top for a gorgeous seasonal garnish.

☯ vegans will enjoy this soup without the cream!

serves 8 - 10

8 cups (2 L) vegetable stock (p. 35)
5 Anaheim chiles
1 1/2 lbs (675 g) tomatillos
2 tbsp (30 mL) vegetable oil
1 yellow onion, diced
10 garlic cloves, minced
2 tsp (10 mL) salt
1 tsp (5 mL) ground coriander
3 tbsp (45 mL) minced oregano
4 jalapeño peppers, seeded and minced
1 medium zucchini, diced
2 medium Yukon Gold potatoes, diced
3 cups (720 mL) corn, fresh or frozen
1 cup (240 mL) heavy cream
1 tsp (5 mL) cracked pepper
1/2 bunch cilantro, chopped
1/2 bunch scallions, sliced

1 Heat the stock and keep it warm while assembling the soup. Pre-heat oven to 400°F. Halve and seed chiles and arrange them on an oiled baking tray. Remove husks from tomatillos, rinse, dry, and rub them with a light coating of oil. Place on a baking sheet with the chiles and roast until the tomatillo and chile skins are slightly charred. Dice the chiles and roughly chop the tomatillos. Set aside.

2 In a soup pot over medium-high heat, heat the oil and sauté onion until translucent. Stir in garlic, 1 tsp (5 mL) salt, coriander, minced oregano and sauté until golden. Add the jalapeños, zucchini, potato and remaining salt and stir to combine. Sauté for several minutes, then pour in warm stock to cover. Bring to a boil, reduce heat and simmer until the potatoes are tender.

3 Add the corn, chiles and tomatillos; simmer 10 minutes. Stir in cream and more stock to thin if necessary. Simmer and season with salt and cracked pepper to taste. Add chopped cilantro and scallions just before serving.

helpful hint ✳

Reduce calories in cream soups by substituting cream with low-fat, soy or rice milk. Reheat gently and do not let the soup come to a boil. Allowing anything other than whipping cream to boil will cause separation.

eastern

eastern inspired soups benefit tremendously from this light vegetable stock scented with Szechuan peppercorns, shiitake mushrooms and lemongrass. As is, this stock is useful for enhancing anything from simple miso soups to a variety of sauces. Add fresh ginger, kaffir lime leaves and extra lemongrass to create an essential backdrop to flavourful Thai soups and sauces.

1 Roughly chop the onion, leek, carrot, celery and scallions. Separate garlic cloves. Cut off the top half of the lemongrass stalk, remove the outer layer and discard. Chop remaining stalk into 3" long pieces. Use the flat of your knife to smash the garlic and lemongrass.

2 Heat oil in a stock pot and add chopped vegetables and salt. Stir to coat and cook for 5 minutes. Add remaining ingredients, except the ginger slices, and set to boil over high heat. Reduce heat to low and simmer for 45 minutes, adding the ginger halfway through.

3 Strain and use the stock immediately, or cool and refrigerate up to 3 days (or freeze up to 2 months).

yields 16 cups (4 L)

1 yellow onion
1 leek
4 celery sticks
4 carrots
1/2 bunch scallions
1 garlic bulb
2 stalks lemongrass
1 tbsp (15 mL) coarse salt
2 tbsp (30 mL) vegetable oil
1/2 bunch cilantro
1 1/2 oz (45 g) dried shiitake mushrooms
2 tsp (10 mL) black peppercorns
2 tsp (10 mL) Szechuan peppercorns
20 cups (5 L) cold fresh water
2" piece of ginger, peeled and sliced

helpfulhint *

Other flavour-enhancing stock additions:
* star anise pods
* fresh fennel
* chopped mushrooms
* kaffir lime leaves
* coriander seeds
* soy or tamari sauce

lonestarminestrone
with corn macaroni 🌀

hearty Italian minestrone soup contains all of the necessary bits and pieces for successful "Southwesternizing". Red kidney beans, corn, peppers, chiles and herbs make a festive pot full of vibrant colour and flavour. Look for corn macaroni at the health food store. Serve with hot buttered corn bread (p. 155) or organic tortilla chips.

serves 8 - 10

10 cups (2 1/2 L) vegetable stock (p. 35)
2 tbsp (30 mL) olive oil
1 yellow onion, diced small
8 garlic cloves, minced
2 tsp (10 mL) salt
4 tbsp (60 mL) minced oregano
2 jalapeño peppers, minced
1/2 tsp (2.5 mL) ground cumin
1 tsp (5 mL) cracked pepper
1 tsp (5 mL) ground coriander
1 tbsp (15 mL) pure chile powder
1 medium yam, peeled and diced
1 sweet red pepper, seeded and diced
1 small zucchini, diced
8 Roma tomatoes, coarsely chopped
1 tsp (5 mL) chipotle purée (p. 38)
1 x 15 oz (425 g) can red kidney beans
1 cup (240 mL) corn, fresh or frozen
1/2 cup (120 mL) dry corn macaroni
chopped fresh oregano and cilantro
asiago cheese (optional)

1 Heat the stock and keep it warm while you prepare the soup. Heat oil in a soup pot over medium-high heat. Add onion and 1 tsp (5 mL) salt; sauté until translucent. Stir in garlic, jalapeños, spices, diced yam and half of the oregano. Cook for 10 minutes, stirring regularly. Add the pepper, zucchini and remaining salt and cook 5 minutes longer. Pour in the warm stock and add chopped tomatoes, chipotle purée and kidney beans. Bring to a boil, reduce heat and simmer for 15 minutes.

2 Add the corn, remaining oregano and corn macaroni (see "hint"); simmer until the pasta is tender. If the soup gets too thick, add more stock or water. Season to taste and serve with chopped fresh herbs, grated asiago cheese and lime wedges.

helpfulhint ✳

If you're not serving the minestrone right away, cook the macaroni separately and add it as you need it, otherwise it will get mushy from sitting in the soup too long.

woodsy**wild**mushroom

with porcini, white wine and cream

heady
wild mushroom flavour gives this soup a sophisticated touch, making it a great opener for a special meal. Garnish with butter-sautéed mushrooms and a sprinkle of fresh chives. Serve with oven-warm foccacia (p. 39), a variety of quality cheeses and a simple field greens salad (p. 8) for a mid-winter treat.

serves 6 - 8

1 Soak porcini mushrooms in boiling water for 1 hour. Strain the liquid through a cheesecloth-lined sieve. Add the soaking liquid to the soup stock and coarsely chop the rehydrated mushrooms. Set aside.

2 Combine stock, potatoes and bay leaves in a pot and heat to a simmer. Cook until the potatoes are tender. Turn off the heat, cover and set aside.

3 Heat a soup pot over medium-high heat and add butter and olive oil. Add all of the mushrooms (including the porcini) and 1 tsp (5 mL) salt. Stir to coat and cover the pan for 5 minutes to let the mushrooms cook down. Uncover and let the mushrooms sear and juices evaporate. Stir in the leeks, carrot, celery, garlic, pepper, thyme and remaining salt; cook for 10 more minutes. Deglaze the pan with wine and reduce the liquid by half.

4 Add stock to the pot and bring to a boil. Reduce heat and simmer for 20 minutes. Remove bay leaves and purée the soup until smooth. Stir in the cream and reheat just before serving. Season with lemon juice, salt and pepper to taste. Serve hot.

1 oz (30 g) dried porcini mushrooms
2 cups (480 mL) boiling water
8 cups (2 L) vegetable stock (p. 35)
2 red potatoes, peeled and chopped
4 bay leaves
2 tbsp (30 mL) butter
2 tbsp (30 mL) olive oil
1 1/2 lbs (675 g) button mushrooms
1/2 lb (225 g) shiitake or portabello mushrooms, chopped
2 tsp (10 mL) salt
3 leeks, whites only, sliced
2 carrots, peeled and finely diced
2 celery sticks, finely diced
8 garlic cloves, minced
1/2 tsp (2.5 mL) cracked pepper
1 tbsp (15 mL) thyme leaves, minced
1 cup (240 mL) white wine
1 cup (240 mL) heavy cream
juice of 1 lemon

African yam & peanut
with ginger and pineapple ☯

silky smooth richness in this soup comes courtesy of peanut butter—there's just enough of it blended in to make this soup luxuriant, rather than cloying. Pineapple, lime and tomatoes add sweetness and tang, while the spices are lively and warming. This soup can handle a generous dose of spice and heat, so arm yourself with a good hot sauce for last minute seasoning. A fruity West Indian habañero hot sauce is perfect.

serves 8

8 cups (2 L) vegetable stock (p. 35)
2 tbsp (30 mL) vegetable oil
1 large yellow onion, diced
2 tsp (10 mL) salt
6 tbsp (90 mL) minced ginger
4 large garlic cloves, minced
1 tbsp (15 mL) ground cumin
2 tbsp (30 mL) ground coriander
1/2 tsp (2.5 mL) cayenne pepper
1 tsp (5 mL) paprika
1 red bell pepper, diced
4 medium yams, peeled and roughly
   chopped
1 x 14 fl oz (398 mL) can water-
   packed pineapple, juice reserved
3 ripe tomatoes, chopped
5 tbsp (75 mL) natural smooth peanut
   butter
I bunch cilantro, chopped
juice of 2 limes, or more to taste
favourite hot sauce, to taste

1 Heat stock and keep it warm on the back burner while you assemble the soup. In a heavy-bottomed soup pot, heat oil over medium heat. Add onion and a pinch of salt; sauté for 10 minutes, stirring occasionally. Next, add garlic, ginger and spices and sauté until soft and golden. Stir in red pepper, yams and salt and continue cooking until they start to stick to the bottom of the pot. Add vegetable stock to cover, bring to a boil, and reduce to a simmer. Cover partially and simmer until the yams are tender.

2 Add pineapple with juice, tomatoes, peanut butter and remaining stock and simmer 30 minutes. Purée the soup until smooth, either directly in the pot with a hand blender, or in batches using a food processor.

3 Return soup to the pot and simmer for a final 10 minutes. Season to taste with more salt, pineapple juice and/or hot sauce. Just before serving, add chopped cilantro and fresh lime juice.

helpful hint ✳

For best flavour, use whole cumin and coriander seeds and lightly toast them in a hot dry skillet until golden and fragrant. Grind in a coffee or spice grinder.

summer**harvest**chowder

with corn, tomatoes and basil

take advantage of seasonal garden offerings with this summery soup. A light touch of cream pulls everything together and balances the heat of the chiles, the sweetness of the corn and the acidity of the tomatoes. Serve with the painted desert salad (p. 16) and fresh cornbread (p. 155) for a late summer patio dinner.

☯ omit the cream for a vegan soup.

serves 8

1 Heat the vegetable stock and keep it warm while preparing the soup. If using fresh corn in the soup (highly recommended!), add the stripped cobs to the stock and remove before using.

2 Heat olive oil or butter in a soup pot and sauté onion with 1 tsp (5 mL) salt, until soft and golden. Add garlic, cracked pepper, oregano and half of the basil; sauté 5 minutes. Stir in potatoes, jalapeños, red pepper, corn and remaining salt. Sauté briefly, then add warm stock to cover and bring the soup to a boil. Reduce heat and simmer until the potatoes are tender.

3 Stir in cream and return the soup to a light simmer. Add tomatoes, remaining basil and cilantro. Heat through, season to taste and serve.

8 cups (2 L) vegetable stock (p. 35)
2 tbsp (30 mL) olive oil, or butter
1 medium yellow onion, diced
2 tsp (10 mL) salt
6 garlic cloves, minced
1/2 tsp (2.5 mL) cracked pepper
1 tsp (5 mL) dried oregano
1/2 cup (120 mL) chopped basil
4 small red potatoes, diced
3 jalapeño peppers, seeded and
   minced
2 red peppers, diced
4 cups (960 mL) corn, fresh or frozen
1 cup (240 mL) heavy cream
3 ripe tomatoes, seeded and diced
1/4 cup (60 mL) chopped cilantro
fresh lime juice to taste

helpful**hint**

The leaves and stems of cilantro and other leafy herbs often hide considerable amounts of sand and grit. Rinse thoroughly in a bowl or sink full of cold water. Hold the stems and swirl the bunch in the water to loosen the dirt. Shake off excess water and dry on paper towels.

creamybroccoli
with almond-Romano pesto

more often than not, creamy broccoli soups are drab, in both flavour and appearance, making them rather forgettable and, at worst, reminiscent of hospital stays. In contrast, this lively recipe is well-seasoned with fresh herbs and full of green goodness. A final swirl of fresh herb pesto takes it over the top.

serves 6

6 cups (1.5 L) vegetable stock (p. 35)

2 tbsp (30 mL) vegetable oil

1 yellow onion, diced

6 garlic cloves, minced

1 tbsp (15 mL) minced fresh thyme

1 1/2 tsp (7.5 mL) salt

1/4 tsp (1.2 mL) red chile flakes

1 large potato, peeled and diced

4 broccoli stalks (2 cups florets
    reserved)

1/2 lb (225 g) spinach, stemmed

1 cup (240 mL) heavy cream

1/2 tsp (2.5 mL) cracked pepper

pesto

1/2 bunch Italian parsley, stemmed

1/2 cup (120 mL) toasted, sliced
    almonds

2 garlic cloves

1/2 cup (120 mL) grated Romano
    cheese

1/4 cup (60 mL) olive oil

salt and pepper, to taste

1 Heat stock and keep it warm while preparing the soup. Heat oil in a soup pot over medium-high heat and sauté the onion until translucent. Add garlic, salt, thyme and chile flakes and sauté until golden. Stir in broccoli and potato; cook for several minutes. Add warm stock to cover; bring to a simmer and cook, partially covered, until the broccoli and potatoes are just tender.

2 Stir in the spinach leaves and turn off the heat. Let the soup rest until the spinach wilts, then purée until smooth. Reheat the purée, add cream and more stock to thin, if necessary. Season to taste with salt and pepper.

3 Meanwhile, bring a small pot of water to a hard boil. Add the salt and reserved broccoli florets and blanch until just done and bright green (about 1 minute). Strain immediately and plunge the florets into a bowl of ice water. Let them cool off, then strain and spread out on a clean, dry towel to drain. Set aside.

4 To prepare the pesto, place the parsley, almonds, garlic and cheese in a food processor and pulse to combine. Add the olive oil and purée, stopping short of making it completely smooth. Blend in salt and pepper to taste.

5 Serve the soup hot, with a swirl of pesto in each bowl and garnished with broccoli florets.

caramelized**red**onion

with port, slow-roast tomatoes and fresh herbs

leisurely caramelized onions, concentrated roasted tomatoes and sweet, rich port wine combine beautifully, dispelling any myths that a good onion soup requires beef stock. The result is a rich and deeply satisfying soup, sophisticated enough for a special occasion. Ladle over Parmesan or Gruyère toasts. Slice a baguette, sprinkle with grated cheese and bake until golden and crispy.

serves 6 - 8

- 1 recipe slow-roast tomatoes (p. 47)
- 8 cups (2 L) vegetable stock (p. 35)
- 4 tbsp (60 mL) extra virgin olive oil
- 6 large red onions, thinly sliced
- 1 garlic bulb, minced
- 2 tsp (10 mL) salt
- 2 tbsp (30 mL) minced thyme
- 4 tbsp (60 mL) minced basil
- 1/2 tsp (2.5 mL) cracked pepper
- 1/2 tsp (2.5 mL) red chile flakes
- 1 tbsp (15 mL) brown sugar
- 1 cup (240 mL) port wine
- 2 tbsp (30 mL) balsamic vinegar
- chopped fresh basil or Italian parsley

1 Prepare slow-roast tomatoes at least 3 hours before beginning soup preparation, or one or two days in advance. Heat stock while preparing the soup and keep it warm on the back burner.

2 Heat olive oil in a soup pot and stir in onions and salt. Sauté over medium heat, stirring occasionally, until the onions are soft and lightly golden. Add minced garlic, herbs, chile flakes, pepper and sugar and continue to sauté gently until the onions are broken down completely. Deglaze the pan with port and let it reduce until syrupy.

3 Remove skins from the roasted tomatoes and chop the flesh coarsely. Add tomatoes, balsamic vinegar and stock to the soup. Bring to a boil, reduce heat and simmer, partially covered, to marry the flavours. Taste and season with more salt, pepper or balsamic vinegar. Just before serving, stir in extra chopped herbs.

helpful**hint**

If port is unavailable, substiute a rich full-bodied red wine.

roasted butternut squash

with ancho chiles, orange zest and pumpkin seeds ☯

winter squash soups are warming and filling enough to be the main meal attraction on a cool, blustery night. This soup is richly flavoured with smoky ancho chiles, roasted peppers, garlic, fresh sage and spices. Orange juice and zest add a fresh touch and complement the sweet squash perfectly. This recipe is very similar to the roasted yam soup (p. 121), but the flavour is so different—try both and see for yourself.

serves 8

10 cups (2.4 L) vegetable stock (p. 35)

3 lb (1.4 kg) butternut squash

2 red pepper, roasted and peeled
(p. 50)

1 garlic bulb

4 Roma tomatoes

3 tbsp (45 mL) vegetable oil

2 tsp (10 mL) salt

1 yellow onion, diced

2 tbsp (30 mL) ancho chile powder

1 tsp (5 mL) ground coriander

2 tbsp (30 mL) minced sage

zest and juice of 1 orange

1 tsp (5 mL) chipotle purée (p. 38)

cracked pepper to taste

1/4 cup (60 mL) pumpkin seeds,
toasted

1 Pre-heat oven to 375°F. Refer to the "helpful hint" for squash roasting tips. Separate garlic cloves and remove skins. Core the tomatoes. Toss the garlic and tomatoes with 2 tsp (10 mL) oil and 1/2 tsp (2.5 mL) salt. Place on a parchment-lined baking sheet and roast until the garlic is golden and tomato skins begin to char (about 20 minutes).
Note: the peppers, tomatoes and garlic can be roasted on the same baking sheet at the same time. The squash should be placed on a separate pan as it will take much longer to roast.

2 Heat the remaining oil in a soup pot and add the onion and remaining salt. Sauté until translucent. Add the chile powder, coriander and sage; sauté 5 more minutes. Roughly chop all of the roasted vegetables and add them to the pot along with enough stock to cover. Bring to a boil; reduce heat and simmer 15 minutes.

3 Purée the soup until smooth using a hand blender or food processor. Gently reheat the soup to a simmer and add the orange zest, juice, chipotle purée and more stock to thin if necessary. Season with salt and cracked pepper. Simmer several minutes to blend the flavours and serve hot, garnished with toasted pumpkin seeds.

helpful hint ✳

To make an easy job of prepping and roasting squash, cut it in half lengthwise, scrape out the seeds and place cut side down on an oiled baking tray. Bake in a 375°F oven until a sharp knife easily slides through the flesh. Cool and scoop out the soft flesh.

blackbean**soup**

sweet & spicy style ☯

glossy black beans cooked to a purée make this soup appear rather dark and evil, but one taste will calm any fears. This thick, intensely flavoured soup was chosen as a favourite from among countless black bean soups that we've made over the years. A lively garnish of mango (p. 98), tomatillo (p. 53), or tomato salsa (p. 44), looks striking against the dark, smooth background.

serves 8

1 Drain and rinse the soaked beans and place them in a soup pot. Heat a small skillet and toast the cumin, coriander and dried oregano until fragrant. Grind the spices (see "hint") and add them to the beans, along with the onion, garlic, jalapeños and bay leaves. Cover with cold water by 2 inches. Bring to a boil; reduce heat and simmer gently, partially covered, until the beans are very tender (approx. 1 hour). Check the water level and add more to cover if it gets low. Add salt to the pot about 15 minutes before the beans are finished cooking.

2 Stir in the tomatoes, **re**barbecue sauce and cracked pepper. Simmer for about 20 minutes to marry the flavours. Using a hand blender or food processor, purée the soup until smooth. Reheat and add more water to thin if necessary. Before serving, season with lime juice, cilantro and salt to taste.

3 cups (720 mL) black beans,
soaked overnight
1 tbsp (15 mL) cumin seed
1 tbsp (15 mL) coriander seed
1 tbsp (15 mL) dry oregano
1 large yellow onion, diced
6 garlic cloves, minced
3 jalapeño peppers, seeded and
roughly chopped
2 bay leaves
1 tsp (5 mL) salt
1 x 28 fl oz (796 mL) can diced
tomatoes
1 cup **re**barbeque sauce (p. 51)
1/2 tsp (2.5 mL) cracked pepper
juice of 1 lime juice
1/4 cup (60 mL) chopped cilantro

helpful**hint** ✳

Buy two coffee grinders, one for coffee beans and the other for spices. Your "better half" may not appreciate cumin-flavoured coffee first thing in the morning! Isn't that right Emilie?!

tortilla**soup**
with avocado, corn and asiago

feast your eyes on this dazzling soup. Sweet morsels of vivid yellow corn, ruby tomatoes and cilantro leaves float in a delicate piquant broth, crowned by a stunning garnish of creamy avocado, shavings of asiago cheese and strips of crisp corn tortillas. Shortly after serving, the tortilla strips will gradually disintegrate and release their soothing masa flavour into the broth. Very yummy.

☯ omit the asiago cheese for a vegan soup.

serves 8

8 cups (2 L) vegetable stock (p. 35)
2 tbsp (30 mL) vegetable oil
2 yellow onions, finely diced
1 tbsp (15 mL) salt
10 garlic cloves, minced
2 tbsp (30 mL) minced oregano
4 jalapeño peppers, seeded and minced
3 cups (720 mL) corn kernels, fresh or
    frozen
2 large red peppers, seeded and finely
    diced
1/2 tsp (2.5 mL) liquid smoke
2 tsp (10 mL) chipotle purée (p. 38)
4 corn tortillas, yellow or blue
2 avocados, diced
1/2 bunch cilantro, stemmed
asiago cheese, shaved with a potato
    peeler
1 lime, cut into thin wedges

1   Heat the stock and keep it warm on the back burner while preparing the soup. In a heavy-bottomed soup pot, heat oil over medium heat. Add onion and 1 tsp (5 mL) salt and sauté until translucent. Stir in the garlic, oregano, half of the minced jalapeños and another 1 tsp (5 mL) salt; sauté 5 minutes.

2   Pour the hot stock into the pot and bring to a gentle boil. Simmer 20 minutes. In the final 5 minutes, stir in the corn, red peppers, remaining jalapeños, the remaining salt, liquid smoke and chipotle purée. Simmer until the corn is tender. Meanwhile, prepare the garnishes and season the soup with salt and pepper to taste.

3   To make tortilla strips, slice each tortilla into long strips 1/4" thick. Toss gently with a light coating of oil, a pinch of salt and chile powder (optional). Spread the strips out on a baking sheet and bake in a 350°F oven until crisp (5 minutes). Remove from the oven and let cool until ready to serve.

4   To serve, ladle the broth into bowls and divide the diced avocado, cilantro leaves and asiago shavings among the servings. Arrange 8 tortilla strips in a teepee in the center of each bowl. Serve immediately with a bowl of lime wedges on the side.

borscht

with porcini mushrooms and white beans

ruby red chunky borscht is always popular among the regular stream of lunch hour customers seeking a hot soup and fresh salad to sustain them through the rest of the day. The addition of porcini mushrooms imparts a meaty flavour reminiscent of traditional ham bone-based borscht recipes found throughout the "old country". Serve with black pumpernickel bread swathed with fresh dill and chive butter.

1 Heat vegetable stock. Soak porcini mushrooms in 2 cups (480 mL) stock for 1 hour. Strain the mushrooms and add the soaking liquid to the remaining stock. Finely chop the porcini and set aside. Peel and dice the beets and carrots.

2 Heat oil and/or butter in a soup pot over medium heat. Add onion, 1 tsp (5 mL) salt and bay leaves; sauté until the onion is soft and translucent. Add the chopped porcini and carrots and sauté 10 more minutes. Stir in the beets, cabbage and another teaspoon of salt. Add stock to cover and bring to a simmer. Cook until vegetables are tender.

3 Add the tomatoes, beans, balsamic vinegar and half of the herbs and simmer for 20 minutes. Before serving, season with lemon juice, remaining herbs, cracked pepper and more salt if necessary. Serve with a dollop of sour cream or crème fraîche.

serves 6 - 8

10 cups (2.5 L) vegetable stock (p. 35)
1 oz (30 g) dried porcini mushrooms
4 medium beets
2 carrots
2 tbsp (30 mL) oil or butter
1 large onion, diced
2 tsp (10 mL) salt
2 bay leaves
2 cups (480 mL) chopped red cabbage
4 ripe Roma tomatoes, chopped
1 x 15 oz (425 g) can white kidney beans
3 tbsp (45 mL) balsamic vinegar
juice of 1 lemon
2 tbsp (30 mL) chopped dill
2 tbsp (30 mL) chopped parsley
sour cream or crème fraîche (p. 108) for garnish

helpful**hint** ✳

Shred cabbage like a pro! Quarter the head, cut out the core and separate each quarter into three layers. Flatten each layer on the cutting board with your palm and slice long, thin shreds.

chunkywintervegetable

with blue cheese-pumpernickel toast

forget about cooking for a few days when you have a batch of this soup
sitting in your fridge. On its own, or with a salad, this hearty soup makes a substantial
meal that continues to improve for a day or two after it's made. The blue cheese toast
is a nice savoury and crispy contrast to the smooth sweetness of the root vegetables.

☯ vegans can replace blue cheese with roasted garlic (p. 158).

serves 8

8 cups (2 L) vegetable stock (p. 35)

2 tbsp (30 mL) vegetable oil

1 leek, mostly white parts, chopped

1 large yellow onion, chopped

4 bay leaves

1/4 tsp (1.2 mL) red chile flakes

1 tbsp (15 mL) salt

8 garlic cloves, minced

2 tbsp (30 mL) chopped sage leaves

2 tbsp (30 mL) thyme leaves

1 acorn squash, 1/2" cubes

1 turnip or rutabaga, 1/2" cubes

2 carrots, half moon slices

1/2 small Savoy cabbage, shredded

1 x 15 oz (425 g) can white kidney
    beans

4 tbsp (60 mL) nutritional yeast (Red
    Star or engevita)

1 bottle (355 mL) dark beer

1 tsp (5 mL) cracked pepper

4 tbsp (60 mL) apple cider vinegar

8 thin slices dark pumpernickel bread

1/2 cup (120 mL) crumbled blue cheese

1 Warm the stock while preparing the soup. Heat oil in a soup
pot and add the leek, onion, bay, chiles and half of the salt.
Sauté until onions are translucent. Add the garlic, herbs and
sauté several more minutes. Next, stir in the vegetables,
remaining salt and sauté, stirring occasionally, for 10 minutes.
Add the stock and bring to a boil. Reduce heat and simmer
until the vegetables are tender.

2 Add the remaining ingredients and simmer on low to let the
flavours mingle. Season to taste.

3 Prepare the pumpernickel toasts just before serving. Toast
the bread lightly, crumble the blue cheese on top and melt
under the broiler. Serve immediately with hot soup.

Tuscan white bean
with rosemary and kale 🌀

here is a soup that you'll never tire of. It is simple, flavourful and wholesome as can be. The beans and kale combine to make this soup rich in iron and folic acid. Drizzle extra virgin olive oil and sprinkle freshly grated Parmesan on top of each serving. Accompany with rosemary-garlic foccacia (p. 39) or a crusty multigrain sourdough loaf.

serves 8

1 Drain and rinse the soaked beans and place them in a pot with bay leaves, 2 tsp (10 mL) rosemary and cold water. Bring to a boil, reduce heat and simmer until the beans are tender. In the last 15 minutes of cooking, add 2 tsp (10 mL) salt to the beans.

2 When the beans are tender, heat olive oil in a soup pot and add the onion, remaining 1 tsp (5 ml) salt and chile flakes. Sauté until the onions are lightly golden, then add the garlic and the remaining rosemary. Cook several minutes, then add the cooked beans and their cooking liquid. Bring to a simmer, add the tomatoes and simmer gently for 20 minutes.

3 Meanwhile, remove the stems from the kale, tear or roughly chop the leaves and rinse well in cold water. Add the leaves to the soup and cook until wilted. Season the soup to taste with balsamic vinegar, cracked pepper and more salt. Garnish with fresh garden herbs if you like.

2 cups (480 mL) cannellini beans, soaked overnight
10 cups (2.4 L) water
4 bay leaves
1 tbsp (15 mL) salt
1 tbsp (15 mL) minced rosemary
2 tbsp (30 mL) olive oil
1 yellow onion, diced
8 garlic cloves, minced
1/4 tsp (1.2 mL) red chile flakes
4 ripe Roma tomatoes, seeded and diced
1/2 tsp (2.5 mL) cracked pepper
2 tbsp (30 mL) balsamic vinegar
1 small bunch kale, or spinach

helpfulhint ✳

Add 1/2 cup (120 mL) orzo or other small pasta shapes for a thick and hearty minestrone-style soup.

Vietnamese**hot**&**sour**

with pineapple, tamarind & mint

discovering the cuisines of Southeast Asia has brought a whole new dimension to our cooking. The **re**bar kitchen is now regularly stocked with exotic items like kaffir lime leaves, galangal and palm sugar. Thai dishes are especially popular, but Vietnamese flavours also strike a chord. Unfortunately, Vietnamese vegetarian dishes are impossible to find in restaurants where often so-called "vegetarian" soups are made with meat stock. We struggled to capture the authentic flavours in a vegetable base but found that the addition of fish sauce makes a tremendous difference, and so, we highly recommend using it if your diet allows. Replace fish sauce with all soy if not.

☯ omit fish sauce and use all soy for a vegan soup.

serves 6 - 8

8 cups Asian stock (p. 127)

1 pod star anise

2 oz (60 g) chopped galangal or ginger

4 tbsp (60 mL) minced lemongrass

2 oz (60 g) tamarind

1 cup (240 mL) boiling water

1/3 cup (80 mL) fish sauce

2 tbsp (30 mL) soy sauce

1 oz (30 g) palm sugar, or brown sugar

2 tsp (10 mL) sambal oelek

1/2 fresh, ripe pineapple, peeled, cored
   and cut into 1-inch chunks

1 cup (240 mL) fresh pineapple juice

4 tomatoes, roughly chopped

4 cups sui choy, chopped in 1" squares

1 bunch scallions, sliced

1/4 cup (60 mL) chopped mint

1/4 cup (60 mL) chopped Thai basil or
   cilantro

1 In a soup pot, bring the stock, galangal, lemongrass and star anise to a boil. Reduce heat and simmer gently for 30 minutes. Strain, discard the solids and keep the stock warm.

2 Pour boiling water over the tamarind and soak for 20 minutes. Strain through a fine mesh sieve, scraping as much pulp from the large seeds as possible. Add the tamarind pulp, fish sauce, soy sauce, sugar and sambal to the stock. Simmer 10 minutes, then add the pineapple, pineapple juice and tomatoes and simmer to heat through. Add sui choy and half of the scallions and herbs. Simmer a few more minutes until the sui choy is just tender and still bright green. Divide the remaining scallions and herbs evenly among serving bowls and ladle the hot soup over top. Serve immediately with fresh lime wedges and fish sauce or soy sauce on the side for seasoning.

curriedchickpea
with tomatoes, ginger and cilantro ☻

working with cooks of diverse ethnic backgrounds can be a great cultural and culinary education. Harbans worked with us for several years, specializing in North Indian cuisine. Her silent skilled movements through the kitchen seemed to hold a magic that could not be conveyed through a recipe, so we kept a close eye on her while she cooked and tried to pick up some of her secrets. Here is a simple and delicious soup that puts our education to the test. Serve with grilled whole wheat chapathi or pita bread.

serves 8

1 Heat the oil in a soup pot and add onion, 1 tsp (5 mL) salt and bay leaves. Sauté until the onions are soft and golden. Meanwhile, place the garlic, ginger, jalapeños, pepper and tomatoes in a food processor and pulse until the vegetables form a rough purée. Set aside.

2 Next, grind the cumin and coriander seeds. Add these and all remaining spices to the sautéed onions and continue cooking and stirring for 5 minutes. Add the vegetable purée and another teaspoon of salt and simmer until small blobs of oil pool on the surface. Add the chick peas and stock and bring to a simmer. Cook several minutes, then add the chutney and coconut milk. Using a potato masher, gently mash the chickpeas against the bottom of the pot to break them up slightly and thicken the soup. Simmer and season to taste with salt and cracked pepper. Add chopped cilantro just before serving.

8 cups (2 L) vegetable stock (p. 35)
2 tbsp (30 mL) vegetable oil
1 yellow onion, finely diced
2 tsp (10 mL) salt
2 bay leaves
8 garlic cloves
3 tbsp (45 mL) minced ginger
2 jalapeño peppers, seeded
1 red pepper
6 ripe tomatoes
1 tsp (5 mL) cumin seed
1 tsp (5 mL) coriander seed
1 tsp (5 mL) paprika
1 tsp (5 mL) garam masala
1/4 tsp (1.2 mL) cracked pepper
1/8 tsp (.5 mL) turmeric
3 cups (720 mL) canned chick peas
1/4 cup (60 mL) prepared mango chutney
1/2 can coconut milk
1/2 bunch cilantro, minced

lentil & splitpea
with mint-mango chutney ☯

legumes are often neglected in the North American diet. This is unfortunate because they are an excellent source of dietary fiber, folic acid, potassium and a good source of iron, protein, magnesium, thiamine, zinc and copper. Serve this gently spiced soup with a spoonful of chutney and fresh hot chapathi.

serves 8

1 cup (240 mL) yellow split peas
3/4 cup (180 mL) brown lentils
3/4 cup (180 mL) red lentils
2 tbsp (30 mL) vegetable oil
1 tsp (5 mL) black mustard seed
1 yellow onion, diced
2 bay leaves
4 garlic cloves, minced
1/4 cup (60 mL) minced ginger
1 tsp (5 mL) salt
1/2 tsp (2.5 mL) red chile flakes
1 tsp (5 mL) cuminseed, ground
2 tsp (10 mL) coriander, ground
1 tsp (5 mL) sweet paprika
1/4 tsp (1.2 mL) turmeric
2 carrots, diced
8 cups (2 L) vegetable stock (p. 35),
   or water
cracked pepper to taste
juice of 2 lemons

1 Combine split peas and lentils in a bowl and soak in cold water for one hour. Meanwhile, heat oil in a soup pot over medium-high heat and add mustard seeds. When they start to turn grey and pop, add the onion and bay leaves and sauté until the onion is soft. Add garlic, ginger, salt and chiles and cook 5 minutes. Stir in the remaining spices and cook for several minutes, stirring often and adding small amounts of stock to prevent sticking. Add the carrots and sauté until tender.

2 Strain and rinse the legumes well. Add them to the pot, along with 6 cups stock or water. Bring to a boil, reduce heat and simmer, partially covered, until the peas and lentils are soft and broken down (about 30 minutes). Add more liquid to cover if necessary. Purée the soup with a hand blender or in a food processor. Reheat in the pot and season with salt, cracked pepper and lemon juice. Add more stock to thin if necessary.

mintmangochutney

1/2 cup (120 mL) mint,
   stemmed and packed
1/2 bunch cilantro
2 scallions
1 garlic clove, chopped
1/2 jalapeño pepper
juice of 1 lime
1/2 cup (120 mL) prepared
   mango chutney (Major
   Grey's)

Combine all ingredients into the bowl of a food processor or blender and purée until smooth. This chutney is best freshly prepared, but can be stored in the refrigerator for up to one week.

coolbeetandcucumber
with fresh dill, beet greens and buttermilk

beat the heat with a chilled soup when summer temperatures soar and the electric fan affords no comfort. Cool and refreshing beets, cucumber, buttermilk and yogourt combine to make a gorgeous fuschia-hued soup that is easy to make and tastes best eaten outdoors, under the shade of a willow on a sweltering summer day.

serves 4 - 6

1 Cut greens from the beetroot and wash both well to remove any clinging dirt. Peel beets, quarter and thinly slice. Place in a pot and cover with cold water by 1-inch. Bring to a boil. Add salt, partially cover and reduce heat. Simmer until the beets are just tender.

2 While the beets are simmering, finely shred the beet greens with their stems. When the beets are tender, stir the greens and sugar into the pot. Cover and turn off the heat. Let stand 10 minutes. Uncover and cool to room temperature; then chill thoroughly before proceeding. (This step can be prepared up to 2 days in advance, or frozen for 1 month.)

3 In a large bowl, combine the beets, greens and cooking water with buttermilk, yogourt, lemon and pickle juice. Season with salt, cracked pepper, sugar or more lemon to get the right balance for your taste. Chill the soup for at least one hour before serving.

4 To serve, stir in the cucumbers, scallions and dill and taste one more time to adjust the seasoning. Serve in chilled bowls.

2 small beet bunches, with greens
water to cover
1 tbsp (15 mL) salt
2 tbsp (30 mL) sugar
3 cups (720 mL) buttermilk
1 cup (240 mL) yogourt, kefir or sour cream
2 - 3 lemons, juiced
1/4 cup (60 mL) pickle juice
lots of cracked pepper
1/2 long English cucumber, 1/4" dice
1 bunch scallions, minced
1/4 cup (60 mL) minced fresh dill

helpfulhint ✳

Serve this soup in the traditional Polish style. Place a peeled, hard-cooked egg in the bottom of each bowl and break it up with a fork. Ladle the soup over and serve with a side dish of hot boiled new potatoes smothered with butter, fresh dill and cracked pepper.

Bonnie'sspringtonic
with stinging nettle tops

remote Gulf Island retreats don't get any better than a visit to Bonnie Olesko's spread on Lasqueti Island. (Bonnie is Audrey's childhood friend and "sister" from her Portland days.) A typical spring visit to Bon's "Mystic Ridge Farm" involves a nettle-picking excursion, trying to fall asleep to the ear-splitting song of mating frogs and a friendly visit with the barnyard creatures big and small. We don't get up there often enough, but Bonnie's supply of herbal tinctures behind the juice bar always remind us that she's not all that far away.

🌓 choose olive oil & vegetable stock options for a vegan soup.

serves 4

3 tbsp (45 mL) butter or olive oil

1 large onion, diced

2 cups (480 mL) packed young
   nettle tops

2 large potatoes, scrubbed and
   chopped

1 tsp (5 mL) sea salt

1/2 tsp (2.5 mL) white pepper

1 garlic clove, minced

4 cups (960 mL) milk or vegetable
   stock (p. 35)

1 Heat oil or butter in a heavy-bottomed soup pot over medium heat. Add onion and sauté until translucent. Add nettles, potatoes, salt and pepper. Add a bit of stock or water, cover and cook until the potatoes are soft, adding more liquid as necessary.

2 Add garlic and milk (or stock) to the pot and heat to a simmer. Using a hand blender or food processor, briefly blend the soup. Reheat and season to taste with more salt and/or white pepper. Garnish with chopped fresh nettle bits and serve with hearty black bread.

helpfulhint ✳

Harvest tender nettle tops in early spring as the plants emerge in mineral rich areas such as maple and old 1st and 2nd growth Douglas fir forest floors. Dried and crushed they can be added to fresh pasta, soups, breads or tea. Ginger, coconut milk or other Asian flavours go well with this assertive green.

Thaidragonbowl
with rice noodles, vegetables and red curry-coconut broth

steaming bowls of noodles, vegetables and broth are a meal in a bowl. This recipe is very flexible and the character of the dish will change each time you make it because the flavours are so dependent on what you put in your stock, the availability of aromatics and the vegetables you choose to use. This version is lovely in summer when tomatoes and sugar peas are fresh. Try adding mushrooms, carrots and napa cabbage in winter. We use tofu, but shellfish or chicken would also be delicious. For a lower fat version, omit the coconut milk, or try "lite" coconut milk.

☯ replace fish sauce with all soy for a vegan soup.

1 Heat the stock to a simmer and add the minced lemongrass, ginger and garlic; simmer 15 minutes. Strain the stock through a sieve to remove the solids and return the liquid to the pot.

2 Stir curry paste, sugar, soy and fish sauces into the broth and simmer 5 minutes. Add coconut milk, if using, and lime juice. Taste and correct the seasoning to your liking.

3 While the broth is simmering, add the rice noodles, tofu and kaffir lime leaves; cook until the noodles are tender, about 5 minutes. Halfway through this time, add the snow peas. When the noodles are cooked, add all of the remaining ingredients. Serve immediately in large bowls with lime wedges, sambal oelek, fish and soy sauce on the side.

dragonbowladditions

❊ replace Thai basil with fresh mint
❊ add chopped bok choy or baby bok choy leaves
❊ top with a stack of bean sprouts
❊ replace red with home-made green curry paste (p. 48)
❊ sprinkle with finely sliced Thai bird chile rounds
❊ add sliced oyster or shiitake mushrooms
❊ garnish with fried shallots, garlic or lotus root rounds
❊ add whole prawns or scallops

serves 4

8 cups (2 L) Asian (p. 127) or vegetable (p. 35) stock
3 lemongrass stalks, trimmed and minced (see instruction #1 on p. 118)
3 tbsp (45 mL) minced ginger or galangal
3 garlic cloves, minced
1/2 tsp (2.5 mL) red curry paste
1 oz (30 g) palm sugar
3 tbsp (45 mL) soy sauce
1/4 cup (60 mL) fish sauce
1 cup (240 mL) coconut milk (optional)
juice of 1 lime
1/3 lb (150 g) rice noodles, medium width
1/2 block x-firm tofu, cut in small cubes
4 kaffir lime leaves, stems removed & finely shredded
6 oz (180 g) snow peas, trimmed
1 bunch scallions, minced
4 tomatoes, diced
1/4 cup (60 mL) minced cilantro
1/2 cup (120 mL) Thai basil leaves, torn
sambal oelek, on the side

7

sides

one could argue that a full-course vegetarian meal is made up entirely of side dishes. In many ways this is correct, particularly if you are accustomed to a meal centered around meat or fish. When we assemble meatless plates at rebar, we start with a dish that serves as the focus, and then add side dishes and garnishes to balance it. If the focus is rich and cheesy, then we'll present it with a fresh and leafy accompaniment. If beans or tofu dominate, the side dish will include a grain and/or vegetables. Sides are not just complements in terms of flavour, but also balance the nutritional make-up, colour and texture of a plate. Here are some recipes that pair up with many of our entrées, lunches and appetizers to create the perfect meal.

Baja baked black beans

with smoky chipotles, brown sugar and cumin

unless you were raised in a country home where mom cooked and baked all day, your experience with baked beans probably extends as far as the can opener. Yet contrary to popular belief, home-spun baked beans are simple to prepare. Most of the time spent involves waiting as the beans cook and bake. In this recipe, the beans bake for only one hour, just long enough to let them soak up their yummy sauce. Accompany with a hot pan of crispy cornbread, oven-baked squash and a salad, or check out the fajita recipe (p. 197) for the ultimate fiesta.

serves 8 - 10

4 cups (960 mL) black beans, soaked
   overnight

1/2 bunch cilantro, coarsely chopped

1 tbsp (15 mL) cumin seed

2 tbsp (30 mL) pure chile powder

1 tbsp (15 mL) dried oregano

6 garlic cloves, peeled and chopped

1 yellow onion, chopped

1 tbsp (15 mL) salt

2 tbsp (30 mL) chipotle purée (p. 38)

1/2 cup (120 mL) brown sugar, firmly
   packed

1 x 5 1/2 oz (196 mL) can tomato paste

1/3 cup (80 mL) red wine vinegar

1 In a large pot, place the soaked beans, cilantro, cumin, chile powder, dried oregano, garlic, and onion. Cover with cold water by one inch. Bring to a boil, reduce heat and simmer until beans are tender (about one hour or longer). Add more water to keep beans covered if necessary. Add 2 tsp (10 mL) salt in the final 15 minutes of cooking.

2 Next, pre-heat the oven to 350°F. Stir the remaining ingredients into the pot. Taste the sauce and season if necessary. Carefully ladle the beans into a large glass baking dish or Dutch oven. Place on a large baking tray (to catch spills), cover with foil and bake. After one hour, remove the foil and check the liquid content. If the beans are still very runny, leave them baking in the oven, and check them every 15 minutes until they reach desired consistency. Let the beans rest for 10 minutes before serving, or refrigerate and reheat as needed.

helpful hint ✳

Add salt to simmering beans only in the final few minutes of cooking. Salt prevents beans from absorbing water, so if you add it too soon they'll take longer to cook and may be unevenly done.

shiitake**brown**rice**pilaf**

with brown basmati, leeks and roasted pecans

mushrooms of the shi, or oak tree, is the English translation of "shiitake", which are highly prized in the Orient for their flavour and reputed medicinal value. Fresh shiitake mushrooms are now widely available. In this dish, they are combined with dried shiitakes to infuse this pilaf with a meaty and rich mushroom essence. Serve with eggplant-tofu satay (p. 57) or teriyaki-glazed salmon and braised Asian greens.

serves 4

1 oz (30 g) dried shiitake mushrooms

2 cups (480 mL) boiling water

2 leeks, mostly white and light green parts

2 garlic cloves, minced

8 oz (240 g) fresh shiitake mushrooms

2 tbsp (30 mL) vegetable oil

3/4 tsp (4 mL) salt

1 cup (240 mL) brown basmati rice

1/2 cup (120 mL) pecans, roasted and roughly chopped

4 scallions, minced (for garnish)

1 Soak dried mushrooms in hot water for at least 30 minutes. Strain and reserve the soaking liquid (you'll need 2 cups – 480 mL). Finely mince the soaked mushrooms and set aside.

2 Quarter the leek whites lengthwise and chop into 1/2" dice. Place in a colander and run cold water over them to remove any clinging grit. Stem the fresh shiitake mushrooms and slice them thinly.

3 In a medium-sized pot, heat the oil and sauté the leeks, garlic and minced soaked shiitakes with 1/2 tsp (2.5 mL) salt until the leeks are soft. Add rice and continue to sauté to toast the rice grains. Add 2 cups of the reserved mushroom-soaking liquid, the remaining salt and bring to a boil. Cover, reduce heat to very low and let the rice steam for 45 minutes. Turn off the heat and allow the rice to sit for an additional 10 minutes. No peeking!

4 Before serving, heat another tablespoon of oil in a skillet and sear the sliced shiitakes until golden. Deglaze the pan with a splash of white wine or balsamic vinegar and season with salt and pepper to taste. Turn the cooked rice into a serving dish and gently stir in the sautéed mushrooms and roasted pecans. Garnish with finely minced scallions and serve hot.

braised winter greens
with garlic and balsamic vinegar ☯

"**eat** your greens" we always say, and we mean it! Kale is one of our favourites—
an excellent source of chlorophyll, calcium, iron and vitamin A. Chard, nettles, spinach,
rapini and many varieties of oriental greens are also loaded with vitamins and minerals, and
are an essential part of any healthy diet focused on getting nutrients form the source.
Cooking techniques for all varieties are straight-forward in order to prevent nutrient loss.
Steaming and braising are some preferred methods, while spinach and chard may be
added directly to hot foods, particularly soups and pasta, in the very last step of preparation.
To take a break from rich foods or holiday feasting, braised greens and a bowl of plain
steamed rice restore harmony to an overworked system. This nutritious side dish is simple
to prepare, can be served with many foods, and is a welcome change from salads in winter.

serves 2

1 large bunch green kale, Swiss or
  ruby chard
1 tbsp (15 mL) olive oil
2 garlic cloves, minced
1/4 tsp (1.2 mL) red chile flakes
1/4 tsp (1.2 mL) salt
1 tbsp (15 mL) balsamic vinegar or
  fresh lemon juice
cracked pepper to taste

1 Stem the greens and place the leaves in a clean sink with cold
water to cover. This should loosen any dirt. Lift them out of the
water and into a large colander to drain. Rinse again if the
greens are particularly gritty.

2 Heat a wok or large skillet over medium-high heat. Heat the oil
and then add garlic, stirring until lightly golden. Add the chiles,
and then the greens, all at once. Toss with a pair of tongs,
sprinkle with salt and cover for several minutes to allow the
volume to steam down. Uncover and continue to toss over
high heat until the greens are wilted. Add vinegar or lemon juice.

3 Remove greens from the pan with a pair of tongs and return
the pan to the burner. Reduce any juices left behind over high
heat and drizzle over the greens. Crack pepper over top and
serve immediately.

sweetcornsalsa

with red pepper, jalapeño and lime

relish a "relish" or a "salsa"? Years spent writing out menus and describing food in the written form has taught us some valuable lessons about the power of language in sales. A good example is the use of the term "relish" as a menu descriptive. For years, this "sweet corn salsa" has been served alongside enchiladas, a staple menu item. During one of our biannual menu revamp sessions, we decided to rename this side dish to "sweet corn relish". Suddenly, our popular enchiladas were not selling!

When the connection was finally unearthed, we promptly reverted to the original "salsa". Sure enough, sales resumed. Just one of many human behaviour experiments that we're carrying out from the **re**bar kitchen! Whatever you choose to call it, this makes a colourful and fresh-tasting side to complement any meal. We like to serve it at room temperature, but some of our customers prefer it hot.

yields 4 cups (960 mL)

1 Toss corn with the oil and 1/2 tsp (2.5 mL) salt and spread out on a baking sheet. Roast in a 350°F oven for 10 minutes. Let cool.

2 Meanwhile, prepare and measure the other vegetables, herbs and spices. Combine everything, including the corn, in a bowl and toss it well. Season to taste and serve.

3 1/2 cups (900 mL) corn, fresh or frozen
2 tsp (10 mL) vegetable oil
1 tsp (5 mL) salt
1 red pepper, finely diced
1/2 small red onion, finely diced
1 jalapeño pepper, seeded and minced
1/4 cup (60 mL) cilantro, stemmed and chopped
1/2 tsp (2.5 mL) ground cumin
1/2 tsp (2.5 mL) pure chile powder
1 tbsp (15 mL) fresh lime juice
4 shots Tabasco sauce, or more to taste

bakedyams

with honey, lime and butter

whole yams baked in the oven are sweet and delicious on their own. Here they're baked until puffy on the outside and creamy soft inside. Then they're mashed with butter to enrich the nutty taste, honey to enhance sweetness and fresh lime juice to brighten the flavours. Try this dish as an alternative to mashed potatoes. At the restaurant we serve it alongside shrimp-corn cakes (p. 61)—their crispy pumpkinseed crust is a nice contrast to the creamy texture of the yams.

serves 6 - 8

3 lbs (1.35 kg) yams
1/4 cup (60 mL) butter
2 tbsp (30 mL) honey
juice of 2 limes
1 1/2 tsp (7.5 mL) salt

1   Pre-heat oven to 400°F. Wash yams and poke each one here and there with a fork. Place on a baking tray with sides and add a cup of water to the tray (this will keep the yams from drying out). Roast up to one hour, depending on the size of the yams, until they are puffy and very soft. Remove and cool them to a comfortable handling temperature.

2   Peel the yams, place in a bowl and add all of the ingredients. Mash until well combined and season to taste. For a silkier texture this can be done in a food processor. To reheat, spread in a baking dish and bake for 15–20 minutes, until heated through. Serve hot.

greenrice

with cilantro and spinach

Mexican rice dishes come in a variety of colours, but this green rice (or arroz verde) recipe is a favourite. It has been adapted from the combined volumes of Mexican cookbooks that we regularly refer to, and in which we have yet to find a recipe that actually delivers the promised colour and flavour. So naturally, we've loaded this recipe with enough chlorophyll to guarantee bright emerald grains and exceptionally fresh flavour. Try it as a side to any Mexican, Caribbean or Indian-inspired meal. It's delicious with enchiladas (p. 201) or with grilled, spice-rubbed salmon.

serves 4 - 6

1 Carefully wash spinach, cilantro, parsley and jalapeños. Place in a blender with salt and 1 cup (240 mL) stock. Blend to liquify and set aside.

2 Heat a rice pot at medium-high and add the oil or butter. Heat and add onion with a pinch of salt; sauté until translucent. Add the garlic and rice and sauté for a few minutes, stirring often, until the rice turns lightly golden. Add the contents of the blender and the remaining stock to the rice; stir well to combine. Turn up the heat and bring to a boil. Cover, reduce heat to very low and cook for 15 minutes. Turn off the heat and let the rice stand covered (no peeking!!) for another 10 minutes. Gently fluff the rice with a fork, turn out into a serving dish and toss gently with minced chives. Serve immediately.

1 bunch spinach, stemmed
1 bunch cilantro
1/2 bunch Italian parsley
2 jalapeño peppers, one seeded
1 tsp (5 mL) salt
2 1/4 cups (540 mL) vegetable stock
   (p. 35) or water
2 tbsp (30 mL) olive oil or butter
1 small yellow onion, finely diced
2 garlic cloves, minced
1 1/2 cups (360 mL) jasmine, or
   other long grain white rice
4 tbsp (60 mL) minced chives

helpfulhint ✳

If you don't already own one, a good quality, medium-sized pot with a heavy bottom is the key to success in cooking rice of any variety. Like most things, you get what you pay for, and a good pot is an investment that will give you years of great service ... and great rice!

Yukon gold and yam gratin
with smoked cheddar & chiles

cast aside the low-fat tricks and revel in this fabulous full-cream version of scalloped potatoes laced with chipotle chiles and smoked cheese. Alternate layers of Yukon Golds and yams give the dish a natural buttery warmth. The smoky heat of the chiles cuts through the richness of the potatoes and cream. Conversely, the cream and potatoes tame the heat of the chiles and allow them to impart their outstanding flavour. A final (optional) flourish of smoked cheese gives this dish a distinctive edge.

serves 6 - 8

3 cups (720 mL) whipping cream
1 tbsp (15 mL) chipotle purée (p. 38)
3 large Yukon Gold potatoes
3 large yams
1 tsp (5 mL) salt
cracked pepper
1 cup (240 mL) grated smoked
    cheddar cheese

helpful hint ✳

Slicing a round vegetable can be awkward and dangerous. A safe way to slice vegetables with rounded edges is to stabilize them on the cutting board by cutting a small slice off any side to create a flat surface. Rest the cut side on the board and slice away with a firm confident grip.

1   Combine whipping cream and chipotle purée in a bowl and whisk thoroughly to blend. Set aside.

2   Peel yams and scrub the potatoes. Slice them as thinly as possible. If you have a mandoline, it will be perfect for this job, otherwise a sharp knife and a bit of concentration are required.

3   Heat the oven to 350°F. Butter an 8" square baking dish and pour enough of the cream/chipotle mixture to just cover the bottom. Alternately overlap 2 layers of yams, sprinkle with salt and pepper and cover with some of the cream mixture. Top with 2 layers of potatoes, season with salt, pepper and cream. Repeat layering the yams, seasonings, cream and potatoes until the ingredients have been used up, ending with a layer of cream, salt and pepper.

4   Place the dish on a baking sheet, cover with foil and bake for 1 hour. Remove the foil and continue baking until the potatoes are soft and most of the cream has been absorbed. In the last 15 minutes of baking, sprinkle grated smoked cheddar over top and return to the oven until the cheese is melted and golden.

5   Let the gratin sit for at least 15 minutes before serving. This will allow any remaining liquid to be reabsorbed by the potatoes and yams. This dish can also be made a day or two in advance. Reheat, covered in the oven, divide into squares and serve hot.

plain&fancycornbread

straight out of the oven and into your mouth is how this cornbread should be served. Make it plain as is, or jazz it up by adding to the batter: a cup of shredded aged cheddar and fresh corn kernels; roasted red peppers and minced chives; blueberries and lemon zest; or just a spoonful of chipotle chile purée (p. 38). No excuses for ignoring this recipe will be accepted, it's just too easy!

yields a 9" x 9" square pan

1 Pre-heat the oven to 400 °F. Combine all of the dry ingredients in a medium sized bowl. In a smaller bowl, whisk together the remaining ingredients.

2 Add the wet mix to the dry mix and fold them together until just blended. Pour the batter into a buttered baking pan and bake for 25 minutes, or until an inserted toothpick comes out clean.

1 cup (240 mL) cornmeal
1/2 cup (120 mL) unbleached flour
1/2 cup (120 mL) whole wheat flour
2 tbsp (30 mL) brown sugar
2 tsp (10 mL) baking powder
1 tsp (5 mL) baking soda
1/2 tsp (2.5 mL) salt
1 cup (240 mL) buttermilk
2 eggs, lightly beaten
5 tbsp (75 mL) melted butter

maplepecanbutter

(yields 1/4 cup - 60 mL)
3 tbsp (45 mL) unsalted butter, softened
2 tsp (10 mL) roasted pecans, ground
2 tsp (10 mL) maple syrup
1/8 tsp (.5 mL) ground cinnamon

Mix together all of the ingredients until well combined and serve, or refrigerate until ready to use.

balsamic roasted shallots
with brown sugar and rosemary

candy-sweet roasted shallots make a great little side dish that is easy to prepare and complements a variety of foods. Serve alongside lasagna, a tart or shepherd's pie. They're especially good with the grilled polenta appetizer (p. 60), and they also make a delicious pizza or foccacia topping. Of course you can always toss them with spaghettini, sundried tomatoes, braised rapini and Romano cheese.

yields 2 cups (480 mL)

8 oz (240 g) shallots, peeled and halved
1 tbsp (15 mL) olive oil
2 tbsp (30 mL) balsamic vinegar
1 tbsp (15 mL) brown sugar
1/2 tsp (2.5 mL) salt
1/4 tsp (1.2 mL) cracked pepper
1 tsp chopped rosemary

1 Pre-heat the oven to 350°F. Toss all of the ingredients together in a small glass baking dish and cover tightly with foil. Bake for 45 minutes, or until the shallots are soft and caramelized. Serve warm.

YukonGoldcowpokes
with sage-lime aïoli

roasted potatoes are a great low-fat substitute when a craving for french fries overwhelms you. The Yukon Gold is an ideal roasting potato—just a little bit of oil and salt crispens the outside, while the yellow flesh inside is creamy and sweet. These are very popular at the restaurant, among patrons and staff alike. In fact, when the "pokes" come out of the oven and are cooling on the baking racks, it's only a matter of minutes before gaps appear as passing staff sneak a "poke" here and there! These are terrific served hot out of the oven with aïoli and **re**barbecue sauce (p. 51).

☯ replace aïoli with seasoned tofu mayo for a vegan dip.

1 Pre-heat the oven to 400°F. Slice the potatoes in half lengthwise, then slice 3/4" thick wedges (while baking, the wedges need to stand on their skins, cut side up, so a solid base is required to keep them from toppling over.)

2 Toss wedges with the oil and coarse salt. Arrange them cut side up on a baking tray, leaving space between each 'poke. Roast for 20 minutes, or until golden and tender. Serve hot.

3 To make aïoli, put the egg and egg yolk in a blender or food processor and blend for 15 seconds. Add lime juice and garlic and blend for another 15 seconds. While the motor is running, slowly drizzle in the blended oils, starting drop by drop and working up to a thin, steady stream. Stop the motor when all of the oil is incorporated and the emulsion is thick. Add lime zest, sage and salt and blend briefly to combine. Season to taste, transfer to a clean container and refrigerate until ready.

serves 4

2 large, or 4 medium Yukon Gold potatoes
1 tbsp (15 mL) vegetable oil
1 tsp (5 mL) coarse salt

sage-lime aïoli
(yields 3/4 cup - 180 mL)
1 whole egg
1 egg yolk
1 tbsp (15 mL) fresh lime juice
2 garlic cloves, minced
1/3 cup (80 mL) olive oil
1/3 cup (80 mL) vegetable oil
1/8 tsp (.5 mL) minced lime zest
1 tbsp (15 mL) chopped fresh sage
1/4 tsp (1.2 mL) salt

helpfulhint ✳

Since aïoli is made with raw egg, please take extra care to ensure that it is refrigerated at all times. Use it up while it's fresh and throw out any leftovers after 2 days.

wholeroastedgarlic ☯

prepare yourself for a real treat if you haven't discovered roasted garlic yet. Most of us wouldn't consider eating an entire garlic bulb at one sitting, but prepared in this way, it's difficult to stop at just one. Luckily nothing could be easier to make. Baked whole in the oven, the cloves transform into mild, buttery versions of their formerly pungent selves. They are ready to pull from the oven when their nutty aroma envelops you in the kitchen. Fully roasted, the soft cloves will readily squeeze out of their skins or be scooped out with a knife. Spread on warm bread, or mash into a paste and use to season vinaigrettes, mashed potatoes, bean spreads, soups and sauces.

serves 2

2 garlic bulbs
2 tsp (10 mL) olive oil
pinch of salt
pinch of cracked pepper

1 Pre-heat oven (or toaster oven) to 400°F. Using a sharp knife, slice the top off the garlic bulb, just enough to expose the tops of the garlic flesh. Center each bulb on a square piece of aluminum foil. Drizzle with olive oil and sprinkle with salt and pepper. Wrap the bulbs securely and pop them into the oven.

2 After 45 minutes you should start to smell the sweet roasting aroma, but depending on the size of your bulb, it may need a bit more time. Test by slipping the sharp point of a paring knife into one of the cloves. If it slides in effortlessly, or the bulbs are starting to poke out of their skins, then the garlic is ready to serve. Plan to serve one bulb per person.

helpfulhint ✳

If you want to serve these hot, they can be roasted well ahead of time and heated up in the microwave for 30–45 seconds just before serving.

crackedwheatpilaf
with vegetables and fresh herbs ☯

golden grains of cracked wheat, or bulghur, make a delicious nutty pilaf when plumped with flavourful stock and studded with radiant vegetables and savoury herbs. Use to fill baked stuffed vegetables (peppers, zucchini, tomatoes) and top with melted feta cheese and toasted pine nuts. Or pack the pilaf into a small mould or cup and invert it onto the center of a plate. Surround with a spring vegetable ragoût or an assortment of steamed vegetables drizzled with herbed butter sauce. Leftovers can be served the next day at room temperature as a healthy lunch salad.

serves 4 - 6

1 Heat vegetable stock and keep warm. Dice the fennel, zucchini, peppers and carrots into 1/8" cubes and set aside.

2 Heat the olive oil and butter in a medium-sized pot. Add onion and garlic and sauté over medium heat until soft and golden. Add bulghur, 1 tsp (5 mL) salt and bay leaf. Sauté stirring for several minutes to toast the grains.

3 Turn up the heat and stir in the diced vegetables and savory. Sauté for a several minutes, then add the white wine. Let the wine be absorbed and then add the warm stock and the remaining salt. Bring to a boil, stir, cover and reduce heat to low. After 25 minutes, uncover and check to see if all of the stock is absorbed and the bulghur is tender. If not, cover and continue to steam for several more minutes. Fluff with a fork and gently stir in parsley. Season to taste and serve.

2 cups (480 mL) vegetable stock (p. 35)
1 tbsp (15 mL) olive oil
1 tbsp (15 mL) butter
1 small red onion, finely diced
4 garlic cloves, minced
1 1/2 cups (360 mL) bulghur
2 tsp (10 mL) salt
1 bay leaf
1/2 fennel bulb
1 small red pepper
1 small zucchini
2 carrots
2 tsp (10 mL) dried savory
1/2 cup (120 mL) white wine
1/2 bunch Italian parsley, minced

helpfulhint ✳

Several commercial brands of vegetable bouillion make a fine substitute for homemade stock in many recipes. Check your local health food store and read the label to make sure it doesn't contain MSG

☯ – a vegan recipe

8

pasta

Julia Child once wrote/said that she never serves pasta to guests because it shows that you don't know how to cook. This may be so in the glamorous world of the culinary elite, but as we mere mortals (particularly vegetarian mortals) all know, pasta is a life saver. When guests are coming and you're stumped, pasta is the easiest and safest way to go. No, you don't have to be a genius in the kitchen to make a great pasta, but there is no better way to please the majority. Include a freshly baked bread and a lovely salad and no one will dare question your cooking skills!

Depending on the dish, we use both fresh and dried pasta. A pasta machine at home is a must-have for real pasta lovers. Even if you don't use it very often, when you do, your meal will be extra special. Fresh pasta is also widely available in supermarkets and delis. Good quality dried pasta will yield excellent pasta dishes. Try substituting regular pasta with whole wheat and organic varieties. Check specialty food markets or visit your local Italian foods shop for the best brands.

Audrey's deluxe mac & cheese
with crispy pine nut-herb crust

comfort food is Audrey's forte in the kitchen. She does wonders with simple, clean ingredients, giving them her special touch and achieving spectacular flavour. Some cooks just have a knack for making something as basic as macaroni and cheese a dish to get excited about. Here is a jazzy adult version that is loaded with garlic, fresh herbs and a crispy crust. Kids will love this one too.

serves 10

6 cups dry pasta shapes, we use
   serpentini
1/4 cup (60 mL) olive oil
1 large yellow onion, minced
2 tsp (10 mL) salt
8 garlic cloves, minced
1/3 cup (80 mL) chopped oregano
2 tbsp (30 mL) chopped thyme
1/2 cup (120 mL) chopped Italian parsley
1/4 cup (60 mL) butter
3 1/2 cups (840 mL) milk
1/4 cup (60 mL) unbleached flour
4 cups (960 mL) grated aged white
   cheddar
4 cups (960 mL) fresh breadcrumbs
1 cup (240 mL) grated Parmesan
1/2 cup (120 mL) pine nuts

helpful hint ✳

For a delicious variation, substitute the cheddar cheese with a mix of fontina and mozzarella, or asiago and Monterrey Jack.

1 Cook pasta in boiling, salted water until just done. Strain and toss with a light coating of olive oil. Set aside or refrigerate. (This step can be done one day in advance.)

2 Meanwhile, heat 1 tbsp (15 mL) olive oil in a small skillet and sauté onion for 5 minutes. Add half of the minced garlic, 1/2 tsp (2.5 mL) salt and sauté until the garlic turns golden. Transfer to a small bowl and stir in half of the chopped herbs. Set aside.

3 Next, make a roux for the cheese sauce. Gently heat the milk and keep it warm. Set a saucepan over medium heat and melt the butter. Sprinkle in flour and whisk constantly as the flour and butter turn golden. Gradually add the warm milk and 1 tsp (5 mL) salt and whisk thoroughly. Heat until the sauce thickens (about 10 minutes). Add the sautéed onion/herb mix, grated cheese and stir until the cheese melts. Season to taste.

4 Finally, make the topping. Combine the breadcrumbs with the remaining garlic, herbs, Parmesan, pine nuts, 1/2 tsp (2.5 mL) salt, plenty of cracked pepper and the remaining 3 tbsp (45 mL) olive oil. Mix together thoroughly.

5 Pre-heat the oven to 350°F. To assemble, combine the noodles and cheese sauce in a large bowl and mix well. Pour into an oiled 8" x 12" baking dish. Scatter the topping over the entire surface, working some of it into the noodles. Bake uncovered until golden and bubbly (about 45 minutes). Serve piping hot.

spaghettini all'arrabbiata
with whole wheat pasta, fresh basil and garlic crumbs

chileheads will love this simple pasta and tomato sauce dish, generously seasoned with fresh garlic, sweet basil and red hot chile flakes. Whole wheat pasta boosts nutritional value and the crispy garlic breadcrumbs add a textural suprise.

☯ use dried spaghettini for a vegan pasta dish.

serves 4

1 Heat a saucepan over medium heat. Add olive oil and heat until a piece of onion sizzles on contact. Sauté onion with 1/2 tsp (2.5 mL) salt for 10 minutes, stirring often. Add garlic, bay leaves, chile flakes and sauté another 5 minutes. Deglaze the pan with red wine and let it reduce until thick and syrupy. Add the fresh and canned tomatoes, basil, pepper and remaining salt. Simmer gently, partially covered, for up to one hour. Meanwhile, put a large pot of water on to boil to cook the pasta.

2 Before serving, season the sauce with more salt, pepper, fresh basil and/or chiles to taste. Add sugar to balance acidity, if required. To thicken, stir in a few tablespoons of tomato paste.

3 To serve, cook spaghettini until al dente. Drain and return the pasta to the pot. Toss with half of the arrabbiata sauce and transfer to a serving dish. Serve remaining sauce on the side along with grated Parmesan, chopped fresh basil and crispy garlic breadcrumbs to sprinkle on top.

2 tbsp (30 mL) olive oil
1 yellow onion, diced
1 1/2 tsp (7.5 mL) salt
6 garlic cloves, minced
2 bay leaves
1/2 tsp (2.5 mL) red chile flakes, or more to taste
1 cup (240 mL) red table wine
1 x 28 oz (796 mL) can whole or diced tomatoes
4 Roma tomatoes, seeded and diced
10 fresh basil leaves, coarsely chopped
1/2 tsp (2.5 mL) cracked pepper
1 lb (450 g) whole wheat spaghettini

crispy garlic crumbs

1 cup (240 mL) fresh breadcrumbs
4 garlic cloves, minced
1/4 tsp (1.2 mL) salt
1/4 tsp (1.2 mL) cracked pepper
2 tbsp (30 mL) olive oil
Combine all of the ingredients in a small bowl and mix well. Spread onto a baking sheet and bake in a 325°F oven until golden and crispy (10 minutes).

wildmushroomravioli
with leeks, cranberries and citrus-sage cream

festive winter holidays often leave vegetarians feeling shortchanged at the family table. Here is a special main course pasta that everyone will love. Look for fresh wild mushroom ravioli at specialty markets. A more standard filled ravioli, such as three cheese or spinach, will do in a pinch. Accompany with garlic-braised winter greens (p. 150) and a warm rustic loaf for a full course feast.

serves 4

2 cups (480 mL) butternut squash,
    1/4" dice
2 tbsp (30 mL) dried cranberries
1/4 cup (60 mL) white wine
1 tbsp (15 mL) butter
2 tbsp (30 mL) olive oil
1 1/2 lb (675 g) assorted mushrooms
    (portabello, oyster, shiitake or
    chanterelle), sliced
4 garlic cloves, minced
2 large leeks, white and light green
    parts only
4 shallots, minced
1 bay leaf
1 tsp (5 mL) salt
1 1/4 cup (320 mL) white wine
juice of 1 orange
juice of 1 lemon
1 tsp (5 mL) orange zest
1 tsp (5 mL) cracked pepper
1 1/2 cups (360 mL) whipping cream
3 tbsp (45 mL) minced sage
3 tbsp (45 mL) minced chives
1 lb (450 g) wild mushroom ravioli
Parmesan cheese for garnish
4 tbsp (60 mL) hazelnuts, roasted,
    skinned and chopped

1 Prepare the squash and lightly steam it until just tender. Place the cranberries in a small bowl and cover with wine. Set aside.

2 Begin heating a large pot of water for the ravioli. In a large skillet, heat butter and 1 tbsp (15 mL) olive oil. Add the sliced mushrooms and a pinch of salt. Stir and cover the pan to let the mushrooms cook down. Remove the lid, add garlic and sauté until the mushrooms are golden and tender. Transfer to a bowl and set aside.

3 Heat the remaining olive oil in the skillet and add leeks, shallots, salt and bay leaf; sauté until soft. Next, add the wine, citrus juices, zest and pepper. When the liquid has reduced by half, add the cream and bring to a full simmer. Meanwhile, start cooking the ravioli.

4 When the sauce has thickened slightly, add the steamed squash, cranberries, sautéed mushrooms and fresh herbs to heat through. Season with salt and pepper. Drain pasta, toss with butter or olive oil to lightly coat, and serve topped with sauce, grated cheese, hazelnuts and extra minced chives.

poppyseedpapparadelle
with mushroom-sweet pepper ragoût

although we tend to shy away from vegetarian cooking that tries to simulate meat, this dish will remind you of a beefy Hungarian goulash. Poppyseed butter adds unexpected crunch to the smooth, extra-wide papparadelle egg noodles. Substitute some wild mushrooms, such as chanterelles or morels, for the regular mushrooms to give this home-style dish a touch of elegance.

☻ replace butter with olive oil and use eggless pasta (vegan).

serves 4 - 6

1. Heat the butter and olive oil in a wide-bottomed pot over medium heat. Add onion and 1/2 tsp (2.5 mL) salt; sauté until the onion is soft and golden. Add garlic, chile flakes, dill and paprika; sauté 5 more minutes. Turn up the heat and add the mushrooms and remaining salt. Stir and cover. When the mushroom juices begin to cook off, stir in the peppers and deglaze the pan with wine. Let the wine reduce for a few minutes, then stir in soy sauce, balsamic vinegar and half of the chopped herbs. Simmer partially covered for 30 minutes. Add all but 2 tbsp (30 mL) of the remaining herbs to the ragoût just before serving.

2. Meanwhile, cook the pasta in a large pot of salted boiling water. Prepare the poppyseed butter by mixing the butter and seeds together thoroughly. Strain the pasta and toss with poppyseed butter. Serve noodles topped with ragoût, a dollop of sour cream and sprinkle with reserved herbs.

1 tbsp (15 mL) butter
1 tbsp (15 mL) olive oil
1 large yellow onion, diced
2 tsp (10 mL) salt
8 garlic cloves, minced
1 tsp (5 mL) red chile flakes
1 tsp (5 mL) dried dill weed
2 tbsp (30 mL) Hungarian paprika
2 1/2 lb (1.2 kg) button mushrooms
3 red peppers, 1/2" dice
1 1/2 cups (360 mL) red wine, Merlot
1 tsp (5 mL) cracked pepper
2 tbsp (30 mL) soy sauce
1 1/2 tbsp (22.5 mL) balsamic vinegar
1/4 cup (60 mL) chopped parsley
1/4 cup (60 mL) chopped dill
1 lb (450 g) papparadelle noodles
1/4 cup (60 mL) butter, softened
1 tbsp (15 mL) poppyseeds
sour cream or crème fraîche

helpfulhint ✳

If you've ever wondered how to use seitan, or wheat gluten, this is your dish! Cut seitan into strips and add it to the ragoût just before adding the wine. You just may fool a meat eater or two!

teriyaki soba

with Japanese eggplant, oyster mushrooms and nori threads ☯

wholesome buckwheat noodles give this otherwise light dish some hearty substance. The earthy soba also provide an interesting contrast to the delicate taste of the sea imparted by the nori. Japanese eggplant and mushrooms absorb the flavourful teriyaki sauce, which is nearly fat-free. In all, this dish is substantial, yet surprisingly clean tasting, leaving you feeling restored, rather than heavily sated. With any luck, you'll have room for dessert!

serves 4

1 lb (450 g) buckwheat soba noodles
2 tbsp (30 mL) vegetable oil
2 Japanese eggplant
1/2 lb (225 g) oyster mushrooms
6 oz (180 g) snow peas
1 small head sui choy, chopped
1 bunch scallions
1 tbsp (15 mL) sesame seeds, toasted
1 sheet nori seaweed (see hint)

teriyaki sauce

2 tbsp (30 mL) minced ginger
1 cup (240 mL) soy sauce
4 tbsp (60 mL) mirin
4 tbsp (60 mL) brown sugar
1 tbsp (15 mL) sesame oil
1 tbsp (15 mL) rice wine vinegar
1/2 tsp (2.5 mL) Shichimi Togarashi
   (Japanese hot chile powder)

helpful hint ✳

To cut nori threads, slice a sheet of nori in half and using a very sharp knife, make fine, thin slices. If your knife is not sharp enough, try using a pair of scissors to cut the strips.

1 Put a large pot of water on to boil to cook the noodles. Meanwhile, prepare the teriyaki sauce by whisking together all of the sauce ingredients in a small pot. Bring to boil and simmer 5 minutes. Set aside.

2 Next, prepare the vegetables. Slice the eggplant in half lengthwise and cut 1/4" thick half-moon slices. Remove thick stems from the oyster mushrooms and slice the larger mushrooms in half. String the snow peas. Chop sui choy into 1" x 2" rectangles. Slice scallions into 1-inch lengths on the bias.

3 When the water is boiling, add the noodles and 1 tbsp (15 mL) salt. Strain when tender (about 8 minutes), toss with a light coat of sesame oil and keep warm.

4 While the noodles cook, stir-fry the vegetables. Heat a wok on high, add oil and heat. Add eggplant and mushrooms and stir constantly while sautéing. If the vegetables start to stick, add a bit of water (or sake) to the pan. When the eggplant and mushrooms are almost cooked, add remaining vegetables and continue tossing them while they fry. Add enough sauce to coat and cook until the snow peas are just done. Remove the vegetables with a pair of tongs and return the wok to the burner. Reduce the pan liquids over high heat until a thick sauce remains.

5 To serve, spoon vegetables over hot noodles, drizzle sauce over top and sprinkle with sesame seeds and a stack of nori threads.

kungpaonoodles
with peanuts and wok-fried vegetables

lively kung pao is a Chinese sauce often used in chicken and pork dishes. Here crisp young spring carrots, snap peas, baby corn and other goodies are quickly wok-fried and seasoned with kung pao—an intense blend of ginger, garlic, chiles and the sweet barbecue flavour of hoisin. Star anise and sesame oil add a rich, exotic touch. If you can find them, use thick fresh Shanghai noodles which will soak up the tasty sauce. Roasted peanuts are a traditional garnish, but cashews or whole almonds are also great.

☯ use dry, eggless pasta for a vegan dish.

serves 4

1 Begin by making the sauce, which can be done several days in advance. Combine all of the ingredients, except cornstarch, in a pot and gently bring to a boil. Reduce heat, cover partially and simmer for 15 minutes. In a small bowl, mix the cornstarch with 1 tbsp (15 mL) water and whisk the slurry into the simmering sauce. Cook until mixture thickens slightly (10 minutes). Remove the star anise and set the sauce aside, or refrigerate, until ready to use.

2 Before beginning preparation of the vegetables, put a large pot of water on to boil the noodles. Thinly julienne the onion and cut the broccoli into florets. Peel the stem and cut in half-moon slices. String the snow peas and leave them whole. Slice the carrots into 1/2" thick half-moon slices. Cut the butt ends from the baby choys and separate the leaves. Slice the larger leaves in half lengthwise. Drain the water chestnuts and the baby corn. Slice baby corns in half lengthwise. Slice scallions into 1-inch lengths. Wash, stem and chop the cilantro roughly. Coarsely chop the roasted nuts.

3 Just before starting the stir-fry, begin cooking the noodles and have a colander ready in the sink for draining them. Heat the wok over high heat, swirl in the oil and add the onion. Fry, stirring constantly, until golden. Add the carrots and broccoli; stir-fry for 3 minutes. Then add the peas, baby corn, water chesnuts, bok choy, scallions and 1/2 cup (120 mL) of sauce. Stir well and cover until the vegetables are cooked but still crisp (about 5 minutes). Uncover and stir in the cilantro. Serve immediately over hot noodles and garnish with roasted nuts.

kung pao sauce

2 tbsp (30 mL) minced ginger
4 garlic cloves, minced
1/4 cup (60 mL) soy sauce
1/4 cup (60 mL) hoisin sauce
1 tbsp (15 mL) brown sugar
2 tbsp (30 mL) dry sherry
2 tsp (10 mL) sesame oil
1 pod star anise
2 tsp (10 mL) sambal oelek
1/2 tsp (2.5 mL) cracked pepper
1/2 cup (120 mL) vegetable stock (p. 35), or water
1 tbsp (15 mL) cornstarch

noodles and vegetables

1 lb (450 g) fresh Shanghai noodles
2 tbsp (30 mL) peanut oil
1 medium yellow onion
1 bunch broccoli, in florets
6 oz (180 g) snow peas
6 young carrots
4 heads baby bok or Shanghai choy
1 small can water chestnuts
1 can baby corn
1 bunch scallions
1/2 bunch cilantro
4 tbsp (60 mL) roasted peanuts

rebar linguine
with balsamic-glazed roasted vegetables

quick preparation makes this pasta a standard both at home and at the restaurant. This recipe is a veteran of our menu and is regularly requested by customers. Preparation is simple, the presentation is lively and the flavours never fail to please. It's a great meal to serve when you have guests and want to spend minimal time in the kitchen. If you're reasonably efficient, or have a helping hand, this dish can be on the table in thirty minutes. With a bottle of red, a warm baguette and a simple salad, you'll have plenty of time to be a social butterfly and gracious host.

serves 4

4 small zucchini
4 Japanese eggplant
3 sweet bell peppers, assorted colours
1 fennel bulb
1 large red onion
1 garlic bulb
3 tbsp (45 mL) olive oil
1 tsp (5 mL) salt
1/2 tsp (2.5 mL) cracked pepper
1 tsp (5 mL) red chile flakes
1/2 cup (120 mL) Kalamata olives, pits
  removed
1 cup (240 mL) chopped basil, loosely
  packed
2 tbsp (30 mL) balsamic vinegar
1 lb (450 g) linguine
Parmesan or Romano cheese

☯ use dry linguine and omit the cheese for a vegan dish.

1 Pre-heat oven to 425°F. Heat a large pot of water on the stove to boil the pasta.

2 Slice zucchini and eggplant into 1/8" thick half-moon slices. Halve, seed and cut peppers into 3/4" dice. Slice thick strips of fennel and red onion. Separate, peel and slice the garlic cloves in half lengthwise. Place all of the vegetables in a large bowl and toss with olive oil, salt, pepper and chile flakes. Spread out evenly on two baking sheets and roast in the oven until golden and tender (about 20 minutes). Stir the vegetables halfway through.

3 When the vegetables are just about cooked, start to cook the pasta. Salt the pasta water and cook the linguine until al dente. Strain and toss with a light coat of extra virgin olive oil.

4 When the vegetables are ready, remove them from the oven and put them back into a large bowl with the olives, basil and balsamic vinegar. Season to taste with more salt, cracked pepper or balsamic. Toss vegetables with the pasta and serve with freshly grated Reggiano or Romano cheese.

helpful hint ✳

For a slightly different twist, replace the fresh basil with rosemary. Toss 2 tbsp (30 mL) minced rosemary with the vegetables before roasting. Top with crumbled goat's feta cheese or chèvre in place of the Parmesan.

roastedvegetablepasti

with rigatoni, feta and fresh herbs

jumble

up a mess of roasted vegetables, pasta, cheese and fresh herbs, bake it with a crispy crust and you get pasticcio! This is an "everything but the kitchen sink" kind of dish, yet delicious and impressive nevertheless. Substitute feta with other favourite cheeses, or try different vegetable combinations. Serve with a spinach salad (p. 31) and dinner is all set! Leftovers are great too.

serves 6 - 8

1 Cook pasta in plenty of salted, boiling water until al dente. Drain and toss with a light coat of olive oil. Set aside.

2 Pre-heat oven to 400°F. Chop red onion, eggplant and peppers into 1/2" square pieces. Cut zucchini into 1/2" thick half-moon slices. In a large bowl, toss vegetables with olive oil, salt, pepper and minced garlic. Spread them out on two lightly oiled baking trays and roast until vegetables are soft and golden (about 15 minutes). Remove the vegetables and reduce the oven temperature to 350°F.

3 In a large bowl, toss together the cooked pasta, roasted vegetables, lemon zest, capers, 2 cups (480 mL) mozzarella, feta cheese and all but 2 tbsp of the chopped herbs. Spoon the entire mixture into an oiled 9" x 13" glass baking dish.

4 Make the topping by combining fresh breadcrumbs with the remaining cup of grated cheese, reserved chopped herbs, a drizzle of olive oil, and salt and pepper to taste. Mix well and spread over the casserole. Bake uncovered at 350°F until bubbly and golden on top (40 minutes).

- 20 oz (600 g) dry rigatoni pasta
- 1 medium red onion
- 1 medium eggplant
- 2 yellow or red peppers
- 2 small zucchini
- 3 tbsp (45 mL) olive oil
- 1 tsp (5 mL) salt
- 1/2 tsp (2.5 mL) cracked pepper
- 4 garlic cloves, minced
- 4 tbsp (60 mL) chopped oregano, basil or mint
- 1/2 bunch Italian parsley, chopped
- zest of 1 lemon
- 2 tbsp (30 mL) capers
- 3 cups (720 mL) grated mozzarella
- 1 1/2 cups (360 mL) crumbled feta cheese
- 2 cups (480 mL) fresh breadcrumbs

helpfulhint ✳

Be extra careful when cutting peppers. The small seeds can get under your knife and cause it to slip, risking a cut finger. To avoid any accidents, thoroughly wipe down your chopping board and knife after seeding, then proceed with chopping or slicing.

portabellofettucine

with arugula pesto, roasted peppers and Romano cheese

peppery arugula leaves make a great pesto for tossing with pasta. The slightly bitter flavour is a nice complement to the sweetness of the vegetables. Grill juicy marinated portabello mushrooms, sweet peppers and red onion on a barbecue or broil them in the oven. Leftover pesto can be used in sandwiches, on pizza, stirred into tomato sauce, a potato soup or spread on crostini and topped with vine-ripe tomatoes.

serves 4

1 lb (450 g) fettucine

4 portabello mushrooms, marinated
   (p. 23) and roasted

2 each red and yellow peppers,
   roasted and peeled (p. 50)

1 tbsp (15 mL) olive oil

1 large red onion, julienned

1 pint cherry tomatoes, halved

1/2 cup (120 mL) chopped fresh basil

1/4 cup (60 mL) arugula pesto

1 cup (240 mL) grated Romano
   cheese

4 tbsp (60 mL) pine nuts, toasted

1 Heat a large pot of water to cook the pasta. Slice the portabello mushrooms and roasted peppers into long, thin strips and set aside.

2 Heat olive oil in a skillet and sauté the onion until translucent. Add the mushrooms, peppers, and cherry tomato halves, toss to heat through and keep warm over low heat. Meanwhile, cook the fettucine.

3 Strain the pasta and toss with enough pesto to liberally coat the noodles. Add the vegetables and basil and toss to combine. Divide among four pasta bowls, sprinkle with Romano cheese and toasted pine nuts.

arugulapesto

2 cups (480 mL) arugula leaves, packed

1/2 cup (120 mL) pine nuts

1/2 cup (120 mL) grated Romano cheese

6 cloves roasted garlic (p. 158)

1 clove fresh garlic

1 tsp (5 mL) salt

1/2 tsp (2.5 mL) chile flakes

1/2 tsp (2.5 mL) cracked pepper

1/2 cup (120 mL) olive oil

Pulse all ingredients, except oil, to form a coarse paste. Add oil and pulse to blend. Keep refrigerated.

padThai
with tofu, bean sprouts and roasted peanuts

upon discovering that it was common among our cook friends to have given up trying to make pad Thai, a favourite Thai noodle dish, we were relieved to know we weren't alone. So we set out to try all the recipes we could find and come out with the best, one that we could rely on at home. This dish is an amalgamation of all the techniques and ingredients that we unearthed in our quest and it's a clear winner!

☯ replace fish with soy sauce and omit the eggs.

serves 4 - 6

1. Start by putting a large pot of water on to boil for blanching the snow peas and soaking the noodles. Once the water starts to boil, add the snow peas for 1 minute, until bright green and just tender. Lift them out with a strainer or slotted spoon. Turn off the heat, add the noodles to the water, cover and let them soak until tender (about 5 minutes). Drain in a colander, rinse with cold water and set aside.

2. Meanwhile, make the sauce by whisking together the ketchup, fish sauce, water, soy, molasses, sambal and pepper. Set aside. Drain tofu and cut the block into 1/2" cubes. Heat 1 tbsp (15 mL) oil in a non-stick skillet, add the tofu and sauté until golden, stirring often. Set aside. Prepare remaining ingredients so that they are all at hand when you begin stir-frying.

3. In a large wok, heat 3 tbsp (45 mL) oil over medium-high heat. Add garlic and crushed chiles and sauté until golden, stirring constantly. Add beaten eggs and scramble until dry and set. Next, add the noodles and keep stirring them around to combine with the egg-garlic mix. The noodles will clump into one big mass, but that's okay; continue stirring them for at least 5 minutes (this is the point where most people give up!)

4. Turn up the heat and add the sauce, tofu, bean sprouts and snow peas. Stir constantly to heat everything through and prevent sticking. After several minutes, add the scallions and cilantro and cook until the whole dish is hot and steamy right through. Divide pad Thai among serving plates, drizzle with fresh lime juice, sprinkle with chopped peanuts and serve extra sambal and fish sauce on the side.

8 oz (240 g) snow peas, halved
1 lb (454 g) package rice noodles, medium width
1/4 cup (60 mL) ketchup or tomato paste
1/4 cup (60 mL) fish sauce
1/4 cup (60 mL) water
1/4 cup (60 mL) soy sauce
3 tbsp (45 mL) Barbados molasses
1 tbsp (15 mL) sambal oelek
1/2 tsp (2.5 mL) cracked pepper
4 tbsp (60 mL) vegetable or peanut oil
1 block extra-firm tofu
8 large garlic cloves, minced
2-3 whole dried red chiles, crushed
3 eggs, beaten
3 cups (720 mL) bean sprouts
2 bunch scallions, sliced
1/2 bunch cilantro, roughly chopped
1 lime
4 tbsp (60 mL) roasted peanuts, crushed

lotuslandlinguine
with wok-fried vegetables and peanut sauce

peanut sauce drizzled over hot noodles and crispy wok-fried vegetables makes a filling and nourishing dinner. Come to think of it, leftovers would make a great lunch salad. Any combination of your favourite seasonal stir-fry vegetables will work here. Add fried tempeh or tofu cubes for a boost of protein.

☯ prepare vegan peanut sauce option and use dry pasta.

serves 4

1 x recipe peanut sauce (p. 40)
1 lb (450 g) linguine noodles
1 tbsp (15 mL) peanut or vegetable oil
1 yellow onion, julienned
2 carrots, half moon slices
1 large red pepper, 1/2" triangles
1 bunch broccoli, florets and stem
  slices
4 oz (120 g) snow peas
4 heads baby bok choy, leaves
  separated
2 bunch scallions, 1-inch long slices
sesame oil

1 Heat a large pot of water for cooking the pasta. In a small pot, gently heat the peanut sauce, adding a bit of stock or water to thin, if necessary.

2 Begin cooking the noodles when you start the stir-fry as they will take about the same amount of time. Have a colander ready in the sink for draining the pasta.

3 Heat a wok over medium-high heat. Add oil and, just before it starts to smoke, add the onion and a pinch of salt. Stir-fry the onion until translucent and then add remaining vegetables in order of their cooking times, beginning with carrots and ending with snow peas, bok choy and scallions. Season lightly with salt and pepper. Continue stirring and tossing the vegetables, keeping them crisp and brightly coloured. If they start to stick, add a splash of water and cover briefly.

helpfulhint ❊

You can also make a nice rich creamy sauce for this dish by stirring the peanut sauce with equal amounts of canned "lite" coconut milk.

4 Toss the drained noodles with a splash of sesame oil. Divide the noodles among serving plates, top with vegetables and drizzle with warm peanut sauce. Garnish with crushed peanuts, freshly chopped cilantro and lime wedges, if desired.

spring**fettucine**
with asparagus, smoked salmon and lemon-vodka cream

local spring asparagus, fresh dill and lemon give this pasta a light, fresh touch, while spinach and capers also help cut through the richness of the cream. Smoked salmon is purely optional in this recipe, though it does combine perfectly with all of these flavours. Fresh shelled peas make a fine vegetarian substitution.

serves 4

1 Bring a large pot of water to boil for the pasta. Snap the tough ends from the asparagus and discard or compost them. Slice the spears diagonally into 1 1/2" lengths. Salt the pasta water and use the boiling water to blanch the asparagus for 1–2 minutes, or until bright green and just barely tender. Shock in ice water, drain and set aside.

2 Melt butter in a large heated skillet. Sauté leeks and garlic until leeks are tender. Add vodka, lemon zest, salt and pepper and simmer until the vodka is reduced by half. Add cream and simmer until slightly thickened. Add asparagus, salmon, capers, spinach and half of the chopped herbs. Cook until the spinach wilts and everything else is heated through. Season to taste.

3 While the sauce simmers, cook the pasta, drain and toss lightly with olive oil. Serve immediately, topped or tossed with the hot sauce. Garnish with reserved herbs, cracked pepper and shaved Parmesan.

1 lb (450 g) bunch asparagus
2 tbsp (30 mL) butter
2 leeks, mostly whites, sliced
4 garlic cloves, minced
1/2 cup (120 mL) vodka
1 1/2 tsp (7.5 mL) lemon zest
1 tsp (5 mL) salt
1/2 tsp (2.5 mL) cracked pepper
1 1/2 cups (360 mL) heavy cream
1/4 lb (115 g) cold smoked salmon,
    thinly sliced
2 tbsp (30 mL) capers
1 large bunch spinach, stemmed and
    roughly chopped
2 tbsp (30 mL) minced dill
2 tbsp (30 mL) minced chives
I lb (450 g) fettucine

helpful**hint** ✳

Purple chive blossoms are edible and make a pretty garnish. Gently pull petals from the blossom head and sprinkle over salads or pasta dishes.

SantaFepastasalad

with roasted corn, candied salmon and feta cheese

Southwestern flavours once again dominate in this dish, giving the potentially ho-hum pasta salad a fresh twist. Roasted peppers, garlic and chipotles combine to make a rich dressing that is bold enough to make you take notice, but doesn't compete with the assertive flavours of fresh sage, roasted corn, feta cheese and smoked salmon. As with most of the recipes in the book, the addtion of salmon is purely optional. Canned chick peas are a fine substitute.

☯ replace salmon with avocado or beans and omit cheese.

serves 6 - 8

dressing

2 red peppers, roasted (p. 50)
4 cloves garlic, roasted (p. 158)
2 tsp (10 mL) chipotle purée (p. 38)
1 shallot, peeled and chopped
2 tsp (10 mL) maple syrup
1/2 tsp (2.5 mL) salt
2 tbsp (30 mL) rice wine vinegar
2 tbsp (30 mL) fresh lime juice
3/4 cup (180 mL) olive oil

salad

4 cups (960 mL) dry fusilli pasta
olive oil
3 cups (720 mL) corn, fresh or frozen
1 tbsp (15 mL) vegetable oil
1/4 tsp (1.2 mL) salt
4 tbsp (60 mL) minced sage
1 bunch scallions, chopped
4 oz (120 g) candied salmon
1 pint cherry tomatoes, halved
2 tbsp (30 mL) pine nuts, toasted
1/2 cup (120 mL) crumbled feta cheese
salt and pepper to taste

1 Begin by preparing the dressing. Seed and peel the roasted peppers. Place them, along with the garlic, shallots and chipotle purée in a food processor and blend until smooth. Add maple syrup, vinegar, lime juice, salt and blend. With the motor running, slowly drizzle in the oil until well incorporated and thickened. Set aside.

2 In a large pot of boiling water, cook the pasta until al dente. Drain and toss with olive oil. Set aside while you prepare the remaining ingredients.

3 Pre-heat the oven to 375°F. Toss corn with oil and salt and evenly spread it out in a small baking pan. Roast in the oven for 10 minutes. Remove and cool. Remove any small bones in the salmon and slice or crumble into bite-sized pieces.

4 To assemble the salad, toss pasta in a large bowl with enough dressing to coat. Add corn, salmon, sage and scallions and toss well. Add more dressing to taste and season with salt and pepper. Just before serving, garnish with cherry tomatoes, crumbled feta cheese and pine nuts. Serve with fresh lime wedges and extra feta on the side.

spinachcannelloni
with sundried tomatoes, fresh herbs and two cheeses

fresh pasta makes an easy job of this recipe. The sauce cooks the pasta as the cannelloni bake, so there is no need to pre-boil the pasta. This dish is a nice alternative to lasagna, perhaps a little more upscale, yet simple to make. For a multi-course dinner, start with Tuscan white bean soup (p. 139), follow with a lightly-dressed salad and accompany with warm rosemary foccacia (p. 39). For dessert, lemon pudding cake (p. 220) with fresh seasonal berries is the ideal finish.

serves 6 - 8

double recipe tomato-sweet basil sauce (p. 45)
1 tbsp (15 mL) olive oil
1 medium red onion, diced
2 tsp (10 mL) salt
6 garlic cloves, minced
1/3 cup (80 mL) sundried tomatoes, not oil-packed
2 large spinach bunches
1 lb (450 g) ricotta cheese
1 1/2 cups (360 mL) fontina cheese
1 tsp (5 mL) lemon zest
1/2 cup (120 mL) mix of chopped basil, oregano, parsley
1/2 cup (120 mL) pine nuts, toasted
salt and cracked pepper to taste
16 x 5" square fresh cannelloni pasta squares

1. Start by making the tomato-sweet basil sauce. While the sauce simmers, prepare the filling. Heat olive oil in a small skillet and sauté the onion with 1 tsp (5 mL) salt until translucent. Add garlic and sauté until golden. Set aside. Pour boiling water over the sundried tomatoes and soak for 15 minutes. Strain and coarsely chop the soaked tomatoes.

2. Wash and stem the spinach. Heat a large pot over medium-high heat. With water still clinging to the leaves, place the spinach into the pot and toss with tongs until the leaves are wilted. Drain and cool in a colander. Squeeze excess water from the spinach and chop coarsely. In a large bowl, combine the spinach, sautéed onion, sundried tomatoes, cheeses, lemon zest, fresh herbs and pine nuts. Mix gently but thoroughly and season with salt and pepper to taste.

3. Pre-heat the oven to 350°F. Lightly oil a 9" x 13" glass baking dish and spread a layer of sauce on the bottom. Place a cannelloni sheet before you and spoon on 1/4 cup (60 mL) filling, spreading it out along the width of the lower edge of the pasta square. Roll it up into a tube and place seam side down on top of the tomato sauce. Repeat with remaining pasta and filling. Spoon sauce over the cannelloni, making sure that all the exposed pasta is sauced. Cover with foil, seal the edges and bake for 30–40 minutes, or until the sauce is bubbling and the pasta is tender. Serve hot, sprinkled with extra grated cheese and chopped herbs.

spinachlinguine
with artichoke heart & sundried tomato salsa

empty vegetable bins in your refrigerator signal the ideal time to whip up this easy pasta. If you're well-stocked with dry goods such as sundried tomatoes, jars of artichoke hearts, capers and olives, then all you need to do is pick some fresh herbs from your garden or at the market. This colourful and flavourful pasta can be ready in minutes. With a simple salad and a warm baguette, an elegant dinner can be had with little effort.

☯ use dry pasta and omit the Parmesan for a vegan dish.

serves 6

1/2 cup (120 mL) sundried tomatoes,
 not oil-packed
1/2 cup (120 mL) Kalamata olives,
 pitted and chopped
3 tbsp (45 mL) capers
3 cups (720 mL) marinated artichoke
 hearts
4 garlic cloves, minced
1/2 cup (120 mL) chopped basil
1/4 cup (60 mL) chopped Italian
 parsley
1 tbsp (15 mL) balsamic vinegar
2 tbsp (30 mL) extra virgin olive oil
1/4 tsp (1.2 mL) salt
1 tsp (5 mL) cracked pepper
1/2 tsp (2.5 mL) red chile flakes
1 lb (450 g) spinach linguine
Parmesan cheese, for garnish
4 small tomatoes, diced

1 Bring a large pot of water to boil for the pasta. Scoop out a cup or two of the hot water and use it to soak the sundried tomatoes in a bowl for 15 minutes. Drain, reserve the soaking liquid and slice the soaked tomatoes.

2 In a medium bowl, combine the sundried tomatoes, olives, capers, artichoke hearts, garlic and herbs. Season with balsamic vinegar, olive oil, salt, pepper and chile flakes.

3 While the pasta is cooking, gently heat the salsa mixture in a saucepan just enough to heat it through. If it starts to stick to the pan, add some of the reserved sundried tomato water. Keep warm. Drain pasta and toss with the salsa until well mixed. Serve topped with grated cheese and chopped fresh tomatoes.

helpfulhint ❋

To boost the vitamin and mineral content of this dish, add chopped spinach, kale or chard to the sauce and wilt just before tossing with the pasta.

Septemberspaghettini
with fresh tomato-basil sauce

more often than not, the least complicated dishes are the most memorable. This basic pasta dish embodies the spirit of the late summer garden with sun-ripe tomatoes, garlic and basil. A nest of spaghettini tossed with sauce, liberally sprinkled with grated Parmigiano Reggiano and washed down with a smooth Chianti is simple and heavenly!

☯ use dry spaghettini and omit the cheese for a vegan pasta.

1 Bring a large pot of water to a boil for cooking the spaghettini. Meanwhile, heat olive oil in a saucepan over medium heat. Add onion and sauté until soft and lightly golden. Add garlic, bay, chiles, salt and pepper and sauté 5 minutes. Stir in tomatoes and simmer gently for 30–45 minutes. Add chopped basil and season to taste.

2 While the sauce simmers, cook the pasta until al dente. Toss noodles with half of the sauce and serve remaining sauce on the side. Top with grated Parmesan cheese and enjoy!

serves 4

2 tbsp (30 mL) extra virgin olive oil
1 small yellow onion, diced
6 garlic cloves, minced
2 bay leaves
pinch red chile flakes
1 tsp (5 mL) salt
1/2 tsp (2.5 mL) cracked pepper
12 ripe garden tomatoes, peeled, seeded and diced (see "hint" p. 120)
2 oz (60 g) fresh basil
1 tbsp (15 mL) brown sugar (optional)
1 lb (450 g) spaghettini
Parmesan cheese for garnish

helpfulhint ✳

Serve pasta in the traditional Italian style. Don't rinse the pasta once you've drained it, but return it to the pot and add enough sauce to coat. Transfer to a large serving dish and have remaining sauce and grated cheese on the side.

udon&gingersquash
with miso-shiitake broth ☯

balancing delicate flavours and interesting textures is one of the pleasures of working with Japanese ingredients. This combination of thick udon noodles, creamy roasted kabocha squash, earthy shiitake mushrooms and a light miso broth is at once hearty, clean and visually stunning. Barely poached whole baby bok choy leaves and crisp Asian pear slices add a fresh and lively dimension to this wintery dish.

serves 4

broth

1/2 oz (15 g) piece wakame or kombu
    seaweed

1/2 oz (15 g) dried shiitake mushrooms

6 cups (1.5L) vegetable stock (p. 35),
    or water

2 tbsp (30 mL) minced ginger

2 tbsp (30 mL) tamari

2 tbsp (30 mL) mirin

2 tbsp (30 mL) sake

3 tbsp (45 mL) aka (red) miso

vegetables

1 1/2 lb (675 g) kabocha squash

1 tbsp (15 mL) vegetable oil

2 tbsp (30 mL) minced ginger

1/2 tsp (2.5 mL) salt

8 large fresh shiitake mushrooms,
    sliced

2 pkg udon noodles

1 Asian "Shinko" pear, quartered, cored
    and sliced

4 heads baby bok or Shanghai choy,
    leaves separated

4 scallions, 1/2" long slices

sesame oil, for garnish

1 Place the seaweed and dried mushrooms in a pot and cover with stock or water. Heat gently, partially covered, for one hour, keeping the water just below a simmer. Strain and discard the solids. Set the broth aside.

2 Pre-heat the oven to 375°F. While the stock is simmering, prepare the vegetables. Peel the squash, cut in half and scrape out the seeds. Slice the squash into 3/4" thick wedges. Toss with oil, 1 tbsp (15 mL) ginger and salt. Place on a parchment-lined baking dish and roast the squash until tender and golden (20–30 minutes).

3 Add tamari, mirin and sake and remaining ginger to the reserved broth. Bring to a gentle boil. Add the sliced shiitake mushrooms and simmer 5 minutes. Turn down the heat and whisk in the miso. Add the noodles and cook for 1 minute. Add the pears, bok choy and scallions and simmer until the vegetables are just wilted and heated through. Season to taste.

4 Divide broth, noodles and vegetables among 4 wide serving bowls. Place 3 or 4 hot roasted squash wedges in each bowl, drizzle with sesame oil and serve.

summer**squash**rigatoni

with corn off the cob and jalapeño-vermouth cream sauce

pale green and yellow summer squashes, picked while young, combine with fresh corn and emerald herbs to make this summery pasta light, despite the addition of cream. A bite from the jalapeño pepper and a hint of fresh lime waken the taste buds against the smooth, fresh background. Add chopped zucchini blossoms if you're harvesting from your own plants. Serve with a chilled bottle of Pinot Gris.

1 To make the sauce, heat butter and olive oil in a skillet. Add onion and sauté until translucent. Add salt and garlic; sauté several minutes longer. Add vermouth, lime juice and zest and simmer until the liquid is reduced by half. Add whipping cream and jalapeños and simmer until thickened. Season with pepper and salt to taste.

2 While the sauce simmers, put a large pot of water on to boil the pasta. Slice the zucchini into 1/4" thick coins. (If the zucchini is rather large, cut half-moon slices.) Sauté the zucchini and corn in a splash of olive oil until just tender. Season lightly with salt and pepper and set aside.

3 Cook the rigatoni until al dente. Add the zucchini, corn and spinach to the cream sauce and heat through until the spinach wilts. Drain the pasta and toss with the sauce and vegetables. Stir in the fresh herbs. Serve hot, garnished with asiago and toasted pine nuts.

serves 4

jalapeño - vermouth sauce

1 tbsp (15 mL) olive oil
1 tbsp (15 mL) butter
1 yellow onion, finely diced
1/2 tsp (2.5 mL) salt
6 garlic cloves, minced
1 1/2 cups (360 mL) vermouth
1/4 cup (60 mL) lime juice
1 lime, zested
2 cups (480 mL) whipping cream
2 jalapeño peppers, minced
1/8 tsp (.5 mL) ground white pepper

pasta and vegetables

1 lb (450 g) rigatoni
4 small green zucchini
4 small yellow zucchini
2 cups (480 mL) fresh corn kernels
1 bunch spinach, stemmed and
   coarsely chopped
1/4 cup (60 mL) minced fresh chives
1/2 bunch cilantro, chopped
1 1/2 cups (360 mL) grated asiago
   cheese
1/4 cup (60 mL) pine nuts, toasted

lasagnaRioGrande

with cilantro pesto, roasted zucchini and smoky tomato sauce

anyone who loves the classic veggie lasagna will appreciate this Southwestern variation, full of character and lively flavours. Add fresh corn when in season and use spinach if chard is unavailable. We like to serve this dish topped with a spoonful of tomatillo salsa (p. 53) and a drizzle of crème fraîche (p.108), with SW Caesar salad (p. 26) to start.

serves 8 - 10

1 x recipe cilantro pesto (p. 41)

smoky tomato sauce (see below)

2 lbs (900 g) green or yellow zucchini

3–4 red peppers, roasted (p. 50)

3 bunches Swiss chard

3 cups (720 mL) ricotta cheese

2 eggs, lightly beaten

2 cups (480 mL) grated asiago cheese

1 cup (240 mL) grated Jack cheese

4 fresh lasagna sheets (9" x 13")

smoky tomato sauce

2 tbsp (30 mL) olive oil

1 onion

1/2 tsp (2.5 mL) salt

2 bay leaves

6 garlic cloves

1/2 tsp (2.5 mL) red chile flakes

2 tbsp (30 mL) ancho chile powder

2 x 28 fl. oz (796 mL) canned tomatoes

1 tsp (5 mL) chipotle purée (p. 38)

1 tbsp (15 mL) brown sugar

salt and pepper to taste

helpfulhint ✳

The lasagna sauce, pesto and vegetables can be prepared one day in advance of assembly and baking. Leftover lasagna freezes beautifully for up to 3 months.

1 Begin by preparing cilantro pesto and smoky tomato sauce. To make the sauce, heat a saucepan on medium, add olive oil and heat. Sauté onions, salt and bay leaves until the onion is translucent. Add garlic, chile flakes and ancho powder and sauté several minutes longer. Purée the canned tomatoes and add to the saucepan. Simmer gently for 30 minutes. Season with chipotle purée, sugar, salt and pepper to taste and simmer 10 more minutes. Set aside.

2 While the sauce simmers, prepare the fillings. To roast zucchini, slice 1/4" thick coins on a diagonal. Lay the slices out on a parchment-lined baking tray. Lightly brush each slice with olive oil and sprinkle with salt and pepper. Roast 10–15 minutes, until tender. Peel and slice the roasted peppers into 1/2" thick strips. Remove stems from the chard and wash the leaves well in a colander. Heat a large pot over medium-high heat and add the chard leaves with the water still clinging to them. Toss with tongs until wilted. Remove and cool. Squeeze out excess water and chop coarsely. Stir together the ricotta cheese and beaten eggs and set aside.

3 Pre-heat oven to 350°F. To assemble, lightly brush a 9" x 13" baking dish with olive oil. Spread 1/2 cup (120 mL) sauce over the bottom of the pan, top with a pasta layer and another 1/2 cup sauce. Sprinkle with 1/2 cup grated asiago and top with the chard. Spread on the ricotta mix, followed by another pasta sheet. Spread the pesto over the pasta and layer on the zucchini slices, 1 1/2 cups sauce, 1/2 cup asiago and another pasta sheet. Cover the pasta with 1 cup sauce, top with pepper slices, the final pasta layer, sauce, asiago and Jack cheeses sprinkled over top. Place the pan on a large baking sheet and cover the lasagna with foil, with edges sealed. Bake 45 minutes to one hour, until the cheese is melted, sauce bubbling and pasta tender. Let sit 15 minutes before serving.

bigbarnbowties

with savoy cabbage, sage and brown butter

country farm markets in the fall/winter are a great source for cool weather vegetables that store well and and provide much-needed nutrients. Caramelized sweet savoy cabbage combines with carrots, nutty brown butter, toasted walnuts, Parmesan and earthy sage to make a unique and humble dish. A fruit crumble (p. 226) with pears, apples and cranberries topped with cinnamon ice cream is the ideal finish to this winter-themed meal.

☯ omit brown butter and replace cheese with nutritional yeast.

serves 4

1 Heat a large pot of water to cook the pasta. Heat the olive oil and butter in a large skillet. Add onion and 1/2 tsp (2.5 mL) salt and sauté until golden. Add garlic, chiles and minced herbs and sauté several minutes longer. Stir in the cabbage and remaining salt and cook until the cabbage is well-cooked and slightly browned. Add stock or water to prevent the cabbage from sticking to the pan. Add carrots and continue to sauté until tender.

2 Meanwhile, cook the pasta until al dente and prepare the brown butter. Just before serving, season the vegetables with balsamic vinegar, salt and cracked pepper to taste. Toss in extra fresh herbs if using. To serve, toss the hot noodles with the vegetables, drizzle each serving with brown butter and top with crushed roasted walnuts and grated Parmesan.

1 lb (450 g) farfalle (bowtie) pasta
2 tbsp (30 mL) olive oil
1 tbsp (15 mL) butter
1 large onion, diced
1 tsp (5 mL) salt
6 garlic cloves, minced
1/4 tsp (1.2 mL) red chile flakes
1/3 cup (80 mL) minced sage
1 tbsp (15 mL) minced thyme
8 cups (2 L) chopped savoy cabbage
1/2 cup (120 mL) vegetable stock (p. 35), or water
2 medium carrots, half-moon slices
2 tbsp (30 mL) balsamic vinegar
1/4 tsp (1.2 mL) cracked pepper
1/2 cup (120 mL) walnuts, roasted
1/4 cup (60 mL) brown butter
extra minced sage and thyme
grated Parmesan cheese

brownbutter

1/2 cup (1/4 lb) unsalted butter

Place butter in a small saucepan and melt over low heat. Let the melted butter gently simmer for about 10 minutes, until golden amber in colour. Strain through cheesecloth to remove solids and use immediately, or store refrigerated until ready to use.

helpfulhint ✳

To boost the nutritional value of this dish, serve with soba noodles instead of bowties. The earthy buckwheat flavour pairs well with the wintery vegetables and herbs.

☯ – a vegan recipe

monk's curry

tempeh tacos

☯ Heidi's masala potatoes

roasted vegetable strüdel

savoury bread pudding

pizza verde

☯ Chiang Mai tofu grill

☯ Mount Fuji stir-fry

buckwheat crêpes

blue corn-wild rice waffles

☯ tomato, tofu & cashew stir-fry

corn dance cakes

Parmesan-corn risotto cakes

fajitas

Wanda's roasted yam pierogi

border paella

roasted potato pizza

enchiladas con calabacitas

☯ bhangra burrito

three sister's burrito

entrées

variety

variety in weekend menu offerings have been a tradition at **re**bar for years—it's quite possible that no two menus have been alike. While certain themes carry over from one menu to the next, the constant change helps challenge the popular belief that a vegetarian menu is boring. The key is thinking seasonally, so that a dish like the wintery buckwheat crêpes with roasted portabello mushrooms, Swiss chard and caramelized onions in a lemon-tarragon cream sauce is transformed in the summer to a cornmeal crêpe with fresh corn, spinach and roasted peppers in a fresh tomato-basil sauce. The same applies to filling a phyllo strüdel, or preparing vegetables for a stir-fry; that is, be free to experiment and twist the elements of a basic recipe by using the best seasonal produce. Then there are side dishes, garnishes, sauces and salads that all contribute a certain character to a plate, lending balance in flavour, texture and colour. The range of ingredients and combinations create countless possibilities—this is where the creativity and versatility of a "well-seasoned" cook becomes most evident.

monk's curry

with Japanese eggplant, potatoes and tofu

homemade curry paste is the key to the most delicious Thai curries. This **re**bar favourite requires a quick shopping trip to Chinatown to pick up the irreplaceable flavours of kaffir lime, galangal, palm sugar, fish sauce and lemongrass. If you aren't fortunate enough to have an Asian market two blocks away, lime leaves and galangal can be bought and stored frozen. Palm sugar, if sealed, will last indefinitely. Fish sauce and lemongrass stock the shelves of most supermarkets. Serve this curry on perfect jasmine rice (p. 194) with chile-lime dip (p. 64) on the side.

serves 4

1 recipe sesame-baked tofu (p. 42)

1 x 398 mL can coconut milk

4 tbsp (60 mL) green curry paste (p. 48)

6 fresh (or frozen) kaffir lime leaves, stemmed and shredded

1/4 cup (60 mL) stock, or water

2 red potatoes, 1/8" thick quarter-moon slices

1 tbsp (15 mL) palm, or brown sugar

2 tbsp (30 mL) soy sauce

4 tbsp (60 mL) fish sauce (optional)

2 Japanese eggplant, half-moon slices

1/2 lb (225 g) oyster mushrooms, sliced

4 baby bok choy, leaves separated

2 bunches scallions, 1-inch long slices

juice of 1 lime

1/3 cup (80 mL) Thai basil leaves or cilantro, chopped

1/4 cup (60 mL) peanuts, roasted and chopped

☯ replace fish sauce with all soy for a vegan dish.

1 Heat a wok over medium heat and add 1/3 can coconut milk. Heat to a simmer and add the curry paste. Work the paste into the coconut milk to thoroughly combine. Add lime leaves and stock and bring to a boil. Add the potatoes, cover and cook at a gentle simmer until the potatoes are just tender.

2 Stir in the palm sugar, soy and fish sauce (if using), eggplant, mushrooms and remaining coconut milk. Cover and continue to simmer until all the vegetables are tender.

3 Turn up the heat and add the tofu, bok choy and scallions. Simmer until the bok choy wilts and the sauce reduces and thickens.

4 Just before serving, stir in the lime juice, basil or cilantro and season to taste with more fish or soy sauce. Serve with jasmine rice garnished with roasted peanuts, chopped fresh cilantro and lime wedges.

tempeh**tacos**
with two salsas and crunchy cabbages

travels in Mexico and across the Southwestern states have left us hooked on fish tacos. Chased with frosty margaritas made with fresh lime and quality tequila, a fish taco feast has become a regular event when visiting Audrey at her home. In the search for a comparable vegetarian rendition, tempeh wins hands down over beans and tofu. Good quality corn tortillas, freshly made salsas and crispy shredded cabbages are traditional accompaniments that combine to make this meal simple, fresh and muy bien!

☯ omit cheese or replace with vegan cheese for a vegan dish.

serves 3 - 4

1. Prepare the salsas and set aside. Slice the tempeh rectangle in half lengthwise. Slice halves crosswise into 1/4" thick batons. Heat oil in a skillet and add the tempeh. Fry until golden brown on all sides and set aside.

2. Re-heat the skillet and brush it with oil. Fry the tortillas, one or more at a time, depending on the size of your pan. Cook one side until small bubbles appear on the underside. Flip, sprinkle with cheese and cook briefly until the cheese begins to melt. Transfer to a plate and cover with a clean kitchen towel until all of the tortillas are cooked. Alternately, eat the tortillas fresh as they are cooked (this will prevent them from sitting around too long and getting crispy as they cool.)

3. To assemble, load each tortilla with shredded cabbage, a few tempeh sticks, top with salsas and sprinkle with hot sauce and a squeeze of fresh lime juice.

1 x recipe fresh-cut tomato salsa (p. 44)
1 x recipe mango salsa (p. 98)
1 x 8 oz (227 g) pkg 7-grain tempeh
1 tbsp (15 mL) vegetable oil
1/2 small green cabbage, finely shredded
12 good quality corn tortillas (we use Que Pasa)
2 cups (480 mL) shredded aged white cheddar, or Jack cheese
lime wedges
hot sauces

Heidi's masala potatoes
with fresh coconut chutney ☯

many stories of chef Heidi's travels in India have circulated through the **re**bar kitchen. Colourful tales are Heidi's trademark, rivalled only by her skill in perfecting authentic Indian cuisine. She serves this dish stuffed inside a crisp dosa—a South Indian lentil crêpe—whose creation requires patient practise. To make things simpler for the rest of us, we suggest you serve these yummy potatoes with plain steamed basmati rice and chutney, or buy yourself a very good Indian cookbook!

serves 4

2 tbsp (30 mL) ghee or vegetable oil
1 tsp (5 mL) black mustard seeds
1 tsp (5 mL) cumin seed
1 tsp (5 mL) urad dal
1 tsp (5 mL) channa dal
1/2 tsp (2.5 mL) asafetida (optional)
1 dried red chile, crushed
1 cup (240 mL) diced onion
3 ripe tomatoes, seeded and chopped
4 - 6 fresh or dried curry leaves
1 tsp (5 mL) turmeric
1 tsp (5 mL) salt
4 large potatoes, peeled and cubed
1 bunch cilantro, stemmed and minced

1 Heat a heavy-bottomed medium pot over medium-high heat. Heat the oil or ghee and add the mustard seeds. As the seeds begin to turn grey and pop, add the cumin seeds and two types of dal. Keep stirring until the dal begin turning reddish, then add the curry leaves, asafetida and chile. Stir once or twice, then add the shallots. Sauté until the shallots are golden, turning down the heat and adding a little water to the pan as necessary to prevent burning. Add the tomatoes, turmeric and salt. Simmer, stirring frequently, until the tomatoes have broken down and given off most of their liquid and the oil floats on top in little pools.

2 Next, add the chopped potatoes and just enough water to cover. Bring to a boil, reduce heat, cover and simmer. Stir occasionally and simmer until the potatoes are not quite fully cooked. Remove the cover, turn up the heat a little and allow the potatoes to simmer until fully cooked and most of the water is evaporated. Fold in the chopped cilantro, taste for salt and serve immediately.

fresh coconut chutney

1 1/4 cup (300 mL) grated fresh coconut
4 scallions, chopped
1 tbsp (15 mL) minced fresh ginger
1 1/2 jalapeño peppers
1 cup (240 mL) cilantro leaves, packed

1 tsp (5 mL) light brown sugar
1/4 tsp (1.2 mL) salt
1 tbsp (15 mL) fresh lime juice
1 tbsp (15 mL) vegetable oil
1 tsp (5 mL) black mustard seeds

Place the scallions, ginger, jalapeños, cilantro, salt and brown sugar in the bowl of a food processor and pulse briefly. Add the grated coconut and process until everything is ground up small, but not puréed. Transfer to a bowl. In a small skillet, heat the oil and mustard seeds over medium heat. As soon as the seeds begin to turn grey and pop, pour them over the chutney. Add lime juice, stir and season with salt to taste.

roasted vegetable strüdel

with bocconcini cheese, olives and fresh thyme

Lizzy is one of our "old-timer" servers whose flaming red hair and flamboyant personality often gets her mistaken as **re**bar's owner. She's entertaining to work with and loves to have fun with the customers—a character that you won't soon forget. It's people like Lizzy that make our restaurant special. Speaking of special, here is a dish that shows up on our weekend special dinner menu. Lizzy always said that you can wrap anything in phyllo and people will order it (although she didn't quite use those words!)

☯ leave out cheese and use only olive oil for vegan strüdel.

serves 6

1 red onion, 1/2" dice
8 garlic cloves, halved
2 red peppers, 1/2" dice
2 Japanese eggplant, 1/4" thick slices
1 medium zucchini, 1/2" thick half
   moon slices
2 tbsp (30 mL) olive oil
1/2 tsp (2.5 mL) salt
1/4 tsp (1.2 mL) cracked pepper
1 1/2 tbsp (22.5 mL) minced thyme
1/4 cup (60 mL) Kalamata olives,
   pitted and chopped
2 balls bocconcini cheese, diced
1/2 cup (120 mL) pine nuts, ground
1 package phyllo pastry
2 tbsp (30 mL) melted butter
2 tbsp (30 mL) olive oil

1 Pre-heat oven to 400°F. In a large bowl, toss together the prepared vegetables with olive oil, salt, pepper and half of the thyme. Spread the vegetables out in a single layer on a parchment-lined baking sheet (you may need two). Roast for 15 minutes, stirring halfway through. The eggplant should be soft and lightly golden. Let the vegetables cool, then toss with the remaining thyme, olives and bocconcini. Season with more salt and pepper to taste. Reduce oven temperature to 350°F.

2 Gently unravel phyllo pastry and cover with plastic wrap. Lay a barely damp cloth over the plastic (this will prevent the pastry from drying out). Combine the melted butter and olive oil in a small bowl. On a clean, dry work surface, lay a sheet of phyllo out in front of you. Using a pastry brush, paint a light coat of the butter/oil mix over the sheet. Dust with ground pine nuts. Lay a second sheet of pastry over top. Handle it as gently as you can but don't worry about small tears (they won't show in the end). Brush butter over the sheet. Repeat with three more phyllo/butter/pine nut layers and try to keep the pastry covered as much as possible as you remove sheets from the stack.

3 Spoon about 1 cup (240 mL) vegetable mix onto the center of the phyllo stack, about 3" away from the edge closest to you. Spread the vegetables out to form a 4" long x 2" wide band. Fold the lower pastry edge up and over the vegetables. Fold in both sides and roll the pastry up to form a log. Place seam side down on a parchment-lined baking sheet. Repeat with remaining filling. Brush the pastries with butter, sprinkle with remaining pine nuts and bake at 350°F until golden (about 20 minutes). Serve piping hot.

helpful hint ✴

The phyllo pastries can be prepared up to one day in advance up to the final step just before baking. Brush the pastries with butter, place on a tray, cover securely with plastic wrap and refrigerate. Remove from the fridge about 30 minutes before baking.

savourybreadpudding
with mixed mushrooms, leeks and Gruyère cheese

no reason to limit this dish to the dinner hour. Serve it for lunch or Sunday brunch with a light salad. Spruce it up for dinner with steamed brussel sprouts tossed in Dijon-shallot butter, or green beans tossed with hazelnut oil and orange zest. Or serve it as a special side dish at a holiday meal (in place of stuffing!) Use a good quality mulitigrain or sourdough bread for best results, and don't hesitate to replace the vegetables and herbs with your favourites, as bread pudding is very forgiving.

serves 8 - 10

3 tbsp (45 mL) butter
3 medium leeks, mostly whites
1/2 tsp (2.5 mL) salt
8 garlic cloves, minced
1 1/2 lb (675 g) assorted mushrooms
   (button, shiitake, oyster, portabello),
   sliced
cracked pepper
1/2 cup (120 mL) Madeira

custard

5 eggs
1 cup (240 mL) whipping cream
1 cup (240 mL) milk
1/2 tsp (2.5 mL) salt
1/2 tsp (2.5 mL) cracked pepper
1 x 1 lb (450 g) multigrain or sourdough
   loaf, cut into 3/4" cubes
2 tbsp (30 mL) thyme leaves
2 tbsp (30 mL) minced sage
4 cups (960 mL) grated Gruyère
   cheese
minced chives for garnish

1 Heat 1 tbsp (15 mL) butter in a large skillet and sauté the leeks and garlic with a pinch of salt until the leeks are soft. Set aside, then melt the remaining butter in the pan. Add all of the mushrooms, season with salt and pepper, cover and cook until the mushrooms have released their juices. Remove the lid and continue to cook until the mushrooms begin to sear. Deglaze with Madeira and let the liquid evaporate. Stir the mushrooms with the leeks and set aside while you prepare the custard.

2 Beat the eggs in a large bowl. Whisk in the cream, milk, salt and pepper. Stir in the bread cubes, cover and let stand for 1 hour. Stir occasionally to ensure that all the bread soaks evenly. Stir in the herbs, mushroom-leek mixture and half of the grated cheese.

3 Heat the oven to 350°F. Butter a 9" x 13" baking dish and spoon the bread pudding mixture into the pan. Sprinkle with reserved cheese and bake until crusty and golden brown and set in the middle (about 45 minutes). Sprinkle with minced chives, let stand for several minutes, cut into squares and serve hot.

pizza**verde**

with oyster mushrooms, Anaheim chiles and Jack cheese

green pizza? No it's not another Dr. Seuss spin-off, but a feisty Southwestern-style pizza with a base of emerald tomatillo sauce. Grilled oyster mushrooms give this pizza meaty substance and the cherry tomatoes and cilantro are fresh and lively. If you have a barbecue, try grilling the pizza for a delicious smoky finish.

☯ replace Jack with soy cheese for a vegan pizza.

yields 1 x 15" round pizza

1/2 x recipe foccacia (p. 39), or your
    favourite pizza crust
2 tbsp (30 mL) cornmeal
1 x recipe tomatillo-cilantro salsa (p. 53)
1 lb (450 g) oyster mushrooms
1 tbsp (15 mL) olive oil
salt and cracked pepper to taste
2 garlic cloves, minced
6 Anaheim chiles, roasted, peeled,
    seeded and sliced (p. 50)
2 bulbs roasted garlic (p. 158)
1 pint cherry tomatoes, halved
3 cups (720 mL) grated Jack cheese
1/2 bunch cilantro, chopped

1 If using the foccacia recipe, prepare the dough for the crust through the first rising. Punch the dough down and roll it out slightly on a floured board. Let the dough rest for 10 minutes. Transfer to an oiled 15" pizza pan that has been dusted with cornmeal. Stretch the dough out to fit the pan, raising the edges slightly. Cover with a kitchen towel and let the dough rest for 15 minutes before loading on the toppings.

2 Prepare the tomatillo salsa up to 2 days in advance. Separate oyster mushrooms from the main stem and slice the larger ones in half. Heat olive oil in a skillet, add the mushrooms and season with salt and cracked pepper. Sauté several minutes, add the minced garlic and cook until the mushrooms are golden. Deglaze the pan with a splash of wine or balsamic vinegar, cook until it evaporates and then set the mushrooms aside.

3 Pre-heat the oven to 450°F. (If you have a baking stone, place it on the bottom rack of your oven before pre-heating.) Paint the pizza dough with tomatillo salsa to cover the surface and sprinkle with half of the cheese. Top with mushrooms, garlic cloves, chile slices and tomatoes. Sprinkle remaining cheese over top. Reduce the oven temperature to 400°F and bake the pizza on the bottom oven rack (or on a pizza stone) for 15 minutes, or until the crust is golden and cheese melted. Serve with chopped fresh cilantro sprinkled over top.

ChiangMaitofugrill
with wok-fried vegetables and peanut, coconut & kaffir lime sauce ☯

just another stir-fry with peanut sauce transforms into an exotic treat in this recipe, courtesy of Thai basil, kaffir lime, coconut and palm sugar. Fragrant Thai flavours have become staples in our pantry and a welcome addition to our cooking repertoire. If you can't find Thai basil, substitute sweet basil or cilantro. Grow Thai basil in your herb garden or plant a pot on a sunny balcony and enjoy it's sweet, exotic fragrance.

serves 4

peanut - kaffir lime sauce

(yields 2 cups - 480 mL)

1/2 can coconut milk

6 kaffir lime leaves, fresh or frozen

2 tbsp (30 mL) minced ginger

1/3 cup (80 mL) smooth peanut butter

1 tbsp (15 mL) soy sauce

1/8 tsp (.5 mL) Thai red curry paste (we use Thai Kitchen brand)

1/2 oz (15 g) palm sugar

2 tbsp (30 mL) lime juice

1/4 tsp (1.2 mL) salt

1/2 tsp (2.5 mL) sambal oelek

2 tbsp (30 mL) hot water

stir-fry

1 recipe Thai basil-soy tofu (p. 42)

3 tbsp (45 mL) peanut oil

1 yellow onion

2 medium carrots

6 oz (180 g) snow peas

1 large red pepper

1 medium zucchini

1/4 cup (60 mL) peanuts, roasted

Thai basil, or cilantro

1 Begin by preparing the peanut sauce. Gently heat the coconut milk, kaffir lime and ginger in a small pot over low heat. Cover, turn off the heat and let the liquid infuse for one hour. Re-heat and whisk in the remaining ingredients until well blended. Bring to a simmer, season to taste and add more liquid to thin the sauce, if necessary. Keep warm until ready to serve, or refrigerate up to 3 days and re-heat before serving.

2 Prepare the marinated tofu up to 4 hours before serving. Julienne the onion, carrots, snow peas, pepper and zucchini into long, thin strips. Pour the marinade off the tofu and reserve. Heat 2 tbsp (30 mL) oil in a skillet and fry the tofu until golden on both sides. While the tofu cooks, heat the remaining oil in a wok and stir-fry the vegetables until just tender, adding some of the reserved tofu marinade to season.

3 To serve, stack the vegetables over the grilled tofu, with steamed jasmine rice (p. 194) and warm peanut sauce on the side. Garnish with crushed peanuts, chopped herbs and fresh lime wedges.

MountFujistirfry
with spicy red miso-sesame sauce ☯

creative food presentation is a trademark of Japanese cuisine. A
mound of stir-fried vegetables over rice has no place in the Japanese aesthetic, unless
of course the namesake of the dish happens to be a hulking volcanic landmark! This is a
stir-fry with a difference. The flavours are more subtle than the robust Chinese sauces.
Miso adds a sweet richness that makes a lovely base for the sesame and fresh ginger.
Serve over a favourite steamed grain or buckwheat soba noodles.

1. Whisk together all of the sauce ingredients in a bowl and set
aside. Cut the eggplant in half lengthwise and make diagonal
half-moon slices about 1/4" wide. Stem shiitakes and cut
thick slices. String the snow peas and separate the leaves of
the baby bok choy. Slice the larger leaves in half lengthwise.
Slice scallions into 1-inch lengths.

2. Heat a wok over medium-high heat. Add the eggplant and
shiitakes and stir-fry until tender. Add some water (or a
splash of sake) to prevent them from sticking to the wok.
Add the snow peas and tofu and cook 2 minutes. Add bok
choy, scallions and enough sauce to coat the vegetables
liberally; cover and simmer just long enough to wilt the bok
choy. Serve hot over steamed brown rice and sprinkle with
toasted sesame seeds for garnish.

serves 2

red miso - sesame sauce
1/4 cup (60 mL) aka (red) miso
3 tbsp (45 mL) water
2 tbsp (30 mL) soy sauce
2 tbsp (30 mL) mirin
1 tbsp (15 mL) sesame oil
1 tbsp (15 mL) minced ginger
1 garlic clove, minced
1/4 tsp (1.2 mL) red chile flakes

stir-fry
2 small Japanese eggplant
8 oz (240 g) shiitake mushrooms
4 oz (120 g) snow peas
1 x recipe sesame-baked tofu (p. 42)
4 heads baby bok choy
1 bunch scallions
2 tbsp (30 mL) vegetable oil
cooked short grain brown rice or
    other favourite grain/noodle
2 tsp (10 mL) sesame seeds, toasted

buckwheat crêpes
with portabello mushrooms, chard and lemon-tarragon cream

special occasions demand some extra time and effort in the kitchen. This dish is ideal for a turkey-free holiday main course, or any celebratory meal. The crêpes can be made and filled a day in advance and re-heated in the oven to serve. If you're not partial to cream sauces or want a lower-fat alternative, prepare the tomato-basil sauce (p. 45), substituting tarragon for the basil.

serves 4 - 6

crêpes

3 eggs
1 cup (240 mL) milk
1 cup (240 mL) water
2/3 cup (160 mL) buckwheat flour
1 cup (240 mL) unbleached flour
1/2 tsp (2.5 mL) salt
4 tbsp (60 mL) melted butter

filling

6 portabello mushrooms, marinated
   and roasted (p. 23)
2 bunches Swiss chard, thick stems
   removed
1 recipe caramelized onions (p. 36)
3 cups (720 mL) grated Gruyère
   cheese

lemon - tarragon cream

1 tbsp (15 mL) olive oil
1 small yelllow onion, minced
2 garlic cloves, minced
1/2 tsp (2.5 mL) salt
juice of 1 lemon
zest of 1/2 lemon
1 cup (240 mL) white wine
1 1/2 cups (360 mL) whipping cream
2 tbsp (60 mL) minced tarragon
cracked pepper
tarragon sprigs for garnish

1. To make crêpes, beat eggs in a medium bowl. Whisk in the milk and water. Combine the dry ingredients in a separate bowl, add to the liquid ingredients and whisk until smooth. Stir in melted butter that has been slightly cooled. Heat an 8" crêpe pan or non-stick skillet over medium-high heat. Brush with melted butter and ladle on 2 oz of crêpe batter, tilting the pan to cover the bottom with a thin film of batter. When the edges begin to dry, use a rubber spatula to lift an edge and gently flip the crêpe over. Cook on the reverse side just long enough to get a light golden colour. Stack on a plate and repeat wth remaining batter. Prepare crêpes up to 3 days in advance and store in the refrigerator, sealed with plastic wrap, or freeze for up to 1 month.

2. Prepare filling by slicing the roasted mushrooms into 1/2" thick strips. Wilt the chard leaves, squeeze out excess water and roughly chop. To fill, lay a crêpe out before you and spread 2 tbsp (30 mL) caramelized onions in a wide strip in the center of the crêpe. Top with 3 mushroom slices, chard and sprinkle with Gruyère cheese. Roll up the crêpe and place in a buttered glass baking dish. Roll up all of the crêpes and brush the tops with melted butter. Cover with foil and bake in a 325°F oven to heat through (30–40 minutes).

3. While the crêpes bake, prepare the sauce. Sauté onion and garlic with salt in olive oil until soft. Add lemon juice, zest and wine; simmer to reduce the volume by half. Add the cream and simmer until thickened to desired consistency. Add tarragon and season with salt and pepper. Serve drizzled over hot crêpes.

bluecornwildricewaffles

with candied salmon and smoky ancho-tequila cream

wipe off the dust accumulating on the waffle iron in your cupboard and give this delicious dinner entrée a try! Serve with sweet corn-pepper salsa (p. 151) and baked yams (p. 152) for a unique Southwestern feast. The waffles are also delicious served with blueberries and maple syrup! Cook them in advance and pop in the toaster to re-heat.

serves 4

1 Begin by preparing the waffle batter. Mix together the dry ingredients in a small bowl. In another bowl, whisk together the buttermilk, yogourt, eggs and melted butter. Gently mix the wet and dry together until just combined. Fold in the wild rice and let the batter rest while you prepare the sauce.

2 In a large skillet, heat 1 tbsp (15 mL) olive oil and sauté the pepper strips with a pinch of salt until tender. Set aside. Heat the remaining oil and sauté onion with salt until lightly golden. Add garlic and ancho powder and sauté 5 more minutes. Add tequila and simmer until the liquid is reduced by half; then stir in the cream and chipotle purée. Let the sauce gently simmer and reduce while you cook the waffles. Just before serving, add the sautéed peppers and sliced salmon to the sauce to heat through. Season to taste.

3 To serve, place two waffles on each plate, slightly overlapping. Divide the sauce among the waffles. Garnish with minced scallions and serve.

waffles

1 cup (240 mL) blue cornmeal
1/2 cup (120 mL) unbleached flour
2 tsp (10 mL) baking powder
1/2 tsp (2.5 mL) salt
1 1/2 cups (360 mL) buttermilk
1/4 cup (60 mL) plain yogourt
2 eggs, lightly beaten
3 tbsp (45 mL) melted butter
1 cup (240 mL) cooked wild rice

ancho - tequila cream sauce

2 tbsp (30 mL) olive oil
2 large red and/or yellow peppers,
  sliced in 1/4" wide strips
1/2 yellow onion, finely diced
1/2 tsp (2.5 mL) salt
4 garlic cloves, minced
3 tbsp (45 mL) ancho chile powder
1/2 cup (120 mL) tequila
1 1/2 cups (360 mL) whipping cream
1 tbsp (15 mL) chipotle purée (p. 38)
8 oz (240 g) candied salmon, sliced
  in long 1/2"-wide strips
minced scallions, for garnish

tomato tofu & cashew stirfry

with sui choy, Thai basil and tamarind sauce 😊

annual visits to Seattle and Portland are a tradition for Audrey and she always comes home with an account of new restaurants and exciting meals. Some of her detailed descriptions have inspired new dishes at **re**bar, and this is one of those. Based soley on Audrey's taste memories, we tried to recreate a favourite dish from Seattle's Wild Ginger. After many valiant attempts, the dish never materialized, yet something new and delicious did!

serves 2

tamarind sauce

2 tbsp (30 mL) tamarind pulp
1/4 cup (60 mL) dark soy
2 tbsp (30 mL) light soy
2 tbsp (30 mL) minced ginger
2 garlic cloves, minced
2 tbsp (30 mL) lime juice
1 tbsp (15 mL) sambal oelek
1/4 tsp (1.2 mL) cracked pepper
2 oz (60 g) palm sugar
1/2 cup (120 mL) water
2 tsp (10 mL) cornstarch

tomato, tofu & cashew stir-fry

1 tbsp (15 mL) peanut oil
2 shallots, sliced
4 garlic cloves, sliced
1 bunch scallions, sliced in 1 1/2"
    lengths
4 cups (960 mL) sui choy, chopped in
    1-inch squares
4 Roma tomatoes, quartered
1 recipe sesame-baked tofu (p. 42)
1/4 cup (60 mL) cashews, roasted
1/2 cup (120 mL) tamarind sauce
1/4 cup (60 mL) chopped Thai basil
2 tbsp (30 mL) chopped cilantro
steamed jasmine rice

1   Prepare the tamarind sauce up to 3 days in advance. Combine all of the ingredients, except the water and cornstarch, in a pot and bring to boil. Simmer 5 minutes. In a small bowl, whisk the cornstarch and water together and whisk the slurry into the simmering sauce. Let it simmer for several more minutes until it thickens. Set aside.

2   Heat peanut oil in a wok over medium-high heat. Add shallots and garlic and fry briefly until golden. Add scallions and sui choy and fry 2 more minutes. Add tomatoes, tofu, cashews and half of the sauce; briefly simmer over high heat until heated through. (Add more sauce if you would like it saucey.) Do not overcook—the tomatoes should retain their shape and the sui choy and scallions should be just tender and bright green. Toss in the chopped herbs. Serve immediately over steamed jasmine rice.

perfect jasmine rice

2 cups (480 mL) jasmine rice
3 3/4 cups (900 mL) water
1 tsp (5 mL) salt
1 tbsp (15 mL) butter

Place rice in a medium, heavy-bottomed pot. Add cold water, salt and butter. Bring to a boil over high heat; cover and reduce heat to very low for 18 minutes. Remove pot from the heat and let stand, covered for 5 minutes. Fluff grains with a fork and serve. Serves 4 - 6.

corn**dance**cakes

with wild rice, corn and smoked salmon

native American tribes of the Southwest took part in the Corn Dance as a planting ritual to invoke clouds, rain and growth, and as an expression of gratitude to the Creator for providing food. These cakes combine traditional foods from the first nations of the North and South. Serve with baked yams (p. 152), grilled summer squashes and fire-roasted pepper salsa - and be sure to give thanks!

serves 6

1 If using fresh corn, blanch in salted boiling water until tender. Cool and set aside. If using frozen corn, thaw for 10 minutes.

2 Combine corn, wild rice, salmon, scallions and cilantro in a bowl and toss together. In a separate bowl, lightly beat the egg. Whisk in the chipotle purée, milk and melted butter. Stir in the remaining ingredients and blend to form a smooth batter. Combine the batter with the corn mixture and mix well.

3 To cook, heat butter or oil in a skillet over medium heat. Drop spoonfuls of batter onto the skillet and form into round cakes 3" in diameter. Cook until golden on one side, then flip and cook on the other side. Repeat with remaining cakes. Serve hot.

2 cups (480 mL) corn, fresh or frozen
1 cup (240 mL) cooked wild rice
1 cup (240 mL) crumbled hot smoked salmon
1 bunch scallions, minced
2 tbsp (30 mL) minced cilantro
1 egg
1 tsp (5 mL) chipotle purée (p. 38)
1 cup (240 mL) milk
1 tbsp (15 mL) melted butter
3/4 cup (180 mL) unbleached flour
1/4 tsp (1.2 mL) baking powder
1 tsp (5 mL) salt
1/4 tsp (1.2 mL) cracked pepper
2 tbsp (30 mL) butter or vegetable oil

flame roasted pepper salsa

2 1/2 lb (1.2 kg) assorted peppers
1 red onion
1 garlic bulb, cloves separated and peeled
1/2 tsp (2.5 mL) salt
2 tbsp (30 mL) olive oil
1 tbsp (15 mL) lime juice
1 tbsp (15 mL) chopped cilantro
1/4 tsp (1.2 mL) cracked pepper

Roast, seed and peel peppers (p. 50). Peel and slice the onion into four thick slices. Brush both sides with oil. Toss the peeled garlic cloves in a light coating of oil. Sprinkle the onions and garlic with salt and place them on a baking sheet. Roast in a 400°F oven until the onion starts to blacken and the garlic softens. Remove and cool. Dice the roasted peppers, onion and garlic. Combine everything in a bowl and toss well. Season to taste and let sit for 30 minutes before serving.

Parmesancornrisottocakes
with grilled zucchini

summer garden harvests make cooking in the warm months easy and rewarding. In this dish, a fresh corn stock is essential for the full corn essence that infuses the risotto. Sautéed in olive oil, the crispy cornmeal crust contrasts with the creamy risotto within. Serve with sautéed or grilled zucchini rounds, finished with a splash of balsamic vinegar. Garnish with cherry tomato-basil salsa (p. 44) and serve with a soup or salad for a full meal. These also make an ideal side dish for grilled halibut or salmon drizzled with fresh lime juice or for a mess of vegetables grilled on the barbecue.

serves 4

fresh corn stock

4 ears fresh corn, kernels removed
   and reserved

1 yellow onion, chopped

4 garlic cloves, crushed

2 bay leaves

few sprigs fresh oregano, parsley,
   thyme

1 tsp (5 mL) black peppercorns

2 tsp (10 mL) coarse salt

8 cups (2 L) cold water

risotto cakes

1 tbsp (15 mL) butter

1 tbsp (15 mL) olive oil

1 small yellow onion, finely diced

3 garlic cloves, minced

1/2 tsp (2.5 mL) salt

1 cup (240 mL) arborio rice

2 cups (480 mL) fresh corn

1 cup (240 mL) white wine (optional)

1 cup (240 mL) grated Parmesan
   cheese

1 cup (240 mL) fine cornmeal

olive oil

3 medium zucchini, sliced in 1/4" - 1/2"
   rounds

1 Place stock ingredients into a pot and cover with water. Bring to a boil and simmer, partially covered, for 45 minutes. Strain and keep warm (you will need 4 - 5 cups in total).

2 Heat butter and olive oil in a large heavy saucepan and sauté onion and garlic until translucent. Add the rice and cook, stirring until the rice is well coated. Add the corn, season with salt and sauté for several minutes. Pour in the wine and simmer until absorbed. Now start adding warm corn stock, one cup at a time. Keep stirring and add the next cup of stock only when most of the liquid is absorbed and the rice looks creamy. When the rice is tender but the grains still slightly firm to the bite, remove risotto from the heat and stir in the Parmesan cheese. Season to taste and spread the risotto into a baking pan to speed cooling. Cover and refrigerate. The recipe can be prepared up to this point one or two days in advance.

3 To sauté cakes, form the risotto into 2 1/2" round cakes and dredge in cornmeal. Fry in hot olive oil until golden and crispy on both sides. Meanwhile, grill or sauté zucchini rounds, season with salt and pepper and finish with a splash of balsamic vinegar. Serve risotto cakes hot, topped with cherry tomato-basil salsa and grilled zucchini on the side. Garnish with roasted pepper sauce (p. 50) or balsamic syrup (p. 60) for a festive presentation.

fajitas

with all the fixins'

friday night dinners at the restaurant have an air of anticipation and celebration about them. Kitchen and floor staff are wound up and ready for anything, while customers appear more relaxed and festive in spirit. With wine flowing, the fracas of conversation mixes with upbeat jazz, the clamour of juice and cappucino machines and the din of a kitchen in high gear. All this creates an exciting atmosphere for diners and staff. Here is a longstanding favourite from our Friday night specials menu.

☯ leave out the cheese or use soy cheese for vegan fajitas.

serves 4

1 Prepare the required recipes. The black beans and tofu can be prepared up to 2 days in advance. The tortillas and the preparations for the salsas can be started early on the same day you plan to serve them.

2 Before serving, slice sweet peppers and onions into 1/2" wide strips. Set aside while you warm the beans, finish the salsas, bake the tofu and cook off the tortilllas. Just before serving, heat the oil in a skillet and fry the peppers and onions with salt until golden and tender. Season with cracked pepper.

3 This dish is best served buffet style, with all components in separate bowls at center table within everybody's reach. Keep the tortillas warm wrapped in foil and allow each person at the table to build their own fajita.

1 x recipe flour tortillas (p. 43), or
   store-bought
1 x recipe Baja black beans (p. 148), or
   good quality canned refritos
1 x recipe ancho chile-lime tofu (p. 42)
3 sweet peppers
1 large onion, red or sweet Vidalia
2 tbsp (30 mL) vegetable oil
1/2 tsp (2.5 mL) salt
cracked pepper
grated Jack cheese (optional)
avocado-tomatillo salsa
fresh-cut tomato salsa (p. 44)

avocadotomatillosalsa

8 ripe tomatillos, diced
2 jalapeño peppers, seeded and
   minced
2 garlic cloves, minced
1/4 small red onion, minced
2 tbsp (30 mL) chopped cilantro
1 tsp (5 mL) sugar
1/4 tsp (1.2 mL) ground cumin
1/4 tsp (1.2 mL) cracked pepper
1 tbsp (15 mL) fresh lime juice
2 ripe avocados

Combine all of the ingredients, except avocados, and toss together in a bowl. Just before serving, halve the avocados, carefully remove the pits, spoon out the flesh and dice. Add to the tomatillo mix and gently toss to combine. Season to taste and serve immediately or cover with plastic wrap and refrigerate for up to an hour.

Wanda's roasted yam pierogi

with smoked gouda, leeks and caraway

Rachael is our floor manager whose high energy and playful spirit keeps the **re**bar wheels spinning. She calls me the "Pierogi Princess", though I've never made a pierogi for her in my life! To make up for it, I dedicate this recipe to her. The smoked gouda gives these a slight bacon flavour and they taste great smothered with onions browned in butter and a side of sour cream with minced chives. This is an ambitious project, so a pasta machine, a pierogi press, and/or an extra set of hands would be a great help.

yields 6 dozen pierogi

filling

5 lb (2.3 kg) yams
2 tbsp (30 mL) butter
3 large leeks, mostly whites, chopped
1 tsp (5 mL) salt
1 lb (450 g) smoked gouda cheese,
    grated
1/2 cup (120 mL) minced chives
1/2 tsp (2.5 mL) cracked pepper
1/2 tsp (2.5 mL) caraway seed (optional)

pierogi dough

4 cups (960 mL) unbleached flour
3/4 tsp (4 mL) salt
4 egg yolks
1 cup (240 mL) boiling water
2 tbsp (30 mL) vegetable oil

helpful hint

Pierogi freeze beautifully so they can be prepared far in advance of a special holiday (Christmas is a great time for a pierogi pig out!) Line uncooked pierogi on a parchment-lined baking sheet dusted with flour. Freeze until solid and store in heavy duty Ziploc freezer bags. Do not thaw before boiling ... they may take just a few minutes longer.

1 Filling can be prepared one day in advance. Pre-heat oven to 400°F. Scrub the yams and poke them here and there with a fork. Place on an oiled baking pan, add 1 cup (240 mL) of water to the pan and roast in the oven until the yams are very soft and puffy. Cool to handling temperature, peel and mash or purée the flesh until smooth.

2 While the yams roast, heat butter in a skillet, add leeks and salt and sauté until lightly golden and caramelized. Combine leeks, mashed yams, grated cheese and chives. Season with cracked pepper, caraway seeds (if using) and more salt if necessary. Refrigerate until ready to use.

3 To make the dough, mix the flour and salt in a large bowl. Add the remaining ingredients and beat well with a wooden spoon until a smooth dough forms. Cover and let rest at room temperature for 30 minutes. Divide the dough into quarters and roll it out about 1/8" thick, or less. (A pasta machine does this job quite well.) Use a glass with a 3" diameter rim, or a cookie cutter dipped in flour to cut circles out of the dough. Place a good teaspoonful or more of filling in the center of each circle and press the edges firmly to seal. If the dough is a bit dry, dip your finger in water and lightly run it along half the circle edge to help seal. Use the ends of a fork to make a crimped edge if you like.

4 To serve, heat a large pot of water to a boil and add 1 tbsp (15 mL) salt. Cook up to 2 dozen pierogi at a time, without covering the pot, until they begin to rise to the surface (about 5 minutes). Stir occasionally to prevent sticking. Remove with a slotted spoon, drain and toss with melted butter. Serve immediately.

border paella
with sweet peppers, green beans and fresh herbs

late summer garden vegetables make this an ideal rice dish to serve as a main course or a side on barbecue night. If you like, add shrimp or calamari at the last minute and heat through. Serve with corn on the cob and a salad for a "dog days of summer" dinner.

☯ leave out the cheese for a vegan dish.

1 In a large, deep cast iron skillet, heat olive oil and sauté onion until translucent. Add garlic, chile flakes, 1 tsp (5 mL) salt and sauté until the garlic and onions are soft. Add the remaining salt, spices, herbs, peppers and tomatoes and simmer, covered, for 10 minutes. Stir in the rice to coat well.

2 Heat the stock, or water and pour it into the pan. Cover and reduce the heat to low. Cook until the rice is tender and most of the liquid has been absorbed (about 30 minutes).

3 Meanwhile, steam or blanch the beans until tender. Stir into the cooked paella. Season with cracked pepper, fresh herbs and serve garnished with grated cheese and minced scallions. Have your favourite hot sauces on hand!

serves 4 - 6

3 tbsp (45 mL) olive oil
1 large onion, diced
6 garlic cloves, minced
1/2 tsp (2.5 mL) red chile flakes
2 tsp (10 mL) salt
1 tbsp (15 mL) pure chile powder
1 tbsp (15 mL) sweet paprika
2 tbsp (30 mL) minced thyme
2 tbsp (30 mL) minced oregano
2 large red and yellow peppers, diced
4 medium ripe tomatoes, roughly
  chopped
1 1/4 cups (300 mL) arborio rice
3 cups (720 mL) vegetable stock (p. 35),
  or water
1/2 lb (225 g) green beans, trimmed
  and sliced in 1-inch lengths
cracked pepper to taste
1/2 bunch cilantro, chopped
1/2 bunch Italian parsley, chopped
1 bunch scallions, minced
aged cheddar or Parmesan cheese

helpful hint

Stuff paella into sweet peppers, top with goat's feta cheese or aged cheddar, cover and bake until the peppers are tender and cheese is melted. Sprinkle with toasted pine nuts and serve with corn on the cob and chile-lime butter!

roasted**potato**pizza
with lemon-rosemary potatoes, artichoke hearts and feta cheese

topping
a pizza with potatoes may seem like an odd thing to do, but you'll be surprised at how delicious this actually is! Served with a light salad, this makes a substantial dinner. Bake on a rectangular pan and cut the pizza into small squares to serve as h'ors d'oeuvres. Chill a bottle of Retsina and kick off a Greek feast.

yields 1 x 15" round pizza

1/2 x recipe foccacia (p. 39), or your favourite pizza crust

1 x recipe sundried tomato pesto (p. 103)

1 lb (450 g) red potatoes

2 garlic cloves, minced

2 tbsp (30 mL) minced rosemary

juice of 1/2 lemon

1 1/2 tbsp (22.5 mL) olive oil

1/4 tsp (1.2 mL) salt

1/4 tsp (1.2 mL) cracked pepper

1/2 bunch spinach, stemmed and washed

2 x 6 oz liq (170 mL) jars marinated artichoke hearts

2 cups (480 mL) crumbled goat's milk feta cheese

2 cups (480 mL) grated mozzarella cheese

1 If using the foccacia recipe, prepare the dough for the crust through the first rising. While the dough is rising prepare the toppings. Pre-heat oven to 375°F. Quarter the potatoes lengthwise and slice 1/4" thick. Toss with garlic, rosemary, lemon, olive oil, salt and pepper. Spread on a parchment-lined baking sheet and roast 20-30 minutes, until golden brown and tender. Cool and set aside. Slice spinach leaves into 1/2" thick ribbons. Drain artichoke hearts and cut in half lengthwise. Crumble and grate the cheeses.

2 Turn the oven heat up to 450°F. Punch the dough down and roll it out slightly on a floured board. Let the dough rest for several minutes, then transfer to an oiled 15" pizza pan. Stretch the dough out to fit the pan, raising the edges slightly. If the dough bounces back, cover with a kitchen towel and let the dough rest until it will give.

3 To dress the pizza, spread the bottom of the crust with pesto and sprinkle with 1 cup (240 mL) mozzarella cheese. Layer with spinach ribbons, potatoes, artichoke hearts and olives. Sprinkle feta cheese over top, followed by the final cup of mozzarella. Turn the oven temperature down to 375°F and bake the pizza on the bottom rack for 20 minutes, until the cheese is melted and crust golden.

helpful**hint** ✳

Tasty pizza substitutions:

✳ tomato-sweet basil sauce (p. 45) for pesto

✳ anchovies for olives

✳ kale for spinach

✳ sage for rosemary

✳ zucchini for potatoes

✳ fontina for feta

enchiladascon calabacitas

with mesa red sauce and two cheeses

zucchini in combination with sweet corn and bell peppers is sometimes referred to as "calabacitas" in Spanish. Here they are quickly sautéed with spices and tossed with herbs and cheeses to make a fresh summery filling for enchiladas. Serve with green rice (p. 153), fresh-cut salsa (p. 44) and/or Baja baked beans (p. 148).

serves 8

1. Begin by preparing the mesa sauce. Next, prepare the vegetables for the filling.

2. Heat oil in a large skillet and sauté onion until soft. Add the garlic, salt, coriander and chile flakes. Stir and cook for 5 minutes. Add the peppers, jalapeños and zucchini and sauté several more minutes, stirring often. Stir in the corn and cook until the corn is just tender. The goal is to keep the vegetables firm. Work quickly and use high heat. Turn the vegetables out into a large bowl or spread on a tray to let cool. Stir in cilantro, cracked pepper and I cup of each cheese. Set aside.

3. Heat a skillet over medium-high and brush with oil. Working with one tortilla at a time, place the tortilla in the hot pan. When small bubbles appear on the underside, flip it over and heat the other side briefly. Transfer to a plate and cover with a clean kitchen towel. Repeat with remaining tortillas, lightly brushing the pan with oil between each one.

4. Pre-heat oven to 350°F. Lightly oil a 9" x 13" glass baking dish. Ladle just enough mesa sauce into the pan to cover the bottom. Lay one or more tortillas out before you. Spoon about 1/4 cup (60 mL) filling into the center of the tortilla, spreading it out horizontally to reach both sides. Roll the tortilla up from the bottom edge and over the filling to form a cylinder. Place seam side down in the pan. Repeat with remaining tortillas. Spoon mesa sauce over the enchiladas, cover with foil and bake for 20 minutes. Remove foil, sprinkle remaining cheese over top and bake until cheese is melted and golden. Serve hot.

1 recipe "mesa red sauce" (4 cups)
2 tbsp (30 mL) vegetable oil
1 small red onion, diced
4 garlic cloves, minced
1 tsp (5 mL) salt
1 tsp (5 mL) coriander seed, toasted and ground
1/4 tsp (1.2 mL) red chile flakes
1 red pepper, 1/3" dice
4 jalapeño peppers, seeded and minced
1 1/2 lb (675 g) zucchini, 1/3" dice
3 cups corn, fresh or frozen
1/2 tsp (2.5 mL) cracked pepper
2 tbsp (30 mL) minced cilantro
2 cups (480 mL) grated asiago cheese
2 cups (480 mL) grated Jack cheese
20 good quality corn tortillas, we use Que Pasa brand

bhangra**burrito**
with chick pea-potato curry and spinach ☯

unconventional burrito fillings are inevitable in the world of cultural food fusion. In this recipe, the cross-cultural mix makes perfect sense—the filling is pure Indian and the Mexican tortilla that wraps up the curry is a close cousin to the chapathi. The outcome is delicious and makes an ideal lunch or dinner entrée. Serve with mint-mango chutney (p. 142) and steamed basmati rice.

yields 6 burritos

4 garlic cloves

1 oz (30 g) ginger, peeled

1 jalapeño pepper, with seeds

1 red pepper, seeded

6 Roma tomatoes

3 tbsp (30 mL) vegetable oil

1 medium onion, diced

1 tsp (2.5 mL) salt

1/2 tsp (2.5 mL) toasted & ground cumin

1 tsp (5 mL) toasted & ground coriander

1 tsp (5 mL) sweet paprika

1/4 tsp (1.2 mL) turmeric

1/2 tsp (2.5 mL) cracked pepper

1 x 19 fl oz (540 mL) can chick peas

2 lbs (900 g) red potatoes, 1/2" dice

1/2 bunch cilantro, stemmed and chopped

1 bunch spinach, washed, stemmed and sliced into 1/2" thick ribbons

1 Roughly chop garlic, ginger, jalapeño, red pepper and tomatoes. Place in a food processor and pulse to form a coarse purée. Heat 2 tbsp (30 mL) oil in a large saucepan over medium heat and sauté onion with 1/2 tsp (2.5 mL) salt until translucent. Stir in cumin, coriander, paprika, turmeric and pepper and continue to sauté to cook the spices. Add the vegetable purée and simmer gently 5-10 minutes. Add chick peas and cook a further 10 minutes to heat through. Set aside.

2 Meanwhile, pre-heat oven to 350°F. Toss diced potatoes with remaining 1 tbsp (15 mL) oil and 1/2 tsp (2.5 mL) salt. Spread out on a parchment-lined baking sheet and roast the potatoes until lightly golden and soft, about 15-20 minutes. Toss the chick pea mixture with roasted potatoes and chopped cilantro. Season to taste.

3 To roll, lay a tortilla out in front of you and spread 1 cup (240 mL) spinach ribbons topped with 1 cup (240 mL) chick pea curry across the middle of the tortilla. Roll it up into a cylinder and place seam-side down in a lightly oiled baking dish. Repeat with remaining filling, cover with foil and bake 30 minutes to heat through. Serve hot with chutney and rice.

threesistersburrito

with roasted squash, pinto beans and corn

clever companion planting methods by Native American farmers involved interplanting pole beans and squash with corn, using the strength of the sturdy corn stalks to support the twining beans and the shade of the spreading squash vines to trap moisture for the growing crop. Squash, beans and corn were hence referred to as the Three Sisters. The well-being of each crop was believed to be protected by one of the Three Sister Spirits—sisters who would never be apart from one another—sisters who should be planted together, celebrated together and eaten together.

☯ replace cheddar with soy cheese for vegan burritos.

1 Pre-heat oven to 375°F. Peel and seed the squash and chop into 3/4" cubes. Toss cubes with oil, ancho powder, salt, maple syrup and lime juice and spread out in a glass baking dish. Roast until tender, about 20 minutes. Transfer the roasted squash to a large bowl and spread the corn into the same baking dish. Toss with 1 tsp (5 mL) oil and a pinch of salt and roast 10 minutes. Combine the squash and corn and cool. Toss in the beans, cilantro and chipotle purée and season to taste.

2 To roll burritos, lay a tortilla out in front of you and spread 1 cup (240 mL) filling across the middle. Top with 1/3 cup (180 mL) grated cheese and roll the tortilla around the filling to form a cylinder. Place seam-side down on a lightly oiled baking dish and repeat with remaining filling. Spoon sauce over the tortillas and sprinkle with remaining cheddar. Cover the pan with foil and bake 30 minutes at 350°F until heated through. Remove foil for a final 5 minutes to melt the cheese on top. Serve with green rice (p. 153) and fresh-cut salsa of your choice.

yields 6 burritos

3 lb (1.4 kg) butternut squash
1 tbsp (15 mL) vegetable oil
1 1/2 tsp (7.5 mL) ancho chile powder
1/2 tsp (2.5 mL) salt
1 tbsp (15 mL) maple syrup
juice of 1/2 lime
1 1/2 cups (360 mL) corn, fresh or
    frozen
1 x 14 fl oz liq (398 mL) can pinto
    beans, drained and rinsed
1/2 bunch cilantro, stemmed and
    chopped
2 tsp (10 mL) chipotle purée (p. 38)
3 1/2 cups (840 mL) grated aged white
    cheddar cheese
6 whole wheat tortillas
mesa red sauce (p. 52), or other
    favourite red sauce

helpfulhint ✳

This filling also makes great enchiladas. Cut the squash into slightly smaller cubes and follow rolling instructions on page 201.

☯ - a vegan recipe

☯ apple-pecan bars
   chocolate-zucchini cupcakes
   citrus poppyseed cake
☯ chocolate mousse blackout
   carrot-coconut cake
☯ trail bars
☯ power spheres
   apple Danish squares
   peanut butter squares
   chocolate chip cookies
   banana bread
   raspberry-oat bars
☯ vegan fudge brownies
   rebar chocolate cake
   pudding cake
   deep dish fruit pies
   pumpkin-millet muffins
   Bayou chocolate torte
   lime sugar cookies
   oat spice cake
   classic fruit crumble
☯ vegan energy bars
   doggie biscotti

10
sweets

goodies, healthy and decadent are cranked out by our sister bakery "Cascadia" daily, much to the pleasure of **re**bar customers. Some people are confused by the varied selection, ranging from vegan, sugar and dairy-free treats, to the butteriest and chocolatiest confections you can imagine. We've never adopted a hard-line attitude toward food and health (within reason) and so we aim to offer something for everyone. Vegans, celiacs and weight-watchers have every right to indulge in a sweet treat from time to time, and all of us could use a big slice of chocolate cake with a coffee or glass of milk now and then. Flip through the following recipes and you're sure to find something to tickle your particular fancy!

applepecanbars

with oat and rice flours ☯

catering to the specific dietary needs of our customers has always been important to us. We try to ensure that there is always a selection of menu items that are vegan, dairy-free, low-fat, etc. More and more people are discovering that they have an intolerance to wheat. Here is a sweet treat that will keep them happy!

yields 12 bars

1/4 cup (60 mL) vegan margarine
1/2 cup (120 mL) brown sugar
1/4 cup (60 mL) "flax eggs"
1 tsp (5 mL) vanilla
1 cup (240 mL) unsweetened
   applesauce
1 cup (240 mL) oat flour
1/2 cup (120 mL) rice flour
1 tsp (5 mL) cinnamon
1/4 tsp (1.2 mL) allspice
1/2 tsp (2.5 mL) baking powder
1/2 tsp (2.5 mL) baking soda
1/4 tsp (1.2 mL) salt
2 apples, peeled & chopped
1/2 cup (120 mL) chopped pecans

streusel topping;

1/2 cup (120 mL) brown sugar
1/4 cup (60 mL) vegan margarine
3 tbsp (45 mL) oat flour
3/4 cup (180 mL) chopped pecans

1 Pre-heat oven to 350°F. Lightly oil a 9" x 9" baking pan. Cream together the margarine and brown sugar until light and fluffy. Stir in the "flax eggs". Mix in the vanilla and applesauce and set aside.

2 In a separate bowl, mix together the flours, spices, baking soda, baking powder and salt. Add the dry mix to the wet mix and stir to combine. Fold in the apples and pecans and spread into the prepared pan.

3 Prepare streusel topping by combining the ingredients and forming a crumbly mixture with your fingertips. Sprinkle the topping over the entire surface and bake 40 minutes. Cool on a wire rack and cut into 12 bars. These keep well refrigerated for up to 4 days.

helpfulhint ✳

You can buy oat or rice flours, or make them by grinding rolled oats and brown rice in a coffee grinder until finely ground.

flaxeggs

(yields about 1 cup - 240 mL)
1/4 cup (60 mL) flax seeds
3/4 cup + 2 tbsp (210 mL) water

Place the flax seeds in the bowl of a food processor and grind them thoroughly. With the motor running, slowly add the water. Once all of the water has been added, let the processor run for 5 minutes. Measure and use as required. Store extra flax eggs in the refrigerator for up to 5 days.

chocolatezucchinicupcakes

with allspice and cinnamon

early autumn gardens are usually bursting with zucchini the size of small house pets. Next time a neighbour leaves one at your doorstep, put it to good use in this delicious recipe. Extra grated zucchini will freeze well and be ready for future cupcake batches. Kids will be delighted by these at birthday parties, particularly if you let them decorate the tops with an assortment of sprinkles and chocolate curls. This recipe will also yield 20 regular muffin-size cupcakes or fill a 9" x 13" baking pan.

1 Pre-heat oven to 350°F. Lightly grease large muffin pans and line with muffin cups.

2 In a medium bowl mix together the sugar, butter and oil. Beat in eggs, one at a time until well incorporated. Stir in vanilla, buttermilk, zucchini and chocolate chips.

3 In a separate bowl mix together all of the dry ingredients. Add the liquid ingredients and mix until well combined. Spoon batter into large muffin pans. Bake in the center of the oven for 35 minutes, or until a toothpick inserted comes out clean. Cool on a wire rack, while preparing the icing.

4 Beat cream cheese on high until smooth and fluffy. Lightly blend in vanilla and butter. Melt white chocolate over a double boiler and add warm melted chocolate to the cream cheese mixture. Scrape down sides of bowl to incorporate all. Mix on high again until smooth and fluffy. Slowly add icing sugar, scraping down the sides of the bowl occasionally, and beat on high until light and fluffy, about 3 minutes.

yields 9 large cupcakes

1 1/2 cups (360 mL) brown sugar
1/4 cup (60 mL) melted butter
3/4 cup (180 mL) vegetable oil
3 eggs
1 tsp (5 mL) vanilla
1/2 cup (120 mL) buttermilk
2 cups (480 mL) grated zucchini
1 cup (240 mL) chocolate chips
2 cups (480 mL) unbleached flour
1 cup (240 mL) cocoa, sifted
1/2 tsp (2.5 mL) salt
2 tsp (10 mL) baking soda
1 tsp (5 mL) allspice
1 1/2 tsp (7.5 mL) cinnamon

icing

10 oz (300 g) Philadelphia cream cheese (firm block, not spreadable)
1/4 cup (60 mL) unsalted butter, softened
1 tsp (5 mL) vanilla
3 oz (90 g) white chocolate
3 cups (720 mL) icing sugar, sifted

decoratingideas

❊ drizzled melted dark chocolate for a zebra-stripe effect
❊ fresh black berries or raspberries
❊ chocolate curls
❊ orange/lemon zest and chopped candied ginger
❊ chopped pistachio nuts or roasted hazelnuts
❊ crushed espresso beans

citruspoppyseedcake
with lemon, lime and orange

searching for a birthday cake for a non-chocoholic? You need look no further than this tangy, moist and flavourful cake. Earthy poppyseeds add a touch of texture to offset the smooth cream cheese frosting. In all, this cake is a classic with a twist of lively citrus flavours—ideal for special occasions.

yields one 8" cake

1 1/2 cups (360 mL) unsalted butter,
   softened
2 1/2 cups (600 mL) sugar
7 eggs
1 1/2 tsp (7.5 mL) vanilla
3 3/4 cups (900 mL) unbleached flour
2 1/2 tsp (12.5 mL) baking powder
3/4 tsp (4 mL) salt
1 cup (240 mL) milk, room temperature
1/2 tsp (2.5 mL) each, zest of orange,
   lemon and lime
1/3 cup (80 mL) poppyseeds

glaze
1 1/2 cups (360 mL) icing sugar
1/4 cup (60 mL) fresh lemon juice

icing
12 oz (360 g) cream cheese
1/2 cup (120 mL) butter, softened
4 cups (960 mL) icing sugar, sifted

1 Pre-heat oven to 350°F. Lightly grease three 8" cake pans and set aside. Cream the butter and sugar until light and fluffy. Mix in eggs, one at a time, beating each one in well before adding the next. Stir in the vanilla.

2 In a separate bowl, combine flour, baking powder and salt. Add to the butter/sugar mix in three batches, alternating with the milk. Fold in the citrus zest and poppyseeds. Evenly divide the batter among the pans and bake for 45 minutes. Cool completely.

3 Mix together the sugar and lemon juice to make a glaze and brush over the cooled cakes.

4 To make the icing, mix the cream cheese until smooth. Mix in the butter, then the sugar. Whip briefly. Spread filling between each layer of cake. Finish the cake by spreading the icing over the top and sides. Chill to set the icing. If you like, decorate with poppyseeds and long strands of citrus zests curled over the top.

helpfulhint ❄

When using citrus fruits for their zest, try to buy organic fruits. If they're not available, be sure to wash each fruit well with hot water and soap before zesting.

chocolate mousse blackout

with cashews, ginger and silken tofu

heart-smart desserts seldom hold promise for cheesecake lovers, yet this extravagant vegan and wheat-free dessert delivers the goods. The dense and creamy cake is rich like cheesecake but without all the heavy calories, and is, in fact, much simpler to prepare than a traditional cheesecake. We also like the flexibility of this recipe. The choice of nuts and spices in the crust, and options for accompanying sauces, offers a range of outstanding possibilities.

1 Pre-heat oven to 350°F. Grease an 8" springform pan and set aside. Place the Sucanat, spelt flour, cashews, salt, cinnamon and ginger in the bowl of a food processor. Pulse to a fine texture. Add the vegetable shortening and process to blend it in well. Transfer the mixture to a bowl and stir in oil and vanilla. Press the mixture into the prepared pan and bake for 15 minutes. Set aside to cool.

2 Next, prepare the filling. Melt the chocolate in a double boiler. Drain the tofu and purée in a food processor until smooth. Add Sucanat, vanilla and salt, mixing it in well. Add the melted chocolate, mixing until well blended. Pour the filling over the baked crust and bake for 35 minutes, or until firm. Cool completely on a wire rack and refrigerate overnight before serving.

yields one 8" torte

crust

3 tbsp (45 mL) Sucanat
1 cup (240 mL) spelt flour
1/3 cup (80 mL) toasted cashews
1/8 tsp (.5 mL) salt
1/2 tsp (2.5 mL) cinnamon
1/4 tsp (1.2 mL) ginger
1/4 cup (60 mL) vegetable shortening
3 tbsp (45 mL) vegetable oil
1/2 tsp (2.5 mL) vanilla

filling

1 lb (450 g) dark Belgian chocolate
2 1/2 boxes silken extra-firm tofu
3/4 cup (180 mL) Sucanat
1 tsp (5 mL) vanilla
1/8 tsp (.5 mL) salt
2 tsp (10 mL) espresso powder (optional)

helpful hint ✳

If you are not vegan, white granulated sugar is a fine substitute. Also, white unbleached flour can be substituted for the spelt flour and will yield a less crumbly crust due to it's higher gluten content.

carrotcoconutcake

with cream cheese-white chocolate icing

attempts at describing this cake invariably result in absolutes - the sweetest, the moistest, the yummiest. This recipe will adapt well to making cupcakes for a kid's birthday party, or a 9" x 13" slab cake to treat your office-mates.

yields one 8" round cake

1 1/2 cups (360 mL) grated carrots
3/4 cup (180 mL) crushed pineapple
3/4 cup (180 mL) unsweetened coconut
3/4 cup (180 mL) chopped walnuts
1/2 cup (120 mL) chopped dates
3/4 cup (180 mL) vegetable oil
3/4 cup (180 mL) brown sugar
1/3 cup (80 mL) white sugar
3 eggs
2 tsp (10 mL) vanilla
1 1/2 cups (360 mL) unbleached flour
1 1/2 tsp (7.5 mL) cinnamon
2 tsp (10 mL) baking powder
1 tsp (5 mL) baking soda
1/4 tsp (1.2 mL) salt
1 1/2 tsp (7.5 mL) ginger
1/2 tsp (2.5 mL) freshly grated nutmeg
1/2 tsp (2.5 mL) allspice

icing

9 oz (270 g) Philadelphia cream cheese (firm block, not spreadable)
1/4 cup (60 mL) unsalted butter, softened
1 tsp (5 mL) vanilla
3 oz (90 g) white chocolate
3 cups (720 mL) icing sugar, sifted

1 Pre-heat oven to 350°F. Butter and flour two 8" round cake pans and set aside. Combine grated carrot, pineapple, coconut and walnuts in a large bowl. In a mixing bowl, beat the sugars with the eggs. Stir in the vanilla and whip on high until the volume has tripled. On low, pour the oil in slowly to blend in.

2 Combine the remaining dry ingredients and gently stir into the egg mix. Fold in the carrot mixture. Divide the batter among the cake pans and smoothe the tops. Bake 30 minutes, until an inserted toothpick comes out clean.

3 While the cakes cool, prepare the frosting. Beat cream cheese on high until smooth and fluffy. Lightly blend in vanilla and butter. Melt white chocolate in a double boiler over medium heat. Add hot melted chocolate to the cream cheese mixture. Scrape down the sides of the bowl and mix on high again until smooth and fluffy. Slowly add icing sugar, stopping to scrape down the sides now and then. Beat on high until all the sugar is well incorporated and the frosting is light and fluffy, about 3 minutes.

4 Spread bottom layer with one third of the frosting, smoothing it evenly to the edges. Chill 10 minutes. Place the top cake layer on and frost the top and sides as you like. Garnish with toasted coconut, walnuts and/or a decorative piped border. Store refrigerated where it will keep well for up to 4 days.

trailbars

vegan, wheat free

pack these along the next time you hit the trails and need a quick energy boost. These make ideal snacks to pack into kid's lunches. They'll also come in handy stashed in the top drawer of your desk at the office, when you find yourself nodding off at the computer in between coffee breaks.

1 Pre-heat oven to 350°F. Line a 10" x 15" pan with parchment paper and set aside.

2 Working in two batches, place dried fruit and rice flour in a food processor and pulse to a coarse texture. Set aside.

3 Mix together the remaining ingredients in a separate bowl. Combine with the dried fruit mixture and spread evenly onto the prepared pan. Place a sheet of plastic wrap over top and roll the surface smooth with a rolling pin. Remove plastic and bake for 10-12 minutes. Cool and cut into 15 bars. Store in an airtight container, or wrap each bar in plastic wrap.

yields 15 bars

1 cup (240 mL) dried figs
1 1/2 cups (360 mL) dried apricots
1/2 cup (120 mL) dried pineapple
1/2 cup (120 mL) dried papaya
1 cup (240 mL) rice flour
1 cup (240 mL) sunflower seeds
1 cup (240 mL) hazelnuts, roasted &
  coarsely chopped
1 cup (240 mL) rolled oats
2/3 cup (160 mL) flax eggs (p. 206)
1/2 cup (120 mL) applesauce
2 tsp (10 mL) vanilla

helpfulhint

Use up leftover flax eggs in pancake batter! Substitute 1/4 cup (60 mL) flax eggs for every egg required in the recipe.

power**spheres**

with dried fruit and seeds ☯

pop a power sphere when energy reserves are low and you need that extra boost to scale the top of the mountain, or just get you home through rush hour traffic! Kids will love these as after school snacks. In fact, kids of all ages will find these simple and fun to make (with adult supervision of course). There's no baking involved and few dishes to wash for clean-up. Wrap each in plastic and take them to a bake sale.

yields 15 spheres

3/4 cup (180 mL) dried apricots

3/4 cup (180 mL) dried apple

4 brown rice cakes

1 cup (240 mL) unsweetened coconut

1/2 cup (120 mL) sunflower seeds

1/2 cup (120 mL) pumpkin seeds

1/3 cup (80 mL) sesame seeds

1/2 cup (120 mL) rolled oats

1 1/4 cups (300 mL) fruit sweetener

1/2 cup (120 mL) natural peanut butter, slightly warmed

1 In a food processor, pulse the apricots, apples and rice cakes to a fine texture. Transfer to a large bowl and set aside.

2 Next, pulse the coconut, seeds, and oats to roughly combine. Add to the fruit mixture, along with the fruit sweetener and peanut butter. Mix everything together until well combined. Cover and chill the dough for at least 1 hour.

3 Roll the dough into balls, approximately 2 oz (60 g). Roll the balls in toasted sesame seeds to coat, pressing them in slightly. Serve, or wrap in plastic and refrigerate.

helpful**hint**

Bring out the nutty flavours of the seeds and oats by toasting them in a hot, dry skillet first. Toast each seed variety and the oats separately, cool them to room temperature and then proceed with the recipe.

apple Danish squares
old-fashioned

organic apples give these squares extraordinary flavour. They have all the taste of apple pie, but are a bit lighter on the sugar, are easier to carry around with you on trips or to school and are a more casual snack than a piece of pie. Invite grandma over for a cup of tea and a slice - she'll be thrilled!

☯ use all-vegetable shortening for a vegan dessert.

yields 10" x 15" pan

pastry
3 1/2 cups (840 mL) unbleached flour
1 1/4 tsp (6.2 mL) salt
3 1/4 oz (105 g) unsalted butter
7 1/2 oz (225 g) vegetable shortening
1/3 cup + 2 tbsp (110 mL) cold water

filling
3 lbs (1.4 kg) Granny Smith apples
   peeled, cored and sliced
1 cup (240 mL) brown sugar
1/4 cup (60 mL) cornstarch
1 tbsp (15 mL) cinnamon
3 tbsp (45 mL) fresh lemon juice

1 Place flour, salt and butter in the bowl of a food processor fitted with a metal blade. Pulse the mixture until the butter is the size of small peas, about 10 "pulses". Add the shortening and pulse briefly until just incorporated. Drizzle in the cold water and run the machine until pastry begins to hold together when pinched (10-15 seconds). Remove dough from the processor and knead the ball of dough very briefly to smooth it out and hold it together. Wrap well in plastic, flatten into a disc and refrigerate for 1 hour before using. Let the dough sit at room temperature for 10 minutes before rolling out.

2 Sprinkle a generous amount of flour on the bottom of a 10" x 15" baking pan with sides. Divide the pastry in half. Work the pastry with your hands and shape it into a square. Roll it out to fit the dimensions of the pan with a 2" overhang. Gently press the pastry into the pan. Refrigerate for 15 minutes.

3 Pre-heat the oven to 350°F. Slice the apples into a large bowl and toss with other filling ingredients. Pour the apples onto the bottom pastry crust, spreading them out evenly. Return the pan to the fridge while you repeat the same rolling process with the remaining pastry.

4 Brush the edges of the bottom crust with milk and lay the top crust over the apples. Use a fork to seal the layers and a knife or kitchen scissors to trim the excess pastry. Brush the top with milk and poke several holes with the tines of a fork over the surface. Sprinkle with turbinado sugar and bake for 30-40 minutes, or until the crust is golden brown and the apples are bubbling. Rotate the pan halfway through baking. Cool and slice into squares. Serve warm or at room temperature.

peanutbuttersquares

with milk chocolate and oats

lovers of the peanut butter and chocolate combination have their hands full (and sticky) with this sweet treat. These squares are not cakey, but more like a dense cookie square. The icing just takes the whole thing over the top - it's another one of those recipes that customers beg us for. Bake sales will never be the same!

yields 8" x 8" pan

1/2 cup (120 mL) unsalted butter, softened
1/2 cup (120 mL) brown sugar
1/2 cup (120 mL) white sugar
1/3 cup (80 mL) smooth, natural peanut butter
1 egg
1/2 tsp (2.5 mL) vanilla
3/4 cup (180 mL) rolled oats
1 cup (240 mL) unbleached flour
1/2 tsp (2.5 mL) baking soda
1/4 tsp (1.2 mL) salt
4 oz (120 g) milk chocolate, chopped into large chunks

icing

1/2 cup (120 mL) peanut butter
2 tbsp (30 mL) soft butter
1/2 tsp (2.5 mL) vanilla
1 cup (240 mL) icing sugar
1/4 cup (60 mL) heavy cream

1 Pre-heat oven to 350°F. Grease an 8" x 8" pan and set aside. Cream together the butter, sugars and peanut butter until light and fluffy. Add the egg and vanilla and mix well.

2 Combine the oats, flour, soda and salt in a separate bowl. Add this to the butter/peanut butter mix and stir well. Fold in the chocolate chunks. Spread into the prepared pan and bake 25 minutes. Set aside to cool.

3 Prepare the icing by creaming together the peanut butter, butter and vanilla. Blend in icing sugar. Stir in cream until you get a nice spreading consistency, using more if necessary.

4 Ice the cooled squares and decorate with additional melted milk chocolate drizzled over top, if you like. Divide into squares and serve.

chocolate**chip**cookies
with apricots and walnuts

jars of assorted freshly baked cookies line the front counter at **re**bar. These chewy, moist cookies have been a top-seller for years. Once you start making these, you'll never buy supermarket cookies again! Once they are fully cooled, store them in an airtight tin for up to one week (if they last that long!)

1 Pre-heat oven to 350°F. Line a cookie sheet with parchment paper and set aside. Cream together the butter and sugar until light and fluffy. Add eggs one at a time, blending each one in well before adding the next. Blend in the vanilla and set aside.

2 Using a food processor, pulse together the apricots with 1/2 cup (120 mL) flour. Chop them up fine and place them in a large mixing bowl. Mix in the remaining flour, baking powder and salt. Add the wet mix and stir in the walnuts and chocolate chips.

3 Drop heaping tablespoonsful of batter on the prepared baking sheet, leaving room in between to allow for spreading during baking. Bake for 9 minutes, rotating the tray half way through baking. Cool on a wire rack and hide them well!

yields 28 cookies

1/2 cup (120 mL) unsalted butter, softened
1 1/2 cups (360 mL) brown sugar
2 eggs
2 tsp (10 mL) vanilla
1/4 cup (60 mL) dried apricots
1 1/2 cups (360 mL) unbleached flour
1 1/2 tsp (7.5 mL) baking powder
1/2 tsp (2.5 mL) salt
1 cup (240 mL) roasted and chopped walnuts
1 1/2 cups (600 mL) good quality chocolate chips

helpful**hint**

If you don't have a food processor, mince the apricots with a sharp knife. Blend with flour and proceed.

banana**bread**

with wheatgerm and walnuts

moist and sweet bananas are nicely paired with the nutty flavour of toasted wheatgerm and walnuts in this tasty, moist loaf. This bread will freeze very well so keep a loaf stored away for rainy days when friends come over for coffee.

yields one 9" x 5" loaf

2 1/2 cups (600 mL) unbleached flour

2 tsp (10 mL) baking soda

2 tsp (10 mL) baking powder

1/4 tsp (1.2 mL) salt

1/4 cup (60 mL) wheatgerm, toasted

1/2 cup (120 mL) unsalted butter,
   softened

3/4 cup (180 mL) brown sugar

3/4 cup (180 mL) white sugar

4 eggs

3 very ripe bananas

1/4 cup (60 mL) sour cream

3/4 cup (180 mL) walnuts, roasted and
   chopped

1 Pre-heat the oven to 350°F. Butter and flour a 9" x 5" loaf pan. Combine the flour, wheatgerm, baking powder, soda and salt in a small bowl and set aside.

2 In a large bowl, cream together the butter and sugars. Blend in the eggs one at a time until well incorporated. Mash together the bananas and sour cream. Add one third of the flour mix into the creamed sugar/butter mix. Next, stir in the banana mash and mix thoroughly. Add the remainder of the flour and mix on low until well combined, taking care not to overmix. Gently fold in the walnuts.

3 Pour the batter into the prepared pan, smoothing the top, and bake for one hour, or until an inserted toothpick comes out clean. Cool the cake in the pan for 10 minutes, then run a knife along the edges and turn the loaf gently out. Cool on a wire rack.

helpful**hint** ✳

Add or substitute any of these to the batter for a yummy twist:

✳ 1/4 cup (60 mL) flax seeds

✳ chopped dates, raisins or cranberries

✳ toasted pecans

✳ chocolate chips

✳ fresh grated ginger

✳ lemon or orange zest

raspberryoatbars
with walnuts and cinnamon

kids will usually jump at the chance to bake a treat on their own. These easy and very quick-to-prepare bars are a great project for the budding baker! Substitute raspberry and walnuts with your favourite fruit jam/nut combination. We like hazelnuts with blackberry, or apricot jam with almonds.

yields 15 bars

1. Pre-heat oven to 350°F. Lightly grease a 10" x 15" baking sheet and set aside.

2. Place all ingredients, except the egg and raspberry jam, into a mixer or food processor. Mix thoroughly. Remove half of the mixture and set aside. Blend the egg into the remaining mixture and press it into the prepared baking sheet. Bake until firm and lightly browned (about 10 minutes).

3. Remove the crust from the oven and spread the jam evenly over the surface. Sprinkle the top with the remaining crumbly mixture. Bake 10 minutes until golden brown. Cool and cut into 15 bars.

> 3/4 cup (180 mL) unbleached flour
> 3/4 cup (180 mL) whole wheat flour
> 2 cups (480 mL) rolled oats
> 1 1/2 cups (360 mL) walnuts
> 2 tsp (10 mL) baking powder
> 1/4 tsp (1.2 mL) salt
> 1 1/2 tsp (7.5 mL) cinnamon
> 1 cup + 2 tbsp (270 mL) unsalted butter, softened
> 1 1/2 cups (360 mL) brown sugar
> 1 egg, lightly beaten
> 1 cup (240 mL) raspberry jam

helpfulhint ✳

If you prefer, these are delicious made with all whole wheat flour. We use Nunweiler's Organic Whole Wheat at Casacadia - it is finely milled and has a great nutty flavour.

vegan**fudge**brownies ☯

customers have begged for this recipe for years and years, so here it is! This moist cakey brownie is as good as, or possibly better than, the "real" thing. They are so popular that our Cascadia bakers can barely keep up production.

yields 12 squares

1 1/2 cups (360 mL) unbleached flour

1/2 cup (120 mL) cocoa

1 1/2 cups (360 mL) brown sugar

1 1/2 tsp (7.5 mL) baking soda

3/4 tsp (4 mL) baking powder

1 tsp (5 mL) salt

3/4 cup (180 mL) coffee

3/4 cup (180 mL) soy milk

1/3 cup (80 mL) vegetable oil

1/2 cup (120 mL) walnuts, roasted and chopped

1/2 cup (120 mL) carob chips

glaze

7 oz (210 g) dark, Belgian chocolate

5 oz (150 g) vegan margarine

1 Pre-heat oven to 325°F. Prepare a 9" x 9" pan by greasing it and then lining it with parchment paper.

2 Sift together the flour, cocoa, brown sugar, baking soda, baking powder and salt. In a separate bowl, stir together the coffee, soy milk and vegetable oil. Combine the wet and dry mixes and stir to mix well. Stir walnuts into the batter. Pour the batter into the prepared pan, sprinkle the top with carob chips, and bake for 25 minutes, or until an inserted toothpick comes out clean. Cool the cake on a wire rack.

3 When the cake is cool, prepare the glaze. In a double boiler, melt the chocolate and vegan margarine. Whisk together very thoroughly to get a smooth, rather than a streaky finish. Pour the warm glaze over the cake, smoothing it out over the surface. Place the pan in the fridge to set. Divide the pan of brownies into 12 squares and enjoy!.

helpful**hint** ✳

To get a smooth, clean cut when slicing a cake, run a large knife blade under very hot water, pat dry with a clean cloth and slice.

rebarchocolatecake

incurable chocoholics savouring this cake share counter space with wheatgrass-gulping health nuts at **re**bar. You've gotta wonder who is having a better time...

yields one 8" round cake

1. Pre-heat oven to 350°F. Prepare three 8" cake pans with oiled parchment cut to fit the bottom of the pans. Set aside.

2. Combine the sugar, flour, cocoa, baking powder, soda and salt in the bowl of a mixer and whisk on low to combine, making sure it's lump-free. Add the coffee, buttermilk, oil, eggs and vanilla and mix on medium-low for 2 minutes, stopping to scrape down the sides. The batter will be pourable.

3. Divide the batter among the prepared pans and bake for 15 minutes, until an inserted toothpick comes out clean. Let the cakes cool before removing them from the pans and cool completely on a wire rack. Remove parchment papers before assembling.

4. Next, prepare the cake filling. Melt the milk and dark chocolates in a double boiler and stir until smooth. Cool 10 minutes. Cream together the butter, cream cheese and vanilla. Mix the cooled chocolate into the creamed mixture. Next, prepare the ganache by heating the cream and butter to just before the scalding point. Pour the cream over the chopped chocolate and let rest for 3 minutes, then whisk gently (to avoid incorporating air as much as possible) until melted and smooth. Cool slightly.

5. To assemble the cake, place one of the cake layers on a cooling rack with a large baking sheet underneath to catch drips. Evenly spread half of the filling over the layer, then position a second layer on top. Repeat with remaining filling, saving a small amount to thinly spread over the top, and to fill in the sides and make it smooth. Position the top cake layer over the filling. Chill 10 minutes. Next, slowly pour the warm chocolate ganache over the entire cake while carefully spreading it with a large metal icing spatula to make a smooth surface. Carefully transfer the cake onto a plate and into the fridge to set.

1 1/2 cups (360 mL) light brown sugar
1 1/2 cups (360 mL) unbleached flour
1/2 cup (120 mL) Dutch process cocoa
1 1/2 tsp (7.5 mL) baking soda
3/4 tsp (4 mL) baking powder
1/4 tsp (1.2 mL) salt
3/4 cup (180 mL) strong coffee
3/4 cup (180 mL) buttermilk
1/3 cup + 2 tbsp (110 mL) vegetable oil
2 eggs (1 whole egg + 1 egg yolk)
1 tsp (5 mL) vanilla

cake filling

5 oz (150 g) milk chocolate
5 oz (150 g) dark chocolate
1/2 lb (225 g) unsalted butter, softened
1/4 lb (112 g) cream cheese, spreadable
1 tsp (5 mL) vanilla

ganache

1/2 cup (120 mL) heavy cream
1 tbsp (15 mL) unsalted butter
5 oz (150 g) semi-sweet chocolate

helpfulhint ✳

The cake layers can be made up to 2 days in advance, wrapped well in saran and refrigerated until ready to devour.

puddingcake
lemony and sweet

simple and divine, this lemony pudding cake is an ideal dessert for a size-able dinner party. The recipe is easily halved and will also make nice little souflée-like desserts if baked (20 minutes) in individual ceramic ramekins. Drop in a few fresh blueberries and pour the batter over top, or serve with a bowl of fresh berries and whipped cream.

serves 12

3 cups (720 mL) milk
1/2 cup (120 mL) butter
6 egg yolks
2 cups (720 mL) sugar
1 cup (240 mL) unbleached flour
2 lemons, zest and juice
1/4 tsp (1.2 mL) salt
6 egg whites

1 Pre-heat the oven to 350°F. Scald the milk and butter and set aside. Butter a 13" x 10" oval baking dish and set aside.

2 Whisk together the egg yolks, 1 1/2 cups (360 mL) sugar, flour, lemon juice, zest and salt. Whisk the scalded milk into the egg yolk mixture.

3 In a separate bowl, whip the egg whites until foamy. Slowly add 1/2 cup sugar and whip until the mixture is slightly stiff and glossy. Do not over-whip! Add 1/3 of the egg white mixture into the egg yolk mixture. Whisk lightly and fold in the remaining whites in two batches. Be gentle and do not over-mix.

4 Pour the batter into the prepared baking dish. Place the dish inside a large roasting pan and add water so that it reaches half way up the sides of the dish. Put into the oven immediately. Bake for 35-45 minutes, or until the top is slightly "springy". Cool and serve.

deepdishfruitpies

brandied peach, sour cherry and bumbleberry

SOMEof us prefer the fruity desserts over the chocolatey ones. Here are three of our most popular fruit pies to serve with ice cream, whipped cream or au naturel.

🌓 use all vegetable shortening for vegan pies.

yields one 10" deep dish pie (halve the recipe for an 8" pie)

1 Place flour, salt, sugar and butter in the bowl of a food processor fitted with a metal blade. Pulse the mixture until the butter is the size of small peas, about 10 "pulses". Add the shortening and pulse briefly until just incorporated. Drizzle in the cold water and pulse until the dough holds together when squeezed with your fingertips (only about 10 more "pulses"). Try not to add too much water or overprocess, or your pastry will be tough. Remove dough from the processor and gather it together into a ball. Knead the dough very briefly to smooth it out and hold it together. Wrap well in plastic, flatten into a disc and refrigerate for 1 hour before rolling it out.
Note: This can easily be done by hand if you don't own a food processor.

2 Pre-heat oven to 350°F. To prepare the fruit fillings, toss the ingredients well to combine, making sure that there are no clumps of thickener. Smooth the filling into a chilled pie pastry shell and top with a lattice. Brush the lattice with milk or egg-wash and sprinkle with coarse sugar.

3 Bake a 10" pie for 40-45 minutes. An 8" pie will need about 25-30 minutes. Make sure the bottom of the crust is browned (we use glass pie plates for easy checking).

pastry
2 cups (375 g) unbleached flour
1/2 tsp (2.5 mL) salt
1/2 tsp (2.5 mL) sugar
3 oz (90 g) cold butter, diced
5 1/2 oz (165 g) vegetable shortening
1/4 cup (60 mL) ice cold water

brandied peach
2 lbs (900 g) peach slices, fresh or frozen
3/4 cup (180 mL) granulated sugar
1/4 cup (60 mL) cornstarch
1 tbsp (15 mL) brandy
1 tsp (5 mL) almond extract

sour cherry
2 1/2 lbs (1.2 kg) sour cherries, pitted
3/4 cup (180 mL) granulated sugar
1/4 cup (60 mL) cornstarch
1 tbsp (15 mL) Triple Sec
1 tsp (5 mL) almond extract

bumbleberry
1/2 lb (225 g) each blueberries, raspberries, strawberries, rhubarb, sliced apples
1 medium orange, zest and juice
1 tbsp (15 mL) lemon juice
3/4 cup (180 mL) granulated sugar
1/3 cup (80 mL) unbleached flour

pumpkin**millet**muffins

with cinnamon, ginger and nutmeg

crunchy millet gives texture to these muffins, which are full of comforting spices and moist pumpkin sweetness. Toasting the millet and pumpkin seeds in a hot dry skillet imparts a wonderful nutty flavour. Serve for brunch with home-made apple butter.

yields 15 large muffins

2 eggs, beaten
1/2 cup (120 mL) vegetable oil
1 cup (240 mL) buttermilk
3/4 cup (180 mL) brown sugar
1/2 tsp (2.5 mL) vanilla
1 1/2 cups (360 mL) pumpkin purée
1/2 cup (120 mL) rolled oats
1/2 cup (120 mL) millet
1/4 cup (60 mL) pumpkin seeds
1 cup (240 mL) unbleached flour
3/4 cup (180 mL) whole wheat flour
2 tsp (10 mL) baking powder
1 1/2 tsp (7.5 mL) baking soda
1/2 tsp (2.5 mL) salt
1/2 tsp (2.5 mL) cinnamon
1/2 tsp (2.5 mL) ground ginger
1/4 tsp (1.2 mL) freshly grated nutmeg

1　Pre-heat oven to 350°F. Grease a large muffin pan and line with muffin cups if you like. Set aside. Combine eggs, oil, buttermilk, sugar, vanilla and pumpkin in a large bowl and mix together, making sure there are no lumps of brown sugar. Stir in the oats. Toast millet in a hot dry skillet until lightly browned and fragrant. Toast the pumpkin seeds and add the millet and seeds to the bowl. Set aside.

2　In a separate bowl, sift the dry ingredients together. Add the dry mix to the wet mix and gently stir to combine. Do not overmix, or the muffins will be dry and tough.

3　Fill muffin cups generously with batter. Sprinkle tops with pumpkin seeds and bake for 25 minutes, or until an inserted toothpick comes out clean.

helpful**hint** ❄

Oat bran would be a good substitute for the oats, and even flax seeds, instead of the millet, in a pinch!

Bayou**chocolate**torte

with bourbon and dark Belgian chocolate

many weekend dinner customers at **re**bar have claimed that this is the best dessert they've ever had! You can get really creative with the addition of coulis or sauces to garnish the cake. This decadent dessert will surely impress guests at a dinner party. The beauty of it all is that it's actually quite simple to make!

serves 8 - 10

12 oz (360 g) dark Belgian chocolate
1 1/3 cups (320 mL) sugar
1/2 cup (120 mL) bourbon
8 oz (240 g) unsalted butter, softened and cubed
5 eggs
2 tbsp (30 mL) flour

1 Pre-heat oven to 350°F. Butter an 8" springform pan. Line the bottom of the pan with parchment paper cut to fit inside. Wrap the outside of the pan with foil so that it won't leak when it is placed in the water bath. Have all ingredients measured and ready to go before commencing.

2 Pulse the chocolate in a food processor until fine. Gently heat the bourbon and sugar until the sugar dissolves (be careful not to ignite it!) Pour the hot syrup over the chocolate while the food processor is running. Add butter, one piece at a time. Add eggs one at a time. Finally, add flour, mixing 15 seconds more.

3 Pour the batter into the prepared pan. Place the pan in a large baking dish. Fill the dish with water halfway up the sides of the springform pan and place in the center of the oven. Bake 25 minutes. Cool the cake completely on a wire rack in the springform pan and refrigerate covered overnight. Invert the cake onto a cookie sheet to remove the parchment and then invert onto a serving platter so that the cake is face up. Serve as is, or in a pool of raspberry coulis, orange crème anglaise or white chocolate whipped cream.

helpful**hint** ✳

The better quality chocolate you use for this recipe, the better your results will be. We use Belcolade from Belgium.

---

raspberry**orange**coulis

2 pints fresh raspberries
1/2 cup (120 mL) sugar
1 cup (240 mL) water
1 tsp (5 mL) orange zest
2 tbsp (30 mL) Grand Marnier

Combine the berries, sugar, water and orange zest in a pot and simmer until the berries collapse and the liquid is syrupy (about 10 minutes). Cool slightly, then strain through a fine mesh sieve. Cover and refrigerate. Whisk in Grand Marnier just before serving.

limesugarcookies
with pumpkin seeds

these sweet melt-in-your-mouth cookies are nicely balanced by the tang of fresh lime and crunch of pumpkin seeds - a unique combination that really works. Serve with coconut gelato and fresh mango after a feast of fajitas (p. 197) or tempeh tacos (p. 185).

yields 11 large cookies

1 cup (240 mL) granulated sugar

1/4 cup (60 mL) unsalted butter

1 tbsp (15 mL) vegetable oil

zest of 1 lime

1 large egg

2 tbsp (30 mL) lime juice

1 3/4 cups (420 mL) unbleached flour

1/4 cup (60 mL) pepitas (pumpkin
   seeds), toasted and roughly chopped

1/2 tsp (2.5 mL) baking soda

1/2 tsp (2.5 mL) salt

1 Pre-heat the oven to 350°F. Cream the sugar, oil, butter and lime zest until light and fluffy. Add eggs and lime juice, and beat together to incorporate.

2 In a separate bowl, mix the flour, pepitas, baking soda and salt. Add the dry mix to the wet mix and stir together well.

3 Using a 2 oz ice scream scoop, or forming 3 tbsp (45 mL) balls, drop the batter onto a cookie sheet, leaving space in between to allow the cookies to spread during baking. Flatten each slightly and sprinkle with granulated sugar. Bake for 8 minutes. Cool on a wire rack.

oatspicecake
with coconut-cashew crown

Billy Hilton is the most tenured of our servers, much loved by staff and customers alike. Customers are particularly impressed when Billy claims that all of the **re**bar recipes are his very own! While he rules his domain during the busiest restaurant hours, Billy does possess other hidden talents. His seasonal home decors are legendary, and we often stop by his apartment to view the latest creation. We asked Billy for an opinion on the oat spice cake, and he recommends serving this moist, rich cake during holiday time on a festive platter surrounded by a holly garnish. Move over Martha!

serves 8 - 10

1 Pre-heat oven to 350°F. Lightly grease a 9" springform pan and set aside. Combine the oats, butter, sugar and boiling water and blend together thoroughly. Set aside.

2 In a separate bowl, combine the flour, baking soda and spices. Add the dry mix to the wet mix and fold them together gently. Pour the batter into the prepared pan and bake for 25 minutes, or until a knife inserted into the middle comes out clean.

3 To make the topping, toast the coconut until lightly golden and fragrant. Combine all of the ingredients in a saucepan and heat the mixture until the butter melts and all is well blended. Pour the mixture over top of the baked cake while it's still in the springform pan. Carefully place the cake under the broiler for about 2 minutes, until the topping turns golden brown. Keep a close eye on it, it will caramelize very quickly! Cool and serve.

2 cups (480 mL) rolled oats
2/3 cup (160 mL) unsalted butter, softened
1 cup (240 mL) brown sugar
1 1/2 cups (360 mL) boiling water
1/2 cup (120 mL) unbleached flour
1 tsp (5 mL) baking soda
1 tsp (5 mL) cinnamon
1 tsp (5 mL) allspice
1/4 tsp (1.2 mL) salt

topping

1 cup (240 mL) brown sugar
1/2 cup (120 mL) unsalted butter
1/2 cup (120 mL) whipping cream
2 cups (480 mL) coconut, toasted
1 1/2 cups (360 mL) cashews, roasted

classicfruitcrumble

with a few "not-so-classic" options

season to season, fruit crumble is the easiest and most flexible dessert you can make. Depending on your menu, your mood and seasonal availability of fruit, this recipe is wonderful and limitless. Serve with ice cream, whipped cream or rice milk.

serves 6 - 8

2 1/4 lbs (1 kg) fruit (apples, peaches, berries, rhubarb, or any combination)

1/3 cup (80 mL) sugar, or more depending on choice of fruit

2 tbsp (30 mL) cornstarch

2 tbsp (30 mL) lemon juice

topping

3/4 cup (180 mL) unsalted butter

1/2 cup (120 mL) brown sugar

1 cup (240 mL) unbleached flour

1/2 cup (120 mL) rolled oats, or other grain

1/4 tsp (1.2 mL) salt

1/2 cup (120 mL) nuts or seeds of choice

☯ replace butter with vegan margarine.

1 Pre-heat the oven to 350°F. Chop or slice the fruit into a large bowl. Stir in the remaining filling ingredients. Pile the fruit mixture into a 11" x 7.5" oval dish, or a 6 cup casserole.

2 Prepare the crumbly topping by mixing together all of the ingedients with your fingertips to get a nice chunky texture. Cover the fruit with the topping and bake for 40 minutes, or until the topping is browned and the fruit is bubbly and hot. Serve warm or at room temperature and hide leftovers from crunchy-topping thieves!

fruit&toppingcombos

fruit	topping
strawberry, rhubarb, mango	almonds, 7-grain cereal
blueberry, nectarine, orange zest	cornmeal, pecans
apple, pear, cranberry	pepitas, millet, cinnamon
peach, plum, apricot	sunflower seeds, flax meal
blackberry, apple, lemon zest	hazelnuts, barley flakes

vegan**energy**bars

with carob, almonds and applesauce ☯

definitely not just for vegans, these bars are a healthy home-made version of the popular energy bars that are stocking shelves everywhere. The grain, fruit, nut and seed combination supplies just about everything you need for days when you have to skip a meal or are more active than usual and need some extra fuel.

1 Pre-heat oven to 350°F. Prepare a 9" x 13" pan by lining it with parchment paper and spraying it with vegetable oil spray. Set aside.

2 Combine the wet and dry mixes in separate bowls. Mix them together thoroughly and evenly spread the mixture onto the prepared pan. Bake 18 minutes. Cool and divide into bars. Wrap and store in the refrigerator.

yields 15 bars

dry mix

2 cups (480 mL) 7-grain cereal
1/2 cup (120 mL) raisins
1/2 cup (120 mL) chopped prunes
1/2 cup (120 mL) whole almonds, coarsely chopped
1/2 cup (120 mL) sunflower seeds
1/2 cup (120 mL) carob chips
1 1/4 cups (300 mL) unbleached flour
2 tsp (10 mL) cinnamon
1 tsp (5 mL) baking soda
1/2 tsp (2.5 mL) salt

wet mix

1/2 cup (120 mL) vegetable oil
2/3 cup (160 mL) brown sugar
1/3 cup (80 mL) "flax eggs" (p. 206)
1 cup (240 mL) applesauce
1 tsp (5 mL) vanilla

doggie biscotti
with cornmeal, kelp powder and peanut butter

treat your best friend to a batch of these healthy dog snacks. Your pet pooch also deserves to eat well and too often commercial dog treats contain long lists of ingredients of unknown origin, while "gourmet" snacks tend to be overpriced for what they are. Many of the dry ingredients in this recipe are interchangeable. Don't leave out the garlic or brewer's yeast though—they help keep the fleas away! These make great gifts for all the hounds in your life, big or small.

1 In a large bowl, combine all of the dry ingredients from the flour through to the salt. In a separate bowl, mix together all of the remaining wet ingredients.

2 Blend wet with dry until well combined. Form into 2 separate balls and shape each into an oval-shaped log, approximately 3 1/2" wide. Place on baking tray lined with parchment paper and bake at 250°F for approximately 35-45 minutes, until golden brown. Let logs cool, then cut them into slices at an angle (as in "real" biscotti) and place slices on baking tray and bake at 325°F for 6 minutes. Turn them over and bake for another 6 minutes. Let cool before storing.

serves 6 big dogs & 14 small ones

1 cup (240 mL) unbleached flour
3/4 cup (180 mL) oat flour
1 cup (240 mL) whole wheat flour
1 cup (240 mL) cracked wheat
1/2 cup (120 mL) cornmeal
1/2 cup (120 mL) rye flour
1/2 cup (120 mL) wheat germ
1/4 cup (60 mL) milk powder
1 tbsp (15 mL) kelp powder
2 tsp (10 mL) brewers yeast
3/4 tsp (4 mL) salt
1 cup (240 mL) vegetable stock (p. 35)
  or water
1/2 cup (120 mL) hot water
1 egg, lightly beaten
2 tbsp (30 mL) honey
3 tbsp (45 mL) peanut butter
4 garlic cloves, minced
1/2 carrot, grated
1 tbsp (15 mL) vegetable oil

drinks

instructions for juicing couldn't be any easier, provided you own a juicer and/or a blender. A home juicer is necessary for making pure fruit or vegetable juices because they separate the pulp from the natural juices. When looking for a juicer to buy, look for one with a good motor, the fewest parts to clean and one that ejects the pulp outside of the machine. For smoothies, a blender is all you need.

We recommend that you use organic produce when possible, to avoid pesticide and herbicide residues. Wash all produce first and remove any bruised or moldy areas. Peel all citrus fruits. If you're not using organic, peel all fruits and vegetables before juicing or, at the very least, wash with a produce cleaning solution. We don't recommend storing fresh juices for any length of time due to rapid nutrient loss to oxidation, so drink up right away and revitalize, rejuvenate and restore!

atomizer

cucumber, pineapple, apple

kitchen staff at **re**bar favour this juice because it's not too sweet and is very refreshing and thirst quenching. It's also great for the complexion, promoting skin elasticity. Of course, we all want to look our best while we toil in the hot kitchen! And if that isn't reason enough to love this juice, it is also high in potassium, which is good for stress reduction. Lord knows we could all use some of that now and then.

yields 12 oz (360 mL)

1/3 of a cucumber (4 1/2 oz - 135 g)
2 pineapple spears (4 1/2 oz - 135 g)
1 1/2 apples
juice above and blend with 3 ice
  cubes

fiesta del sol

cranberry, orange, apple

tart cranberries counter the sweetness of this juice. They also act as a powerful antibacterial and antiviral agent, detoxifying the bladder, kidneys and prostate. Combined with orange, you have a tasty drink rich in vitamin C and pretty and as a Mexican sunset.

yields 12 oz (360 mL)

1/2 cup (120 mL) cranberries,
  fresh or frozen
1 apple
1 orange

liver**quiver**

lemon, grapefruit, garlic, cayenne, olive oil

citrus juices are rich in vitamin C, potassium and calcium. These benefit the liver by detoxifying the blood and improving the absorption of minerals, among other things. Raw garlic is a powerful antibiotic and antiviral, while cayenne is one of the highest botanic sources of vitamin C (it will also make you sweat!) This combination is great medicine during the cold and flu season.

yields 12 oz (360 mL)

1/2 lemon
1 1/2 grapefruit
1 garlic clove
1 tbsp (15 mL) olive oil
3 pinches cayenne

rio**luna**

fennel, celery, apple

women will appreciate this juice because it's a powerful stomach tonic, promoting digestion and soothing symptoms of PMS and menopause. Fennel also aids in releasing endorphins from the brain into the bloodstream which calms anxiety and frayed nerves.

yields 12 oz (360 mL)

1 celery stalk (1 1/2 oz - 45 g)
1/3 fennel bulb (4 oz - 120 g)
2 apples
3 ice cubes

atomicglow

ginger, strawberry, apple

soothing

ginger has long been used as a tonic for the gastrointestinal tract, helping to relieve nausea and motion sickness. For pregnant women, fresh ginger can offer relief from morning sickness. This juice is high in B complex, potassium and ellagic acid, a cancer-fighting compound found in strawberries and apples.

yields 12 oz (360 mL)

2 apples
6 strawberries
1/2 oz (15 g) ginger
3 ice cubes

AmourdeCosmos

strawberry, grapefruit, pear

Victoria

has it's share of colourful characters and this trend has roots in our city's history. The eccentric Amour de Cosmos (born William Alexander Smith), came to Victoria via San Francisco during the gold rush era and began his career as editor of a newspaper, where he became notorious for his attacks on the government. He was MP for Victoria and in 1872 became the second premier of B.C., where he was instrumental in the province's entry into Confederation. Big deal you say? Well, we think that anyone who changes their name to Amour de Cosmos deserves to have a juice named after them!

yields 12 oz (360 mL)

1/2 grapefruit
6 strawberries
1 pear
3 ice cubes

double**happiness**
pineapple, strawberry, banana, coconut milk, soymilk

there is a Chinese character meaning double happiness which symbolizes good luck and happiness and often adorns gifts given to newlywed couples. This juice will certainly give you great happiness. It is rich in potassium, protein and vitamin C and best of all, it tastes double yummy! Use all soy milk if you don't have coconut milk.

yields 12 oz (360 mL)

1 banana
6 strawberries
2 pineapple spears (2 oz - 60 g)
4 tbsp (30 mL) light coconut milk
1/3 cup (80 mL) plain soymilk

hyperion
pineapple, pear, orange

fruit juices are excellent for cleansing the body of toxins and giving you energy, making them a perfect drink to start the day. Pineapple is rich in the enzyme bromelain which helps break down animal and plant proteins and improves digestion. Pears are high in pectin and contribute to the cleansing action by promoting the elimination of toxins and wastes in the body. And such a sweet taste for this serious, hard-working juice!

yields 12 oz (360 mL)

3 pineapple spears (4 1/2 oz - 135 g)
1 pear
1 1/2 oranges
3 ice cubes

diablo

parsley, jalapeño, carrot, beet, ginger, garlic

evil brews such as this are bound to be healthy! Parsley is loaded with vitamins, especailly A and C, and is also rich in riboflavin, calcium, iron, magnesium, and potassium. Overall, this is an excellent tonic for increasing energy, lowering cholesterol and cleansing the blood. Be sure to rinse parsley well to wash away hidden grit.

yields 12 oz (360 mL)

4 carrots
1/2 medium beet
1/2 oz (15 g) ginger
1/3 jalapeño pepper, with seeds
1 oz (30 g) parsley
1 garlic clove

Anasazi

red pepper, jalapeño, carrot

ancestors of the modern Pueblo Indians in the U.S. Southwest were the Anasazi, or "Ancient Ones". They inhabited the Four Corners area bordering Colorado, Utah, New Mexico and Arizona, where beautiful red rock mesas dominate the landscape. At sunrise and sunset the rocks are ablaze with rich red and orange hues that inspired the naming of this juice. Sweet red pepper provides this juice with it's lovely colour, plus it's very high in vitamin C and silicon, which strengthens bones, hair, skin and fingernails.

yields 12 oz (360 mL)

1/2 sweet red pepper
1/2 jalapeño pepper (with seeds)
6 carrots

axis**shift**

beet, carrot, apple, ginger

balance
in daily life is essential to an overall feeling of well-being. Keeping that balance isn't always easy, so a juice like this, rich in vitamins and minerals, is guaranteed to shift your axis in the right direction!

yields 12 oz (360 mL)

1/2 medium beet
4 carrots
1 apple
1/2 oz (15 g) ginger

Fellini

celery, broccoli, carrot, garlic

avant
garde film directors have little in common with fresh vegetable juices, so this should dispel any rumours that all the juice names on our menu have great significance. Now this juice does have garlic, and Federico Fellini was Italian, and Italians do love garlic, so it is within the realm of possibility that Fellini would have also loved this juice. And a good thing too, because it's very high in vitamins E and provitamin A, pantothenic acid and copper, making it a powerful antiviral cleanse. Cut!

yields 12 oz (360 mL)

1 broccoli stalk
1 celery stalk
4 carrots
1 garlic clove

Dale Evans

strawberry, banana, soymilk

cowgirls everywhere will recognize this name. This juice is named in honour of Dale Evans, who passed away in 2001 and was one of country music's brightest stars (and wife of Roy Rogers). Audrey must have inherited her love of the torch and twang from her parents, who named their daughter after her - Audrey Dale Alsterberg! This creamy concoction is rich in protein, potassium and ellagic acid, but most important of all, it's very sweet and yummy. Happy trails!

yields 12 oz (360 mL)

1/2 banana
6 strawberries
6 oz plain soymilk
handful of ice cubes

Bootsy Collins

blueberry, banana, orange, yogourt

funk music's most famous bass player is given tribute with this juice. As fans everywhere know, listening to funk music keeps you young. The blueberries in a "Bootsy Collins" have the same effect! Blueberries are rich in antioxidants, which are said to delay the onset of the effects of aging. They are also high in vitamins A and C, ellagic and folic acids, and dietary fibre.

yields 12 oz (360 mL)

2 oz (60 g) blueberries
1/2 banana
orange
4 tbsp (60 mL) plain yogourt

chai

with fresh ginger, cardamom and cinnamon

real Indian-spiced chai is easy to make and so much tastier than the too-sweet commercial chais that have recently flooded the market. Traditionally, it is a very sweet tea, but the beauty of making it yourself is being able to sweeten it to your taste. Buy spices and teas at an Indian grocer for the freshest selection. A few fennel seeds sprinkled in is also a nice touch. Play around and discover your favourite combinations of spices.

serves 4

1 Place water and spices in a pot and bring to boil. Reduce heat, partly cover and gently simmer for 30 minutes. Strain the mixture, discard the solids and return the liquid to the pot. Add the tea bags and let them steep for 5 minutes. Remove the tea bags and stir in the honey and milk. Re-heat, adjust honey and milk levels to taste, and serve.

4 cups water
1 large ginger thumb, peeled and sliced
1 x 3" cinnamon stick
6 cloves
10 cardamom pods, crushed
1/2 tsp (2.5 mL) black peppercorns
3 tea bags, Assam or Orange Pekoe
2 tbsp honey
1 1/2 cups milk, soy or rice

mango**lassi**

mango, banana, lime, yogourt, vanilla

sweet juicy mangoes are great for smoothies. A traditional Indian lassi includes rose water, so add a few drops if you have some on hand. Blend this drink until it's good and frothy. This combination is also delicious with a cup of frozen raspberries blended in.

yields 12 oz (360 mL)

1 ripe mango
1/2 banana
1/2 lime
1/4 cup (60 mL) plain yogourt
1 tbsp (15 mL) vanilla syrup
3 ice cubes

winterzinger

hot lemon, apple, ginger

warm yourself from tip to toe with this delicious steamy drink, rich in vitamins A, C and folic acid. If you feel a cold and sore throat coming on, the anti-inflammatory and anti-viral agents will provide soothing relief. Steam or heat up, but don't let the liquid come to a boil. Toss in a cinnamon stick and stir it all up.

yields 12 oz (360 mL)

1/2 lemon
2 apples
1/2 oz (15 g) ginger
1 cinnamon stick

floofighter

carrot, ginger, lemon, apple, echinacea

vitamins A, B, C, E and zinc are well represented in this juice. With echinacea thrown in the mix, this combination makes a powerful tonic for building and supporting a strong immune system. Think of it as preventative medicine.

yields 16 oz (480 mL)

5 carrots
1/2 oz (15 g) ginger
1/2 lemon
1 apple
1/2 tsp (2.5 mL) echinacea

grasshopper

mint, apple, pineapple and wheatgrass

Ann Wigmore, a pioneer in the wheatgrass juice revolution, gets the nod for this creation. Her work has been the primary influence in shaping the **re**bar philosophy; that is, health and vitality through food. For those at home without access to a wheatgrass juicer, substitute one of the widely available green-food supplements. These chlorophyll-rich products include the micro-algae spirulina and chlorella, and cereal grasses, such as wheat and barley grasses, available in powder or tablet form.

yields 16 oz (480 mL)

4 large fresh mint sprigs
2 apples
3 pineapple spears (4 1/2 oz - 135 g)
3 ice cubes
1 oz (30 g) wheatgrass (p. 243)

wheatgrass

trays of wheatgrass have become a **re**bar symbol; in fact, they have evolved into an important part of the restaurant's decor! Twice a week, flats of fresh wheatgrass are delivered to **re**bar from Metchosin where they end up occupying all available space behind the bar. From here the grass is neatly clipped and expertly handled by our trained juice staff, who extract the precious green elixir with a special wheatgrass juicer. The healing and nutritive properties of fresh wheatgrass are too extensive to list here, so further investigation, particularly into the works of Ann Wigmore, is recommended to anyone interested. Here is a short list of just some of the special attributes of this super food:

wheatgrassjuice:

is one of the richest natural sources of Vitamins A, C and E and the B vitamins

is high in protein and contains all 8 essential Amino Acids

is full of live enzymes which aid in the digestion and metabolization of foods, promote healthy intestinal flora and neutralize and digest toxins in our cells

is rich in chlorophyll, which purifies and enriches the blood

helps rejuvenate aging cells

neutralizes and reverses the accumulation of free radicals in the body

is a good source of calcium, sodium, potassium, magnesium and a wide variety of trace minerals.

glossary

adobo sauce

a mixture of tomato, onion, paprika and vinegar used to marinate canned chipotle chiles.

aïoli

a French mayonnaise-style sauce used for dipping vegetables. Aïoli is prepared with raw eggs; therefore this sauce must be stored in the refrigerator and used within 2 days.

Anaheim chile

a mild, light green chile measuring 5"–7" long. Available fresh or canned. Commonly used to make chiles rellenos.

ancho chiles

a dried poblano chile that tastes earthy and sweet ... like a slightly spicy raisin!

arborio rice

a short-grain Italian white rice used to make risotto.

arugula

also known as "rocket". A peppery, slightly bitter green used in salads and pestos.

asiago cheese

a sharp, creamy Italian cheese.

balsamic vinegar

a sweet, rich vinegar made from the juice of Trebbiano grapes aged in wooden barrels.

basmati rice

a fragrant long-grain Indian rice with a nutty flavour.

bocconcini cheese

fresh mozzarella (not pressed, aged, or seasoned).

brown butter

clarified butter that is cooked to an amber colour; has a rich aroma and sweet, nutty flavour and is used to flavour food, rather than to cook with. See recipe (p. 181).

bulghur

a Middle Eastern grain staple made from wheat that has been steamed, dried and cracked into small pieces.

Cambozola

a soft, very rich German blue cheese (a cross between gorgonzola and blue cheeses).

cannellini beans

a creamy, white variety of kidney bean used in Italian cooking.

caper

the small, green buds of the Mediterranean caper bush, packed in brine and with a salty, piquant flavour.

chèvre

a soft, mild goat's milk cheese.

chiffonade

herbs or leafy vegetables cut into very fine shreds (often used for garnish).

chipotle chiles

smoked jalapeños, most commonly found canned in adobo sauce—very hot and smoky flavour.

clarified butter

"ghee" in Indian cooking—butter from which the water and milk solids have been removed; nice rich taste.

compound butter

softened butter flavoured with herbs, fruit, citrus zest, nuts, etc.

confit

traditionally it is meat (goose, duck or pork) cooked and preserved in its own fat ... in our case it refers to onions, or members of the onion family, slowly cooked with butter and seasonings to a sweet-tasting, jam-like consistency. See recipe (p. 72).

coulis
a thick fruit or vegetable purée.

crème fraîche
slightly soured and thickened cream. See recipe (p. 108).

daikon
a large, white Japanese radish.

extra virgin olive oil
the oil extracted from the first mechanical pressing of olives; does not involve the use of heat or chemicals.

feta cheese
a soft, unripened, white Greek cheese stored in brine. Made from cow, sheep and goat's milks.

fermented black beans
pungent soy beans that have been fermented, dried and salted; an ancient Chinese staple used to flavour sauces.

fish sauce
Thai "nam pla" or Vietnamese "nuoc mam" is a staple Southeast Asian sauce made from salted and fermented anchovies. Store the bottle in the refrigerator once opened.

fontina cheese
a mild, buttery, soft melting cheese.

galangal
a relative of ginger, but with a more perfumed, sour and peppery flavour. If fresh is unavailable, look for frozen galangal in Asian markets.

ganache
a filling or glaze made with chocolate and heavy cream.

genoise
sponge cake made with whole eggs.

Gruyère cheese
a mellow, nutty, Swiss-type cheese.

habañero chile
a fruity, intensely hot West Indian chile ... the hottest!

hijiki
a calcium-rich dried black seaweed; soak in warm water for 30 minutes before using in salads or soups.

Hoisin sauce
a sweet Chinese barbecue sauce made from soybeans, vinegar and spices.

jalapeño pepper
a dark, rich green chile about 2" long used in cooking and to make fresh salsas; can be fairly hot.

jicama
a Mexican root vegetable that is crisp, moist and sweet (a cross between an apple and a potato).

kasha
buckwheat groats.

kaffir lime leaves
a common Thai seasoning with a strong lime-like scent, used in curries, soups and salads. Available fresh, frozen and dried (we prefer fresh or frozen).

lemongrass
an aromatic citrusy tropical grass used in Indonesian and Thai cooking. Use only the bottom 4" of the stalk, after removing the outer layers.

Madeira
a fortified Portuguese red wine.

mesclun
a mixture of young baby salad greens.

millet
a small seed-like grain that is a more nearly complete protein than any other grain; also very digestible.

mirin

a clear, sweet Japanese cooking wine made from sake (rice wine).

miso

a salty Japanese paste used to make soups. Miso is made from cooked, aged and fermented soy beans and often mixed with other grains, such as brown rice or barley, to create different flavours.

mizuna

a sweet, mild Japanese green with narrow, deeply cut leaves, used for salads.

nori

dark green seaweed sold dried in thin sheets. Toasted nori (yakinori) is most commonly used as a wrapper for making sushi. Very rich in protein, vitamins, calcium, iron and other minerals.

orzo

rice-shaped pasta.

parchment paper

heat resistant paper used in cooking ... not edible.

Parmigiano-Reggiano

the finest (and most expensive) quality Parmesan cheese with a full, buttery flavour.

pasilla chile

a dark green chile—hotter than the Anaheim.

pepita

toasted pumpkin seed.

pesto

an Italian sauce traditionally made by pounding fresh basil, pine nuts, garlic, Parmesan and olive oil into a paste.

pico de gallo

a simple, salsa-like relish; means "rooster's beak" in Spanish!

pine nuts

harvested from pine cones; used in Mediterranean and Southwestern cooking.

polenta

cooked cornmeal which is commonly mixed with butter, cheeses, herbs; can be eaten soft (like cream of wheat cereal) or spread on a baking sheet, cut into shapes and baked or fried. See recipe (p. 37).

ponzu

a Japanese dipping sauce made with fresh citrus juices; very low in fat. See recipe (p. 115).

Port

a fortified dessert wine.

radicchio

a ruby red, crisp, slightly bitter member of the chicory family.

raita

a yogourt-based sauce used to cool the fire of spicy Indian food.

rajas

literally "strips"; as in "red pepper rajas", that is, strips or julienne of red pepper.

reduction

a sauce resulting from the slow simmering of liquid (wine, citrus juices, vegetable stock) to thicken and concentrate flavors.

saffron

a thread-like spice that is the dried stamens of crocus flowers; strongly aromatic and exotic flavour.

sambal oelek

a fiery Asian hot chile pepper paste.

serrano chile

a small, very hot (hotter than jalapeño) green chile.

shiitake mushrooms

cultivated Japanese mushrooms with a chewy texture and distinctive earthy flavour; available fresh or dried.

soba noodles

Japanese noodles made from buckwheat and wheat flours.

soy milk

a non-dairy beverage derived from cooked soybeans; contains no lactose and is cholesterol-free.

soy sauce, dark

a rich, black soy sauce that is aged for much longer than regular or light; used in cooking to add a sweet depth of flavour.

star anise

an eight-point star-shaped seedpod with a rich licorice flavour.

Sucanat

a granulated natural sweetener made from dried cane juice.

sui choy

also known as Napa or Chinese cabbage; a big, barrel-shaped head with tightly packed, pale green leaves. More sweet and delicate than regular cabbage, used raw in slaws or stir-fried.

Szechuan peppercorn

a small aromatic seed that looks like a peppercorn.

papparadelle

a long, very wide noodle.

tahini

sesame butter—a spreadable paste made from sesame seeds; rich in calcium.

tamari

Japanese soy sauce that is naturally brewed without the additives and colouring agents found in most commercial soy sauces.

tempeh

a soyfood that is native to Indonesia; a cake of compressed, fermented whole soybeans that is nutty in flavour and slightly chewy in texture.

tofu

a fresh soybean curd that is pressed into custard-like cakes; high in protein, low in calories (147 in 8 oz) and unsaturated fats.

tomatillo

a tangy, pale green, small tomato-like fruit covered with a papery husk; related to gooseberries, not tomatoes.

Thai bird chiles

tiny, extremely hot chiles, used fresh or dried.

udon noodles

Japanese wheat noodles available in various thicknesses, fresh or dried. We use the widely available, fresh vacuum-packed variety.

wasabi

a dried Japanese radish that is mixed with water to form a paste and used as a condiment for sushi, etc. Very pungent and hot—use sparingly!

wild rice

the seed of a wild grass traditionally harvested by native people in North America (not a rice at all!)

suppliers

Alpine Florist & Food Market
1019 Blanshard Ave.
Victoria, B.C. V8W 2H4
250-382-6233

Bagga Pasta
104-2000 Cadboro Bay Rd.
Victoria, B.C. V8R 5G5
250-598-7575

Big Barn Market
1286 MacKenzie Ave.
Victoria, B.C. V8P 5P2
250-477-9495

Cascadia Wholefoods Bakery
1812 Government St.
Victoria, B.C. V8T 4N5
250-380-6606

Caterina Italian Foods
1114 Blanshard St.
Victoria, B.C. V8W 2H6
250-385-7923

Fisgard Market Ltd.
550 Fisgard St.
Victoria, B.C. V8W 1R4
250-383-6969

Island Egg Sales
P.O. Box #1
Westholme, B.C. V0R 3C0
250-383-7337

Lifestyles Markets
180-2950 Douglas St.
Victoria, B.C. V8T 4N4
250-384-3388

Living Foods
5046 Rocky Point Rd.
Victoria, B.c. V9B 5B4
250-474-2490

Mt. Royal Bagel Factory
6-1115 North Park St.
Victoria, B.C. V8J 1E7
250-380-3588

Mystic Ridge Farm
Lasqueti Island, B.C. V0R 2J0
eagle@bcsupernet.com

North Douglas Distributors
602 Barbon Pl.
Victoria, B.C. V8Z 1C5
250-475-3311

PSC Natural Foods
95 Esquimalt Rd.
Victoria, B.C. V9A 3K8
250-386-3880

Que Pasa Mexican Foods
1637 West Fifth Ave
Vancouver, B.C. V6J 1N5
604-737-7659

Rising Star Wholefoods Bakery
9-935 Devonshire
Victoria, B.C. V9A 4T8
250-480-0021

Seed of Life
1316 Government St.
Victoria, B.C. V8W 1Z3
250-382-4343

Self-Heal Herbal Cente
1106 Blanshard St.
Victoria, B.C. V8W 2H6
250-383-1913

Silk Road Aromatherapy & Tea Co.
1624 Government St.
Victoria, B.C. V8W 1Z3
250-382-0006

Snow Cap
2271 Voxhall Place
Richmond, B.C. V6V 1Z5

Thrifty Foods
1590 Fairfield Rd.
Victoria, B.C. V8S 1G1
250-544-1234

Torrefazione Italia
P.O. Box 4100
Vancouver, B.C. V6B 5X4
604-738-7400

The Vitamin Shop
1212 Broad St.
Victoria, B.C. V8W 2A5
250-386-1212

index

about the authors

Never one to do things the easy way, Audrey has surprised even herself with what one is capable of accomplishing, given enough obstinance and enthusiasm. Raising a small family in a "back to the land" setting on a remote island provided the mettle needed to open and operate a restaurant. Since the age of 6, when her mother allowed her to bake a chocolate cake "all by her self", the passion for creating and eating good food took a stronghold. Today she still watches over her restaurant and bakery, while making more time to cook just for fun for friends and family, planning art projects and gardens, travelling and adoring her two Boston terriers.

As a former city girl gone country, Wanda loves to get her hands dirty and when she's not doing that in a kitchen, she's out in the garden, growing her food. Her love of cooking was instilled early in life by Polish immigrant parents who love to cook and love to eat. A vegetarian since 1985, Wanda's cooking has evolved as her knowledge of growing organic food has. Focus on seasonal, local and organic products are now the main influences of her cooking style and she dreams of running a farm growing specialty organic vegetables for restauranteurs. Wanda also loves to climb mountains, run and read anything she can get her hands on, especially if it's about cooking or gardening.